REMEMBERING the DEAD in the ANCIENT NEAR EAST

REMEMBERING THE DEAD IN THE ANCIENT NEAR EAST

RECENT CONTRIBUTIONS FROM BIOARCHAEOLOGY AND MORTUARY ARCHAEOLOGY

EDITED BY

BENJAMIN W. PORTER AND ALEXIS T. BOUTIN

UNIVERSITY PRESS OF COLORADO
Boulder

Published by University Press of Colorado
5589 Arapahoe Avenue, Suite 206C
Boulder, Colorado 80303

 The University Press of Colorado is a proud member of
the Association of American University Presses.

The University Press of Colorado is a cooperative publishing enterprise supported, in part,
by Adams State University, Colorado State University, Fort Lewis College, Metropolitan
State University of Denver, Regis University, University of Colorado, University of Northern
Colorado, Utah State University, and Western State Colorado University.

∞ This paper meets the requirements of the ANSI/NISO Z39.48-1992 (Permanence of Paper).

Library of Congress Cataloging-in-Publication Data

Remembering the dead in the ancient Near East : recent contributions from bioarchaeology
and mortuary archaeology / [edited by] Benjamin W. Porter & Alexis T. Boutin.
      pages cm
   Includes bibliographical references and index.
   ISBN 978-1-60732-324-2 (cloth : alk. paper) — ISBN 978-1-60732-528-4 (pbk. : alk. paper) —
ISBN 978-1-60732-325-9 (ebook)
   1. Human remains (Archaeology)—Methodology—Middle East. 2. Excavations
(Archaeology)—Middle East. 3. Funeral rites and ceremonies—Middle East. 4. Human
skeleton—Analysis. 5. Middle East—Antiquities. I. Boutin, Alexis T. II. Porter, Benjamin W.
   DS56.R456 2014
   939.4—dc23
                            2014001151

Cover and text design by Daniel Pratt

Cover photograph: The Standard of Ur; Reg. No. 1928,1010.3; BM Big No. 121201; PRN.
WCO24764; © The Trustees of the British Museum

This book is dedicated to five very cool kids:
Rosey, Eva, and Charlie Harris
&
Quinn and Desmond Jacobs Porter

Contents

Acknowledgments

This volume grew out of a 2011 Society for American Archaeology session in Sacramento, California, bearing a title similar to the one used for this book. We, the editors, would like to thank Darrin Pratt, Jessica d'Arbonne, Laura Furney, Daniel Pratt, and their colleagues at the University Press of Colorado, who first approached us about organizing this volume. The feedback from the manuscript's two anonymous reviewers helped to sharpen each chapter's arguments as well as the volume's overall themes. We would also like to thank our fifteen contributors whose research appears in the pages to follow. Our home institutions—the University of California, Berkeley, and Sonoma State University—provided logistical support. Boutin would like to thank her Archaeology and the Bible stidents for their editorial assistance. Porter would also like to thank Johns Hopkins University's Near Eastern Studies Department, particularly its chair, Glenn Schwartz, for hosting him during a 2012–13 sabbatical leave, when the final editing and reviewing duties took place. We would also like to thank the Louis J. Kolb Society of Fellows at the University of Pennsylvania for their ongoing support since our graduate school years. We hope this co-authored project reflects the society's rigorous interdisciplinary spirit. Not least, we would like to thank our spouses, Jenny Jacobs and Ben Harris, for partaking in life's most treasured collaborations.

REMEMBERING THE DEAD IN THE ANCIENT NEAR EAST

I

*Bringing Out the Dead in
the Ancient Near East*

Benjamin W. Porter and
Alexis T. Boutin

Intentional burial—a characteristically human behavior that first occurred nearly 100,000 years ago in the Middle East—is one of the most fundamental acts of commemoration. Although some people who lived in ancient Near Eastern societies[1] clearly planned for their funerary treatment prior to their death (e.g., the Egyptian Old Kingdom pyramids at Giza), burial practices were largely decided by the living: how to prepare the body for interment; how to position the body in the burial chamber; what objects to include with the deceased; what ritual acts to perform days, weeks, or even years later. Given the diversity of ancient Near Eastern societies over so many millennia, the Middle East boasts a rich archive in which to investigate how people made deliberate choices to remember and commemorate the dead. And yet for all of the bodies that have been exhumed since Near Eastern archaeology began in the mid-nineteenth century, comprehensive treatments of mortuary contexts are rarely published. Mortuary rituals, the identities of the deceased, or beliefs about the afterlife consequently are interpreted using a single data set—the assemblage with which a person was buried, for instance, or the person's osteological profile, or written commentaries about the deceased. In doing so, scholars paint only part of a much more complex picture of death in the ancient Near East. The dearth of holistic studies integrating these data sets is odd given the sustained scholarly interest in ancient Near Eastern societies' perceptions of death and beliefs about the afterlife (e.g., Baker 2012; Campbell and Green 1995; Kramer 1967; Laneri 2007; Schmidt 1994). This book is a response to the irregular nature in which ancient Near Eastern mortuary

DOI: 10.5876/9781607323295.c001

contexts have been studied in the past. The chapters that follow use evidence from across the region's societies—from Neolithic Turkey to Bronze Age Jordan, from ancient Egypt and Sudan to the Arabian Gulf and Mesopotamia. In each, authors bring at least two different, yet complementary, analytical techniques together to investigate how ancient Near Eastern societies remembered and commemorated the dead. While no chapter offers a perfect vision of collaboration, many demonstrate how teams of researchers with different skillsets—osteological analysis, faunal analysis, culture history and the analysis of written texts, and artifact analysis—offer ways to interpret ancient Near Eastern mortuary contexts in a richer and more robust light.

This chapter prepares readers for the studies to follow, introducing key issues surrounding the investigation of death, memory, and commemoration in ancient Near Eastern mortuary contexts. The chapter begins with a brief survey of the segmented roles that mortuary archaeologists, osteologists, bioarchaeologists, and cultural historians have played in analyses. When these disciplinary genealogies are placed side by side, a clearer vision for intersecting interests and moments of collaboration becomes apparent. The discussion then examines how recent scholarship on social memory in the humanities and social sciences provides a framework for investigating practices of remembering and commemorating the dead in ancient Near Eastern societies. Mortuary contexts, structured depositions shaped by both conscious and unconscious intentions, are sites of memory and are the result of memory work. Different modes of mortuary analysis can shed light on aspects of memory work, whether it is osteological data that can reconstruct the osteobiography of the interred person, the material cultural analysis of objects, or historians and epigraphers building a cultural context around the interment event. This chapter concludes with an overview of the different chapters in this book, illustrating how each speaks to issues raised in broader discussions.

INVESTIGATING MORTUARY CONTEXTS IN ANCIENT NEAR EASTERN SOCIETIES

Mortuary Archaeology

The skewed emphases in the analysis of ancient Near Eastern mortuary contexts are explained by the fact that investigations have developed along distinct disciplinary trajectories that worked in relative isolation from each other. The most dominant trajectory has been mortuary archaeology, whose principal focus has concerned materials associated with the deceased, such as the objects interred with the body or the architectural design of tombs. A glance at the contents of many excavation reports reflects mortuary archaeology's dominance. Each volume will invariably include an individual chapter, often entitled "The Burials," placed alongside other sections on architecture, ceramics, and chronology. Although human skeletal remains may be described in terms of their preservation and deposition in such chapters, the results of osteological analyses often appear in separate chapters, if at all (see below), with no attempt to integrate data and context. The mortuary assemblage receives the bulk of writers' attention for several good reasons. The objects' locations in a sealed context can help to establish chronological sequences (Duday 2006: 37), and, because whole or nearly whole objects are commonly recovered in mortuary contexts, they are valuable assets in designing artifact corpora; these same objects are also ideal specimens for museum displays (Woolley 1937: 81). For more than a century of research, these descriptive reports of human burials have comprised the majority of research on mortuary practices in the ancient Near East (e.g., Delougaz, Hill, and Lloyd 1967; Goffinet 1982; Jean-Marie 1999; Maeir 2004; Thrane 1978; Woolley 1934).

While basic documentation of mortuary contexts remains prevalent, thematic studies—often diachronic and broad in their geographic coverage—have grown more abundant in recent decades. The most common topics use mortuary assemblages to demarcate geographic zones of shared cultural and religious identities (e.g., Bienkowski 1982; Carter and Parker 1995; Gonen 1992) or observe changes in long-term mortuary practices that, in turn, reflect changes in social and political complexity (e.g., Joffe 2003; Keswani 2004; Richards 2005). Mortuary practices also have been regarded as key to understanding ancient Near Eastern symbolic systems and religious beliefs, with ancestor veneration a popular topic of inquiry (Mabry 2003; Pfälzner et al. 2012; Pitard 1996; Salles 1995; Schmidt 1994, 1996; van der Toorn 1994, 1996). Recently, scholars have interpreted elite funerary rituals in the ancient Near East, especially their conspicuous consumption of material wealth (e.g., construction of substantial architecture, disposal of rich and rare grave goods), as acts of memorialization that create and reinforce political authority, in particular by drawing on ancestor ideologies (Matthiae 1979; Morris 2007; Peltenburg 1999; Pollock 2007; Porter 2002; Schwartz 2007). Burials of children (Kulemann-Ossen and Novák 2000), and certain types of grave goods, such as figurines (Marchetti 2000; Pruss and Novák 2000) and weapons (Rehm 2003), have been considered as social or religious symbols. Mortuary archaeology also has been inspired by third-wave feminism and its emphasis on human difference. These approaches explore how one or more facets in the reflecting and refracting prism of social identity—encompassing age, kinship, sex, gender, sexuality, agency, and so on—are reproduced through mortuary practices; however, they remain rare in scholarship on the ancient Near East (e.g., Baker 2012; Croucher 2005).

In the chapters that follow, authors include mortuary assemblages and architecture in their analyses, albeit in different ways and at different intensities. Almost all authorial teams use objects and architecture to supply relative dates, or confirm absolute dates, for interment events. And almost all authors explicitly or implicitly consider objects as "gifts" that the living gave to deceased persons to bring with them into the afterlife. Although this is a common assumption about the role objects play in ancient Near Eastern mortuary rituals, objects likely possessed multiple functions and meanings. While the editors did not plan this arrangement, most mortuary contexts analyzed in this volume may be classified as "vernacular," or nonelite. This is a refreshing change from projects in the region that favor elite contexts, such as the Royal Tombs of Ur, that have received steady attention since their discovery (e.g., Baadsgaard 2011; Cohen 2005; Keith 1934; Molleson and Hodgson 2003; Pollock 2007; Woolley 1934). Yet, consequently, such nonelite contexts often lack the abundant grave goods and elaborate architectural designs that offer themselves up for interpretations. The chapters in this volume nevertheless find much to interpret in even the smallest object and most ordinary structures, finding them to be humble yet evocative acts that the living could muster to commemorate the dead.

SKELETAL AND DENTAL EVIDENCE

The second mode of mortuary analysis is osteology, a field that uses methods from the biological sciences to study human remains. The study of the human body in the ancient Near East traditionally has focused on it as an "objectified entity in physical or biological studies" or viewed its treatment in death as representative of social structures or symbolic systems (Boyd 2002:137). Detailed studies of the osteology of ancient Near Eastern populations have been conducted for much of the time that modern scholars have explored the region (e.g., Buxton and Rice 1931; Charles 1962; Charlier 2000; Keith 1934; Krogman 1949; Kunter 1984). Skeletal data prioritized by these studies include age, sex, metrics (cranial, postcranial, and dental), nonmetric traits, cranial morphology and associated "racial" types, and ad hoc observations (rather than systematic analysis) of paleopathology. As mentioned earlier, osteological data from burials often appear incidentally in excavation reports, or are conspicuously absent. When reports do appear, they are usually appended to, or published separately from, excavation reports discussing the mortuary contexts from which the data were collected. This disconnect between data and context is even apparent in projects whose research designs ostensibly seek such integration (e.g., Hodder 2005; cf. Buikstra, Baadsgaard, and Boutin 2011:11).

Scholars of the ancient Near East are not alone in their inability to integrate mortuary analyses, theoretical developments in archaeology, and interpretations of human skeletal remains (Goldstein 2006). Fortunately, the introduction of bioarchaeological praxis has begun to ameliorate this blind spot through a holistic integration of archaeological and osteological data from ancient Near Eastern mortuary contexts (notably, Perry 2012). Several disciplinary histories of bioarchaeology's origins and research orientations have been published recently (Agarwal and Glencross 2011a; Armelagos 2003; Buikstra and Beck 2006; Buikstra, Baadsgaard, and Boutin 2011) and need not be repeated here. Although the populations and time periods studied are wide ranging and diverse, three primary perspectives have shaped bioarchaeologists' research agendas. The "biocultural" approach to bioarchaeology explores "the effects of localized, proximate conditions on human biologies and the linkage between these contexts and larger historical political-economic processes" (Zuckerman and Armelagos 2011:20). Its investigative scale varies from exploring longer-term adaptive trends (Goodman and Leatherman 1998) to the lived experiences of communities and individuals (Agarwal and Glencross 2011b; Blakey 2001; Sheridan 1999). Clark Spencer Larsen (1997, 2002) defines bioarchaeology as use of the human biological component of the archaeological record to make behavioral inferences that shed light on the history of the human condition. Research by him and other like-minded scholars has produced wide-ranging studies that explore patterns of disease, diet, activity, and demography, among other topics, from a population perspective (e.g., Larsen 2001; Steckel and Rose 2002; Tung 2012; Walker 2001).

The approach taken in this volume, however, follows the method and theory championed by Jane Buikstra (2006), which emphasizes the contextual analysis of human remains from archaeological settings via multiple lines of evidence (iconographic, textual, and ethnographic data in addition to archaeology and osteology). Contemporary social theory is employed to reconstruct human life histories and population structures (e.g., Baadsgaard, Boutin, and Buikstra 2011; Knudson and Stojanowski 2009; Stodder and Palkovich 2012). Accordingly, in the current volume, perspectives from disability studies (Boutin and Porter), postcolonial theory (Smith and Buzon), and the politics of ethnic identity (Pestle, Torres-Rouff, and Daverman) are deployed in support of holistic interpretations of data from mortuary contexts.

Several trends are evident when tracking bioarchaeological research on the ancient Near East. In addition to exploring how memory and commemoration are expressed in funerary practices, each chapter in this volume also engages with these broader areas of inquiry. Human skeletal remains have been a rich data source for correlating health and diet with changes in sociopolitical organization. The introduction of new technologies and methods of food preparation at key moments of growth in social complexity has been inferred from skeletal markers of occupational stress (Molleson 1994) and dental microwear (Alrousan and Pérez-Pérez 2012; Molleson, Jones, and Jones 1993). Long-term, regional changes in subsistence strategy also have been explored via dental pathology alone (Littleton and Frohlich 1989, 1993) and in combination with a variety of skeletal indicators of stress, trauma, and infection (Blau 2007; Littleton 2007; Smith and Horwitz 2007). In the current volume, Campbell and coauthors provide evidence for large-scale feasting and its ties to place- and memory-making, while Smith and Buzon analyze dietarily derived stable isotopes in their investigation of migration during colonial encounters.

The human skeleton also has been used to reveal social differentiation along many axes of identity in ancient Near Eastern societies. The ways that gender intersects with status, behavior, and ancestordom has been studied by means of artificial cranial modification (Lorentz 2008), skeletal markers of occupational stress (Peterson 2002, 2010), bone quantity and quality (Glencross and Agarwal 2011), and postmortem skull decoration (Bonogofsky 2003). Social interpretations of chronological aging and biological maturation across the life course are another growing area of interest, with a particular focus on childhood as embodied by health (Littleton 2011), social roles (Perry 2005), and mortuary treatment (Torres-Rouff and Pestle 2012). Biochemical evidence from bones and teeth has been a productive source for investigating transitional moments such as weaning (Dupras, Schwarcz, and Fairgrieve 2001; Gregoricka and Sheridan 2012; Richards et al. 2003). In the current volume, mortuary and osteological evidence are brought together by Dabbs and Zabecki to explore differences in socioeconomic status in New Kingdom Egypt, while Pestle and coauthors focus on ethnic affiliation at Kish during a period of transition from Sumerian to Akkadian rule.

The issue of analytical scale in bioarchaeology has undergone interrogation lately in an ancient Near Eastern context (Pollock 2011). Many of the studies just reviewed approach assemblages of human skeletal remains in a systematic, yet broad, fashion to produce population-level profiles of characteristics such as age, sex, health, and occupational stress. Such research also can shed new light on how kinship units, whether biological or fictive, were organized (Bentley 1991; Pilloud and Larsen 2011). Finer-grained analyses of individual persons, sometimes termed "osteobiographies" (after Saul and Saul 1989), represent a more recent development (Boutin 2011, 2012; Martin and Potts 2012; Molleson and Hodgson 1993, 2003; Özbek 2005). In the current volume, Boutin and Porter juxtapose the biographies of ancient and modern individuals, and Sheridan and coauthors present skeletal evidence for family and lineage affiliation.

Written Sources and Visual Culture

A third analytical mode that works apart from mortuary archaeology and bioarchaeology consists of cultural historians, art historians, and philologists who study the large, diverse corpus of written sources and visual culture concerning death that was produced by ancient Near Eastern societies. Different genres of written sources, including ritual texts describing how mortuary customs were to be performed, literary texts that ponder death's meaning in myths and lamentations, and even economic texts discussing inheritance and funeral payments, reveal different, although sometimes oblique, insights into ideologies about death, the afterlife, and mortuary practices (Haas 1995; Scurlock 1995; Xella 1995). Visual culture such as public monuments, funerary paintings, and seals and sealings depicts a wide array of information about mortuary customs, including ritual and violent death, funerary banquets, and mythical scenes depicting the underworld, although this evidence is rarely vernacular in design. Elites often sponsored the crafting of such objects that were designed to commemorate authority and reflect the power and wealth that the deceased possessed while alive. Combined, this evidence reveals the diversity of ideologies about death and mortuary practices across the ancient Near Eastern societies, making it impossible to generalize about the region.

Interpreting such written and visual sources with any accuracy poses another challenge. One cannot merely translate and "read" a text, or easily tease out the image's visual program, unfortunately. Their interpretability will always be limited, not only because archaeologists lack living informants to confirm their conclusions, but also because these sources are the products of substantially different societies, both from each other and from the modern ones that scholars inhabit. Discussions of death and its commemoration within written sources should not necessarily be understood as a direct reflection of a society's attitudes, but must rather be interpreted within the context of a specific text. Furthermore, belief and sentiments may exist beyond language, beyond the expressions that writers and artists are capable of representing in text or image. When such challenges are unheeded, scholars are led to think about death in anachronistic fashions that transfer meanings from one cultural and historical milieu with more information to another context with fewer or no sources. One cannot easily extend a stereotypical understanding about, for example, mortuary practices at late second millennium BCE Ugarit, to later societies, such as first millennium BCE ancient Israel, without several caveats. These risks of anachronistic thinking may partly explain why historians and philologists rarely integrate evidence from excavated mortuary contexts into their analyses, as one must first argue that there is an interpretive connection between a text and a particular context.[2] This reluctance, however, does not seem to be shared by mortuary archaeologists and bioarchaeologists, as many use written and visual sources to support their interpretations of contexts. In fact, many authorial teams make these interpretive leaps in the chapters that follow, using written sources and visual culture to paint a historical narrative around the context they investigate, or draw from commentaries about death located in contemporaneous sources.

That the investigation of ancient Near Eastern mortuary beliefs and practices is dispersed across these different fields of inquiry is not entirely surprising. Ultimately, each scholarly trajectory described above requires rigorous training in specialized analytical techniques, whether competency in an ancient language like Akkadian or in the osteological analysis of human remains. There are too many skills and too large a corpus for a single scholar to master in his or her lifetime. Yet the interpretation of mortuary contexts cries out for greater collaboration among these factions. All of the authorial teams in the following chapters are collaborative in nature, and half (Campbell et al., Boutin and Porter, Smith and Buzon) are composed of scholars with expertise in at least two different fields. While this is a strength in the book's contributions, more collaboration—particularly with experts in ancient Near Eastern written sources—is needed in future projects focused on mortuary contexts.

MEMORY WORK IN MORTUARY CONTEXTS

This book emphasizes how mortuary contexts are rich zones for thinking about the ways ancient Near Eastern societies commemorated the deceased, whether they were immediate family members or important leaders. Although popular Western notions of memory consign it to a psychological phenomenon occurring strictly within the minds of persons, social scientific and humanistic research in the latter half of the twentieth century have illustrated that memories need not be strictly personal. Memories, like other aspects of culture, may begin as a sentiment within the body but can often become externalized through memory work, that is, externalized acts expressed through language, bodily practices, and objects that ascribe meaning to an event, a person or group, or place (Connerton 1989; Nora 1989). Memory work is cultural, learned through a person's membership in a society that teaches individuals appropriate rules and traditions. This partly explains why memory work is so diverse through time and between, even within, societies. But despite its predictable differences, memory is a human phenomenon that comes to be shared between people, as several scholars have argued (e.g., Connerton 1989; Halbwachs 1992). An entire realm of scholarship dedicated to social memory, or now less commonly referred to as collective memory, has grown to become an interdisciplinary topic whose literature is too broad to discuss in this volume's introduction (but see, Erll and Nünning 2008; Olick, Vinitzky-Seroussi, and Levy 2011; Radstone and Schwarz 2010).

Cross-cultural investigations reveal wide variation in how the living experience the event of death (Metcalf and Huntington 1991; Parker Pearson 1999; Robben 2005). But despite so many differences in ideologies about the afterlife and the rituals (or lack thereof) designed to prepare the deceased's body for burial or cremation, the one universal aspect is that a person's death is a collective experience for those people left behind. Many pre- and postmortem rituals are public; that is, they are practices that can be observed by a third party and often leave behind physical traces, a monument, a tomb, or a published obituary, for example. But the near universal presence of ritual surrounding death does not explain what compels humans to commemorate their dead. Bronislaw Malinowski, seeking an explanation for death rituals among the Melanesian societies he studied, observed long ago the contradiction in many societies that simultaneously desire to preserve the body and a person's memory, while facing the need to distance themselves physically from the decaying body (Malinowski 1948: 52). Rituals surrounding death, he argued, played a role in mitigating this incongruity, creating a means to mollify both issues. While it is no longer fashionable to think in such universal and functionalist criteria, of course, one must at least recognize that the crisis that death presents to the living motivates different kinds of responses to commemorate and remember the deceased.

Broader social scientific and humanistic research on collective and social memory has inspired archaeologists to consider the role of memory work in different archaeological contexts, from households to monuments and landscapes (Jones 2007; Mills and Walker 2008; Van Dyke and Alcock 2003; Williams 2003). The examination of memory work in mortuary contexts, however, has not always been archaeologists' principal question. While archaeologists have long agreed that the beliefs and behaviors of the living are expressed in a mortuary context's material signature (e.g., Childe 1945, [1944] 1971), they have used such contexts to discuss anything but issues pertaining to social memory. Processual archaeologists (e.g., Binford 1971; Brown 1995; Saxe 1970), for instance, believe that the degree of wealth and effort that a society differentially invests in mortuary ritual reflects the complexity of its social structure. Such mirroring of society in both life and death, however, may be naive, since ritual can invert or skew quotidian practices. Other avenues of inquiry must be pursued to confirm links between social organization and mortuary ritual. Accordingly, scholars have also argued that mortuary practices are a form of ritual communication in which the deceased are powerful symbols idealized and manipulated by the living. Based on his ethnoarchaeological work in Sudan, for example, Ian Hodder (1982: 200) writes that through "distortions, partial expressions and even inversion" mourners can manipulate material symbols to induce a form and meaning in mortuary practices that finds no direct expression in the living society. The symbolic power surrounding the corpse and associated mortuary practices has multiple levels of meaning that do not simply reflect social relations but represent and misrepresent them simultaneously. Thus, body symbolism and mortuary rituals can legitimize sectional interests and (re)constitute the social order (Shanks and Tilley 1982). Ideological beliefs may be operationalized through practices surrounding treatment and disposal of the corpse, thus producing specific material results. While certain social contradictions are ignored or intentionally misrepresented in mortuary activity, many social roles can be preserved in death so that their presence in living society is made to seem natural (David 1992; Rissman 1988).

The ideological realm of representation is not merely a feature of the ritualized world or a mask of everyday reality, however. Human experience encompasses economic and political circumstances, gender and status relationships, and social roles, all of which may be reconstituted within the ritualized world of funerary activity (Parker Pearson 1999). Postprocessual archaeologists have applied this appreciation for the socially recursive quality of mortuary ritual at two scales. On the one hand, research on a diachronic scale (e.g., Cannon 1989; Keswani 2004, 2005; Morris 1992) has focused on how major long-term changes in mortuary ritual articulate with independent social, political, and economic developments, in an attempt to understand the "structure and ideological significance of mortuary ritual within a particular society" (Keswani 2004: 20). On the other hand, funerary rituals have been understood as embodied performances in which the disposal of the corpse and memorialization of the dead provide an opportunity for identities and social memories to be created, maintained, and contested in both personalized and formalized ways (e.g., Gillespie 2001; Joyce 2001; Kuijt 2008; Tarlow 1999).

The applications of such theoretical lenses to mortuary practices in the ancient Near East has grown increasingly common over the past decade, although not nearly as intensive as studies in other areas of the world. Meredith Chesson's research on Early Bronze Age Jordan (Chesson 1999, 2001, 2007), and Lynn Meskell's work on ancient Egypt (Meskell 1999, 2001, 2004; Meskell and Joyce 2003) have led the way in the ancient Near East and Egypt, respectively. Their scholarship investigates how the processes of dying, death, funerary treatment, and ancestor veneration provide new, unique opportunities for the (re)construction of the social identities of the decedent, the persons who survive him or her, and the living community. They have also employed phenomenological approaches to describe collective experiences of emotion and the immediate perceptions of the five senses in mortuary settings. In addition, a small handful of studies have focused on how particular aspects of personhood (e.g., gender, age, social status) were entangled with mortuary rituals and objects (e.g., Bolger 2003; Croucher 2012; Pollock 1991; Savage 2000).

The authors in this volume implicitly build on these earlier works, illustrating how mortuary contexts, as structured depositions, are sites of memory work. Such depositional practices are conceived in terms of strategies of commemoration that involve building mortuary spaces, modifying the body and interring it in a mortuary context—feasting and other events around the interment. The authors combine the different analytical strategies described earlier to identify and interpret memory work in mortuary contexts. Bioarchaeological techniques, for instance, can reconstruct an interred person's osteobiography, his or her life history as recorded in bone. Such information does not just provide the person's sex and age at death. Active or healed pathological lesions may reflect the disease processes or trauma that a person experienced during his or her lifetime and around the time of death, while markers of occupational stress can reveal habitually embodied behaviors, whether quotidian or occupational. Altogether, this information helps reconstruct the kinds of experiences a person had during life, social status, the diseases and disabilities struggled with, and the manner of death. While this osteobiographical information reveals who was being commemorated, mortuary archaeology reveals the strategies used to commemorate a person upon interment and how the memory work was materialized in a structured deposition. Mortuary archaeology pays attention to how commemorative rituals were materialized through architectural construction and objects placed with the individual. Written sources and visual culture, the final analytical strategy, help build a historical and cultural context around the person's life and the commemorative event. Such evidence is not necessarily found in a direct relationship with the burial context and therefore must be used cautiously not to construct false analogies.

BRINGING OUT THE DEAD IN THE ANCIENT NEAR EAST: AN OVERVIEW OF CHAPTERS

In the six chapters to follow, each set of authors examines acts of memory work using a host of interdisciplinary techniques drawn from mortuary archaeology, bioarchaeology, and culture history. In chapter 2, Campbell, Kansa, Bichener, and Lau draw on evidence from mortuary contexts at late Neolithic Domuztepe in southeast Turkey, a fascinating mortuary context containing a minimum of thirty-five disarticulated individuals whose remains were highly processed, suggesting killing, sacrifice, or perhaps even cannibalism. The authors trace patterns of structured deposition of dog remains, feasting materials, and other objects in and around human interments at Domuztepe. They complicate the notion of burial, extending it from a funerary behavior reserved only for humans to one that also includes nonhumans. In chapter 3, Pestle, Torres-Rouff, and Daverman consider evidence from Kish in southern Iraq during the transition from the Early Dynastic III period to the Akkadian period. Written sources describe the late third millennium BCE period as one fraught with conflict, when Akkadian ethnic identities were ascendant over the Sumerian societies that had previously dominated Mesopotamia. The authors' chosen context, Kish's A "Cemetery," is surprisingly homogenous in burial treatment. The authors interpret the similarities either as a suggestion that Akkadian ethnic identity was not as pronounced as previous scholarship had assumed, or as an attempt through memory work to mask biological and ethnic differences between societies.

In chapter 4, Boutin and Porter draw on evidence from the Peter B. Cornwall collection in the Hearst Museum of Anthropology to discuss the commemoration of disability. Working anachronistically, the authors contrast Cornwall, a deaf graduate student who faced institutional discrimination, with a young woman he excavated during his expedition to Bahrain in 1940. Archaeologists know little of Cornwall's life and its challenges compared to other more celebrated archaeologists of his time. His biography does not fit seamlessly with disciplinary archetypes of able-bodied hero-scientists. This lack of commemoration is contrasted with that of the young woman who lived in Dilmun at the turn of the second millennium BCE. Her osteobiography reveals unusually short stature, modified use of one arm, and an awkward gait. A large number of objects were interred with this young woman, many more than in normative mortuary contexts. These case studies, separated in time by four millennia, reveal how disability is a culturally constructed notion, displacing the untested assumption that past societies lacked tolerance for persons with disabilities.

In chapter 5, Sheridan, Ullinger, Gregoricka, and Chesson examine osteological evidence from the Early Bronze Age site of Bab edh-Dhra' located in the Jordan Valley. The settlement likely functioned as a regional burial center, where thousands of bodies were interred, from the mid-fourth millennium to the late third millennium BCE. Despite this continuity, osteological evidence and mortuary contexts indicate that funerary rituals shifted over time to reflect altered settlement patterns and changing social dynamics. Shaft tombs, created by the residents of seasonal campsites during the Early Bronze IA, contained secondary burials of related individuals and represented families from across the community. By contrast, the Early Bronze II-III charnel house—which was associated with a planned, fortified settlement—housed a smaller number of multigenerational families. As population size and investment in land at Bab edh-Dhra' grew, understandings of kinship changed. New ways of commemorating the dead were associated with expanding group identity and membership.

In chapter 6, Smith and Buzon consider how the deceased are remembered during and following periods of colonization. Based on evidence from Tombos in Sudanese Nubia, the authors explore both shorter-term practices commemorating individuals and longer-term cultural memories. They also investigate the ways in which the archaeological record reveals both inscribed (e.g., monuments) and incorporated (e.g., embodied practices) traditions of memorialization. Osteological and archaeological analyses of burials dating to this Egyptian colonial community's founding in 1400 BCE reflect the cultural entanglements between local Nubians and recently arrived colonizers from Egypt. Following Tombos's secession from the Egyptian empire and the establishment of a Nubian dynasty, a new, hybrid identity comprised of intermarriage and syncretic funerary practices can be discerned during the Napatan period. Finally, Dabbs and Zabecki consider remembering and forgetting at the late second millennium BCE site of Tell el-Amarna in Middle Egypt in chapter 7. Their investigation takes places in the enormous South Tombs Cemetery, where all social classes save the most wealthy were interred, but grave goods are rare. For a capital of the New Kingdom, skeletal indicators of physiological stress appear at unexpectedly high frequencies in all demographic and occupational groups. This may reflect the city's rapid construction and occupation by a newly arrived and highly diverse population. The authors suggest that extensive grave robbing shortly after the cemetery's abandonment may not reflect irreverence of the dead, as is frequently assumed, but the respectful remembering and repatriation of deceased loved ones after the city's collapse.

Despite differences in time period and location, these chapters do possess some commonalities that are apparent when placed side by side. As already mentioned, most chapters investigate the mortuary practices of nonelite populations, a refreshing change from previous studies that have focused on the wealthy and powerful in the ancient Near East. More than half of the chapters are concerned with Bronze Age populations, with Campbell, Kansa, Bichener, and Lau's research on the Neolithic; and Smith and Buzon's on first millennium Sudan, being the exception. This bias toward the third and second millennia, unplanned by the editors, suggests that more work on either side of the ancient Near Eastern Bronze Age is needed in future research. Finally, most of the studies presented here fall within the core geographic areas of the ancient Near East, namely, Egypt, the Levant, and Mesopotamia. While the Arabian Gulf and Sudan are represented, the absence of Bronze and Iron Age Turkey, the Caucusus, Iran, and Yemen are conspicuous and call out for more research and publication in traditionally under-represented regions of ancient Near Eastern studies. Despite this overlap, the case studies presented here will hopefully serve as a model for integrating multiple lines of archaeological, osteological, written, and visual evidence in the investigation of ancient Near Eastern mortuary practices.

NOTES

1. Throughout this volume, the ancient Near East is defined broadly to include the area known today as the Middle East, including Egypt and Sudan, from the Paleolithic Era to the late first millennium BCE.

2. Egyptology is exceptional in this regard, as scholars must bring a diverse array of disciplinary knowledge from texts, images, material culture, funerary architecture, and the interred body together to interpret (often elite) mortuary contexts.

REFERENCES

Agarwal, Sabrina C., and Bonnie Glencross. 2011a. "Building a Social Bioarchaeology." In *Social Bioarchaeology*, edited by S. C. Agarwal and B. A. Glencross, 1–11. Chichester, England: Wiley-Blackwell.

Agarwal, Sabrina C., and Bonnie Glencross, eds. 2011b. *Social Bioarchaeology*. Chichester, England: Wiley-Blackwell. http://dx.doi.org/10.1002/9781444390537.

Alrousan, Mohammad, and Alejandro Pérez-Pérez. 2012. "Buccal Dental Microwear as an Indicator of Dietary Habits of the Natufian People of El-Wad and El-Kebarah." In *Bioarchaeology and Behavior: The People of the Ancient Near East*, edited by M. A. Perry, 165–79. Gainesville: University Press of Florida. http://dx.doi.org/10.5744/florida/9780813042299.003.0008.

Armelagos, George J. 2003. "Bioarchaeology as Anthropology." In *Archaeology is Anthropology*, edited by S. D. Gillespie and D. L. Nichols, 27–40. Arlington, VA: American Anthropological Association.

Baadsgaard, Aubrey. 2011. "Mortuary Dress as Material Culture: A Case Study from the Royal Cemetery of Ur." In *Breathing New Life into the Evidence of Death: Contemporary Approaches to Bioarchaeology*, edited by A. Baadsgaard, A. T. Boutin, and J. E. Buikstra, 179–200. Santa Fe: School for Advanced Research Press.

Baadsgaard, Aubrey, Alexis T. Boutin, and Jane E. Buikstra, eds. 2011. *Breathing New Life into the Evidence of Death: Contemporary Approaches to Bioarchaeology*. Santa Fe: School for Advanced Research Press.

Baker, Jill. 2012. *The Funeral Kit: Mortuary Practices in the Archaeological Record*. Walnut Creek, CA: Left Coast Press.

Bentley, Gillian R. 1991. "A Bioarchaeological Reconstruction of the Social and Kinship Systems at Early Bronze Age Bab edh-Dhra', Jordan." In *Between Bands and States*, edited by S. A. Gregg, 5–34. Carbondale: Southern Illinois University.

Bienkowski, Piotr A. 1982. "Some Remarks on the Practice of Cremation in the Levant." *Levant* 14 (1): 80–89. http://dx.doi.org/10.1179/lev.1982.14.1.80.

Binford, Lewis R. 1971. "Mortuary Practices: Their Study and Their Potential." In *Approaches to the Social Dimensions of Mortuary Practices*, edited by J. A. Brown, 6–29. Washington, D.C.: Society for American Archaeology.

Blakey, Michael L. 2001. "Bioarchaeology of the African Diaspora in the Americas: Its Origins and Scope." *Annual Review of Anthropology* 30 (1): 387–422. http://dx.doi.org/10.1146/annurev.anthro.30.1.387.

Blau, Soren. 2007. "Skeletal and Dental Health and Subsistence Change in the United Arab Emirates." In *Ancient Health: Skeletal Indicators of Agricultural and Economic Intensification*, edited by M. N. Cohen and G. M. M. Crane-Kramer, 190–206. Gainesville: University Press of Florida.

Bolger, Diane L. 2003. *Gender in Ancient Cyprus: Narratives of Social Change on a Mediterranean Island*. Walnut Creek, CA: AltaMira Press.

Bonogofsky, Michelle. 2003. "Neolithic Plastered Skulls and Railroading Epistemologies." *Bulletin of the American Schools of Oriental Research* 331 (331): 1–10. http://dx.doi.org/10.2307/1357755.

Boutin, Alexis T. 2011. "Crafting a Bioarchaeology of Personhood: Osteobiographical Narratives from Alalakh." In *Breathing New Life into the Evidence of Death: Contemporary Approaches to Bioarchaeology*, edited by A. Baadsgaard, A. T. Boutin, and J. E. Buikstra, 109–33. Santa Fe: School for Advanced Research Press.

Boutin, Alexis T. 2012. "Written in Stone, Written in Bone: The Osteobiography of a Bronze Age Craftsman from Alalakh." In *The Bioarchaeology of Individuals*, edited by A. L. W. Stodder and A. M. Palkovich, 193–214. Gainesville: University Press of Florida.

Boyd, Brian. 2002. "Ways of Eating/Ways of Being in the Late Epipalaeolithic (Natufian) Levant." In *Thinking through the Body: Archaeologies of Corporeality*, edited by Y. Hamilakis, M. Pluciennik and S. Tarlow, 137–52. New York: Kluwer Academic/Plenum Publishers. http://dx.doi.org/10.1007/978-1-4615-0693-5_8.

Brown, James. 1995. "On Mortuary Analysis—with Special Reference to the Saxe-Binford Research Program." In *Regional Approaches to Mortuary Analysis*, edited by L. A. Beck, 3–26. New York: Plenum Press.

Buikstra, Jane E. 2006. "Preface." In *Bioarchaeology: The Contextual Analysis of Human Remains*, edited by J. E. Buikstra and L. A. Beck, xvii–xx. Burlington, MA: Elsevier.

Buikstra, Jane E., Aubrey Baadsgaard, and Alexis T. Boutin. 2011. "Introduction." In *Breathing New Life into the Evidence of Death: Contemporary Approaches to Bioarchaeology*, edited by A. Baadsgaard, A. T. Boutin, and J. E. Buikstra, 3–26. Santa Fe: School for Advanced Research Press.

Buikstra, Jane E., and Lane A. Beck, eds. 2006. *Bioarchaeology: The Contextual Analysis of Human Remains*. Burlington, MA: Elsevier.

Buxton, L. H. Dudley, and D. Talbot Rice. 1931. "Report on the Human Remains found at Kish." *Journal of the Royal Anthropological Institute of Great Britain and Ireland* 61:57–119. http://dx.doi.org/10.2307/2843826.

Campbell, Stuart, and Anthony Green, eds. 1995. *The Archaeology of Death in the Ancient Near East*. Oxford: Oxbow Books.

Cannon, Aubrey. 1989. "The Historical Dimension in Mortuary Expressions of Status and Sentiment." *Current Anthropology* 30 (4): 437–58. http://dx.doi.org/10.1086/203764.

Carter, Elizabeth, and Andrea Parker. 1995. "Pots, People and the Archaeology of Death in Northern Syria and Southern Anatolia in the Latter Half of the Third Millennium BC." In *The Archaeology of Death in the Ancient Near East*, edited by S. Campbell and A. Green, 96–116. Oxford: Oxbow Books.

Charles, Robert P. 1962. "Contribution a l'étude anthropologique du Site de Ras Shamra." In *Ugaritica IV*, edited C. F. A. Schaeffer, 521–63. Paris: Librairie Orientaliste Paul Geuthner.

Charlier, Christine. 2000. "Tell Beydar: Deux squelettes exhumés en 1994. Rapport anthropologique préliminaire." In *Tell Beydar: Environmental and Technical Studies. Subartu VI*, edited by K. van Lerberghe and G. Voet, 39–53. Turnhout, Belgium: Brepols.

Chesson, Meredith S. 1999. "Libraries of the Dead: Early Bronze Age Charnel Houses and Social Identity at Urban Bab edh-Dhra', Jordan." *Journal of Anthropological Archaeology* 18 (2): 137–64. http://dx.doi.org/10.1006/jaar.1998.0330.

Chesson, Meredith S. 2001. "Embodied Memories of Place and People: Death and Society in an Early Urban Community." In *Social Memory, Identity, and Death: Anthropological Perspectives on Mortuary Rituals*, edited by M. S. Chesson, 100–113. Arlington, VA: American Anthropological Association. http://dx.doi.org/10.1525/ap3a.2001.10.1.100.

Chesson, Meredith S. 2007. "Remembering and Forgetting in Early Bronze Age Mortuary Practices on the Southeastern Dead Sea Plain, Jordan." In *Performing Death: Social Analyses of Funerary Traditions in the Ancient Near East and Mediterranean*, edited by N. Laneri, 109–40. Chicago: Oriental Institute of the University of Chicago.

Childe, V. Gordon. 1945. "Directional Changes in Funerary Practices during 50,000 Years." *Man* 45 (4): 13–9. http://dx.doi.org/10.2307/2793007.

Childe, V. Gordon. [1944] 1971. *Progress and Archaeology*. Reprint. Westport, CT: Greenwood Press.

Cohen, Andrew C. 2005. *Death Rituals, Ideology, and the Development of Early Mesopotamian Kingship: Toward a New Understanding of Iraq's Royal Cemetery of Ur*. Leiden: Brill.

Connerton, Paul. 1989. *How Societies Remember*. Cambridge: Cambridge University Press.

Croucher, Karina. 2005. "Queerying Near Eastern Archaeology." *World Archaeology* 37 (4): 610–20. http://dx.doi.org/10.1080/00438240500418664.

Croucher, Karina. 2012. *Death and Dying in the Neolithic Near East*. Oxford: Oxford University Press.

David, Nicholas. 1992. "The Archaeology of Ideology: Mortuary Practices in the Central Mandara Highlands, Northern Cameroon." In *An African Commitment: Papers in Honour of Peter Lewis Shinnie*, edited by J. Sterner and N. David, 181–210. Calgary: University of Calgary.

Delougaz, Pinhas, Harold D. Hill, and Seton Lloyd, eds. 1967. *Private Houses and Graves in the Diyala Region*. Chicago: University of Chicago Press.

Duday, Henri. 2006. "L'archéothanatologie ou l'archéologie de la mort (Archaeo-thanatology or the Archaeology of Death)." In *Social Archaeology of Funerary Remains*, edited by R. Gowland and C. J. Knüsel, 30–56. Oxford: Oxbow Books.

Dupras, Tosha L., Henry P. Schwarcz, and Scott I. Fairgrieve. 2001. "Infant Feeding and Weaning Practices in Roman Egypt." *American Journal of Physical Anthropology* 115 (3): 204–12. http://dx.doi.org/10.1002/ajpa.1075.

Erll, Astrid, and Ansgar Nünning. eds. 2008. *Cultural Memory Studies: An International and Interdisciplinary Handbook*. Berlin: Walter de Gruyter.

Gillespie, Susan D. 2001. "Personhood, Agency, and Mortuary Ritual: A Case Study from the Ancient Maya." *Journal of Anthropological Archaeology* 20 (1): 73–112. http://dx.doi.org/10.1006/jaar.2000.0369.

Glencross, Bonnie, and Sabrina C. Agarwal. 2011. "An Investigation of Cortical Bone Loss and Fracture Patterns in the Neolithic Community of Çatalhöyük, Turkey Using Metacarpal Radiogrammetry." *Journal of Archaeological Science* 38 (3): 513–21. http://dx.doi.org/10.1016/j.jas.2010.10.004.

Goffinet, M. 1982. "Les Tombes." In *Meskéné-Emar: Dix ans de travaux 1972–1982*, edited by D. Beyer, 137–39. Paris: Éditions Recherche sur les Civilisations.

Goldstein, Lynne. 2006. "Mortuary Analysis and Bioarchaeology." In *Bioarchaeology: The Contextual Analysis of Human Remains*, edited by J. E. Buikstra and L. A. Beck, 375–87. Burlington, MA: Elsevier.

Gonen, Rivka. 1992. *Burial Patterns and Cultural Diversity in Late Bronze Age Canaan*. Winona Lake, IN: Eisenbrauns.

Goodman, Alan H., and Thomas L. Leatherman, eds. 1998. *Building a New Biocultural Synthesis: Political-Economic Perspectives on Human Biology*. Ann Arbor: University of Michigan Press.

Gregoricka, Lesley A., and Susan G. Sheridan. 2012. "Food for Thought: Isotopic Evidence for Dietary and Weaning Practices in a Byzantine Urban Monastery in Jerusalem." In *Bioarchaeology and Behavior: The People of the Ancient Near East*, edited by M. A. Perry, 138–64. Gainesville: University Press of Florida. http://dx.doi.org/10.5744/florida/9780813042299.003.0007.

Haas, Volkert. 1995. "Death and the Afterlife in Hittite Thought." In *Civilizations of the Ancient Near East*, edited by J. M. Sasson, 2021–30. Peabody, MA: Hendrickson.

Halbwachs, Maurice. 1992. *On Collective Memory*, edited and translated by Lewis A. Coser. Chicago: University of Chicago Press.

Hodder, Ian. 1982. *Symbols in Action*. Cambridge: Cambridge University Press.

Hodder, Ian, ed. 2005. *Inhabiting Çatalhöyük: Reports from the 1995–99 Seasons*. Cambridge: McDonald Institute for Archaeological Research/British Institute of Archaeology at Ankara.

Jean-Marie, Marylou, ed. 1999. *Tombes et nécropoles de Mari*. Beirut: Institut Français d'Archéologie du Proche-Orient.

Joffe, Alexander H. 2003. "Slouching Toward Beersheva: Chalcolithic Mortuary Practices in Local and Regional Context." In *The Near East in the Southwest: Essays in Honor of William G. Dever*, edited by B. A. Nakhai, 45–68. Boston: American Schools of Oriental Research.

Jones, Andrew. 2007. *Memory and Material Culture*. Cambridge: Cambridge University Press. http://dx.doi.org/10.1017/CBO9780511619229.

Joyce, Rosemary A. 2001. "Burying the Dead at Tlatilco: Social Memory and Social Identities." In *Social Memory, Identity, and Death: Anthropological Perspectives on Mortuary Rituals*, edited by M. S. Chesson, 12–26. Arlington, VA: American Anthropological Association. http://dx.doi.org/10.1525/ap3a.2001.10.1.12.

Keith, Arthur. 1934. "Report on Human Remains." In *Ur Excavations. Vol. 2: The Royal Cemetery*, edited by C. L. Woolley, 400–409. London: Publications of the Joint Expedition of the British Museum and of the Museum of the University of Pennsylvania to Mesopotamia.

Keswani, Priscilla. 2004. *Mortuary Ritual and Society in Bronze Age Cyprus*. London: Equinox Publishing Ltd.

Keswani, Priscilla. 2005. "Death, Prestige, and Copper in Bronze Age Cyprus." *American Journal of Archaeology* 109:341–401.

Knudson, Kelly J., and Christopher M. Stojanowski, eds. 2009. *Bioarchaeology and Identity in the Americas*. Gainesville: University Press of Florida.

Kramer, Samuel Noah. 1967. "The Death of Ur-Nammu and His Descent to the Netherworld." *Journal of Cuneiform Studies* 21:104–22. http://dx.doi.org/10.2307/1359365.

Krogman, Wilton Marion. 1949. "Ancient Cranial Types at Chatal Hüyük and Tell al-Judaidah, Syria, from the Late Fifth Millennium B. C. to the Mid-Seventh Century A. D." *Türk Tarih Kurumu Belleten* [*Belleten (Türk Tarih Kurumu)*] 13 (51): 407–79.

Kuijt, Ian. 2008. "The Regeneration of Life: Neolithic Structures of Symbolic Remembering and Forgetting." *Current Anthropology* 49 (2): 171–97. http://dx.doi.org/10.1086/526097.

Kulemann-Ossen, Sabina, and Mirko Novák. 2000. "Kûbu und das "Kind im Topf." Zur Symbolik von Topfbestattungen." *Altorientalische Forschungen* 27 (1): 121–31.

Kunter, Manfred. 1984. "Bronzezeitliche Skelettreste aus Mumbaqat, Nordsyrien." *Homo* 35 (3–4): 205–29.

Laneri, Nicola, ed. 2007. *Performing Death: Social Analyses of Funerary Traditions in the Ancient Near East and Mediterranean*. Chicago: Oriental Institute of the University of Chicago.

Larsen, Clark Spencer. 1997. *Bioarchaeology: Interpreting Behavior from the Human Skeleton*. Cambridge: Cambridge University Press. http://dx.doi.org/10.1017 /CBO9780511802676.

Larsen, Clark Spencer. 2001. *Bioarchaeology of Spanish Florida: The Impact of Colonialism*. Gainesville: University Press of Florida.

Larsen, Clark Spencer. 2002. "Bioarchaeology: The Lives and Lifestyles of Past People." *Journal of Archaeological Research* 10 (2): 119–66. http://dx.doi.org/10.1023 /A:1015267705803.

Littleton, Judith. 2007. "The Political Ecology of Health in Bahrain." In *Ancient Health*, edited by M. N. Cohen and G. M. M. Crane-Kramer, 176–89. Gainesville: University Press of Florida.

Littleton, Judith. 2011. "Moving from the Canary in the Coalmine: Modeling Childhood in Bahrain." In *Social Bioarchaeology*, edited by S. C. Agarwal and B. A. Glencross, 361–89. Chichester, England: Wiley-Blackwell. http://dx.doi.org/10 .1002/9781444390537.ch13.

Littleton, Judith, and Bruno Frohlich. 1989. "An Analysis of Dental Pathology and Diet on Historic Bahrain." *Paléorient* 15 (2): 59–75. http://dx.doi.org/10.3406/paleo .1989.4509.

Littleton, Judith, and Bruno Frohlich. 1993. "Fish-Eaters and Farmers: Dental Pathology in the Arabian Gulf." *American Journal of Physical Anthropology* 92 (4): 427–47. http://dx.doi.org/10.1002/ajpa.1330920403.

Lorentz, Kirsi. 2008. "From Life Course to *longue durée:* Headshaping as Gendered Capital?" In *Gender through Time in the Ancient Near East*, edited by D. Bolger, 281–312. Lanham, MD: AltaMira Press.

Mabry, Jonathan B. 2003. "The Birth of the Ancestors: The Meanings of Human Figurines in Near Eastern Neolithic Villages." In *The Near East in the Southwest: Essays in Honor of William G. Dever*, edited by B. A. Nakhai, 85–116. Boston: American Schools of Oriental Research.

Maeir, Aren M. 2004. *Bronze and Iron Age Tombs at Tel Gezer, Israel*. Oxford: Archaeopress.

Malinowski, Bronislaw. 1948. *Magic, Science and Religion and Other Essays*. Glencoe, IL: Free Press.

Marchetti, Nicolò. 2000. "Clay Figurines of the Middle Bronze Age from Northern Inner Syria: Chronology, Symbolic Meaning and Historical Relations." In *Proceedings of the First International Congress on the Archaeology of the Ancient Near East, Rome, May 18th–23rd 1998*, edited by P. Matthiae, A. Enea, L. Peyronel, and F. Pinnock, 839–868. vol. 2. Rome: Dipartimento di Scienze Storiche, Archeologiche e Antropologiche dell'Antichità.

Martin, Debra L., and Daniel T. Potts. 2012. "Lesley: A Unique Bronze Age Individual from Southeastern Arabia." In *The Bioarchaeology of Individuals*, edited by A. L. W. Stodder and A. M. Palkovich, 113–26. Gainesville: University Press of Florida.

Matthiae, Paolo. 1979. "Princely Cemetery and Ancestors Cult at Ebla during Middle Bronze II: A Proposal of Interpretation." *Ugarit-Forschungen* 11:563–9.

Meskell, Lynn. 1999. *Archaeologies of Social Life: Age, Sex, Class et cetera in Ancient Egypt*. Oxford: Blackwell Publishers.

Meskell, Lynn. 2001. "The Egyptian Ways of Death." In *Social Memory, Identity, and Death: Anthropological Perspectives on Mortuary Rituals*, edited by M. S. Chesson, 27–40. Arlington, VA: American Anthropological Association.

Meskell, Lynn. 2004. *Object Worlds in Ancient Egypt: Material Biographies Past and Present*. Oxford: Berg.

Meskell, Lynn M., and Rosemary A. Joyce. 2003. *Embodied Lives: Figuring Ancient Maya and Egyptian Experience*. London: Routledge.

Metcalf, Peter, and Richard Huntington. 1991. *Celebrations of Death: The Anthropology of Mortuary Ritual*. Cambridge: Cambridge University Press.

Mills, Barbara J., and William H. Walker. 2008. *Memory Work: Archaeologies of Material Practices*. Santa Fe: School of Advanced Research.

Molleson, Theya. 1994. "The Eloquent Bones of Abu Hureyra." *Scientific American* 271 (2): 70–75. http://dx.doi.org/10.1038/scientificamerican0894-70.

Molleson, Theya, and Dawn Hodgson. 1993. "A Cart Driver from Ur." *Archaeozoologia* 6 (11): 93–106.

Molleson, Theya, and Dawn Hodgson. 2003. "The Human Remains from Woolley's Excavations at Ur." *Iraq* 65:91–129.

Molleson, Theya, Karen Jones, and Stephen Jones. 1993. "Dietary Change and the Effects of Food Preparation on Microwear Patterns in the Late Neolithic of Abu Hureyra, Northern Syria." *Journal of Human Evolution* 24 (6): 455–68. http://dx.doi.org/10.1006/jhev.1993.1031.

Morris, Ellen F. 2007. "Sacrifice for the State: First Dynasty Royal Funerals and the Rites at Macramallah's Rectangle." In *Performing Death: Social Analyses of Funerary Traditions in the Ancient Near East and Mediterranean*, edited by N. Laneri, 15–37. Chicago: Oriental Institute of the University of Chicago.

Morris, Ian. 1992. *Death-Ritual and Social Structure in Classical Antiquity*. Cambridge: Cambridge University Press. http://dx.doi.org/10.1017/CBO9780511611728.

Nora, Pierre. 1989. "Between Memory and History: Les Lieux de Mémoire." *Representations* 26 (1): 7–24. http://dx.doi.org/10.1525/rep.1989.26.1.99p0274v.

Özbek, Metin. 2005. "Skeletal Pathology of a High-Ranking Official from Thrace (Turkey, Last Quarter of the 4th Century BC)." *International Journal of Osteoarchaeology* 15 (3): 216–25. http://dx.doi.org/10.1002/oa.777.

Olick, Jeffrey K., Verde Vinitzky-Seroussi, and Daniel Levy, eds. 2011. *The Collective Memory Reader.* New York: Oxford University Press.

Parker Pearson, Mike. 1999. *The Archaeology of Death and Burial.* College Station: Texas A & M University Press.

Peltenburg, Edgar. 1999. "The Living and the Ancestors: Early Bronze Age Mortuary Practices at Jerablus Tahtani." In *Archaeology of the Upper Syrian Euphrates: The Tishrin Dam Area*, edited by G. del Olmo Lete, and J.-L. Montero Fenollós, 427–42. Aula Orientalis-Supplementa. Barcelona: Editorial AUSA.

Perry, Megan A. 2005. "Redefining Childhood through Bioarchaeology: Toward an Archaeological and Biological Understanding of Children in Antiquity." In *Children in Action: Perspectives on the Archaeology of Childhood*, edited by J. E. Baxter, 89–111. Arlington, VA: American Anthropological Association. http://dx.doi.org/10.1525/ap3a.2005.15.89.

Perry, Megan A., ed. 2012. *Bioarchaeology and Behavior: The People of the Ancient Near East.* Gainesville: University Press of Florida. http://dx.doi.org/10.5744/florida/9780813042299.001.0001.

Peterson, Jane. 2002. *Sexual Revolutions: Gender and Labor at the Dawn of Agriculture.* Walnut Creek, CA: AltaMira Press.

Peterson, Jane. 2010. "Domesticating Gender: Neolithic Patterns from the Southern Levant." *Journal of Anthropological Archaeology* 29 (3): 249–64. http://dx.doi.org/10.1016/j.jaa.2010.03.002.

Pfälzner, Peter, Herbert Niehr, Ernst Pernicka, and Anne Wissing. 2012. *(Re-) Constructing Funerary Rituals in the Ancient Near East.* Wiesbaden: Harrassowitz.

Pilloud, Marin A., and Clark Spencer Larsen. 2011. "'Official' and 'Practical' Kin: Inferring Social and Community Structure from Dental Phenotype at Neolithic Çatalhöyük, Turkey." *American Journal of Physical Anthropology* 145 (4): 519–30. http://dx.doi.org/10.1002/ajpa.21520.

Pitard, Wayne T. 1996. "Care of the Dead at Emar." In *Emar: The History, Religion, and Culture of a Syrian Town in the Late Bronze Age*, edited by M. W. Chavalas, 123–40. Bethesda, MD: CDL Press.

Pollock, Susan. 1991. "Women in a Men's World: Images of Sumerian Women." In *Engendering Archaeology: Women and Prehistory*, edited by J. M. Gero and M. W. Conkey, 366–87. Oxford: Blackwell.

Pollock, Susan. 2007. "Death of a Household." In *Performing Death: Social Analyses of Funerary Traditions in the Ancient Near East and Mediterranean*, edited by N. Laneri, 209–22. Chicago: The Oriental Institute of the University of Chicago.

Pollock, Susan. 2011. "Making a Difference: Mortuary Practices in Halaf Times." In *Breathing New Life into the Evidence of Death: Contemporary Approaches to Bioarchaeology*, edited by A. Baadsgaard, A. T. Boutin, and J. E. Buikstra, 29–53. Santa Fe: School for Advanced Research Press.

Porter, Anne. 2002. "The Dynamics of Death: Ancestors, Pastoralism, and the Origins of a Third-Millennium City in Syria." *Bulletin of the American Schools of Oriental Research* 325: 1–36. http://dx.doi.org/10.2307/1357712.

Pruss, Alexander, and Mirko Novák. 2000. "Terrakotten und Beinidole in sepulkralen Kontexten." *Altorientalische Forschungen* 27 (1): 184–95.

Radstone, Susannah, and Bill Schwarz, eds. 2010. *Memory: Histories, Theories, Debates*. Bronx: Fordham University Press.

Rehm, Ellen. 2003. *Waffengräber im Alten Orient*. Oxford: Archaeopress.

Richards, Janet. 2005. *Society and Death in Ancient Egypt: Mortuary Landscapes of the Middle Kingdom*. Cambridge: Cambridge University Press.

Richards, M. P., J. A. Pearson, T. I. Molleson, N. Russell, and L. Martin. 2003. "Stable Isotope Evidence of Diet at Neolithic Çatalhöyük, Turkey." *Journal of Archaeological Science* 30 (1): 67–76. http://dx.doi.org/10.1006/jasc.2001.0825.

Rissman, Paul. 1988. "Public Displays and Private Values: A Guide to Buried Wealth in Harappan Archaeology." *World Archaeology* 20 (2): 209–28. http://dx.doi.org/10.1080/00438243.1988.9980068.

Robben, Antonius C.G.M., ed. 2005. *Death, Mourning, and Burial: A Cross-Cultural Reader*. Chichester, England: Wiley-Blackwell.

Salles, Jean-François. 1995. "Rituel mortuaire et ritual social à Ras Shamra/Ougarit." In *The Archaeology of Death in the Ancient Near East*, edited by S. Campbell and A. Green, 171–84. Oxford: Oxbow Books.

Saul, Frank P., and Julie Mather Saul. 1989. "Osteobiography: A Maya Example." In *Reconstruction of Life from the Skeleton*, edited by M. Y. İşcan and K. A. R. Kennedy, 287–302. New York: Alan R. Liss.

Savage, Stephen H. 2000. "The Status of Women in Predynastic Egypt as Revealed through Mortuary Analysis." In *Reading the Body*, edited by A. E. Rautman, 77–92. Philadelphia: University of Pennsylvania Press.

Saxe, Arthur Alan. 1970. *Social Dimensions of Mortuary Practices*. PhD diss., Department of Anthropology, University of Michigan.

Schmidt, Brian B. 1994. *Israel's Beneficent Dead: Ancestor Cult and Necromancy in Ancient Israelite Religion and Tradition*. Winona Lake, IN: Eisenbrauns.

Schmidt, Brian B. 1996. "The Gods and the Dead of the Domestic Cult at Emar: A Reassessment." In *Emar: The History, Religion, and Culture of a Syrian Town in the Late Bronze Age*, edited by Mark W. Chavalas, 141–63. Bethesda, MD: CDL Press.

Schwartz, Glenn M. 2007. "Status, Ideology, and Memory in Third-Millennium Syria: "Royal" Tombs at Umm el-Marra." In *Performing Death: Social Analyses of Funerary Traditions in the Ancient Near East and Mediterranean*, edited by N. Laneri, 39–68. Chicago: Oriental Institute of the University of Chicago.

Scurlock, Jo Ann. 1995. "Death and the Afterlife in Ancient Mesopotamian Thought." In *Civilizations of the Ancient Near East*, edited by J. M. Sasson, 1883–93. Peabody, MA: Hendrickson.

Shanks, Michael, and Christopher Tilley. 1982. "Ideology, Symbolic Power and Ritual Communication: A Reinterpretation of Neolithic Mortuary Practices." In *Symbolic and Structural Archaeology*, edited by I. Hodder, 129–54. Cambridge: Cambridge University Press. http://dx.doi.org/10.1017/CBO9780511558252.013.

Sheridan, Susan G. 1999. "'New Life the Dead Receive': The Relationship between Human Remains and the Cultural Record for Byzantine St. Stephen's." *Revue Biblique* 106 (4): 574–611.

Smith, Patricia, and Liora K. Horwitz. 2007. "Ancestors and Inheritors: A Bioanthropological Perspective on the Transition to Agropastoralism in the Southern Levant." In *Ancient Health*, edited by M. N. Cohen and G. M. M. Crane-Kramer. 207–22. Gainesville: University Press of Florida.

Steckel, Richard H., and Jerome C. Rose, eds. 2002. *The Backbone of History: Health and Nutrition in the Western Hemisphere*. Cambridge: Cambridge University Press. http://dx.doi.org/10.1017/CBO9780511549953.

Stodder, Ann L. W., and Ann M. Palkovich, eds. 2012. *The Bioarchaeology of Individuals*. Gainesville: University Press of Florida. http://dx.doi.org/10.5744/florida/9780813038070.001.0001.

Tarlow, Sarah. 1999. *Bereavement and Commemoration: An Archaeology of Mortality*. Oxford: Blackwell Publishers.

Thrane, Henrik. 1978. *Sukas IV: A Middle Bronze Age Collective Grave on Tall Sukas*. Copenhagen: Det Kongelige Danske Videnskabernes Selskab Historisk-filosofiske Skrifter.

van der Toorn, Karel. 1994. "Gods and Ancestors at Emar and Nuzi." *Zeitschrift für Assyriologie* 84:38–59.

van der Toorn, Karel. 1996. *Family Religion in Babylonia, Syria and Israel: Continuity and Change in the Forms of Religious Life*. Leiden: Brill.

Torres-Rouff, Christina, and William J. Pestle. 2012. "An Exploration of Infant Burial Practices at the Site of Kish, Iraq." In *Bioarchaeology and Behavior: The People of the Ancient Near East*, edited by M. A. Perry, 35–59. Gainesville: University Press of Florida. http://dx.doi.org/10.5744/florida/9780813042299.003.0003.

Tung, Tiffiny A. 2012. *Violence, Ritual, and the Wari Empire: A Social Bioarchaeology of Imperialism in the Ancient Andes*. Gainesville: University Press of Florida. http://dx.doi.org/10.5744/florida/9780813037677.001.0001.

Van Dyke, Ruth M., and Susan E. Alcock, eds. 2003. *Archaeologies of Memory*. Malden, MA: Blackwell. http://dx.doi.org/10.1002/9780470774304.

Walker, Phillip L. 2001. "A Bioarchaeological Perspective on the History of Violence." *Annual Review of Anthropology* 30 (1): 573–96. http://dx.doi.org/10.1146/annurev.anthro.30.1.573.

Williams, Howard, ed. 2003. *Archaeologies of Remembrance: Death and Memory in Past Societies*. Plenum, New York: Kluwer Academic. http://dx.doi.org/10.1007/978-1-4419-9222-2.

Woolley, C. Leonard. 1934. *Ur Excavations. Volume II: The Royal Cemetery*. London: Publications of the Joint Expedition of the British Museum and of the Museum of the University of Pennsylvania to Mesopotamia.

Woolley, C. Leonard. 1937. *Digging up the Past*. Harmondsworth, England: Penguin Books.

Xella, Paolo. 1995. "Death and the Afterlife in Canaanite and Hebrew Thought." In *Civilizations of the Ancient Near East*, edited by J. M. Sasson, 2059–70. Peabody, MA: Hendrickson.

Zuckerman, Molly K., and George J. Armelagos. 2011. "The Origins of Biocultural Dimensions in Bioarchaeology." In *Social Bioarchaeology*, edited by S. C. Agarwal and B. A. Glencross, 15–43. Chichester, England: Wiley-Blackwell. http://dx.doi.org/10.1002/9781444390537.ch2.

2

Burying Things

Practices of Cultural Disposal at Late Neolithic Domuztepe, Southeast Turkey

Stuart Campbell, Sarah Whitcher Kansa, Rachel Bichener, and Hannah Lau

ABSTRACT

Human burial is generally treated as a discrete category of behavior, something that is distinctive and unique. While this may be partially true in contemporary Western society, it was not necessarily the case in the past. This chapter seeks to link patterns of human burial with a wider pattern of burial and structured disposal of things, drawing particularly on the archaeological record of late Neolithic Domuztepe in southeast Turkey. Parallels can be observed in the way in which some animal remains were disposed of, particularly striking with dogs and feasting debris, as well as a broader practice of the deliberate burial of certain types of objects. This suggests a new view, both of the meanings attached to the things buried and of the practice of burial itself, which can in turn inform our understanding of the treatment of human remains in this time period and the close ties of commemoration and remembering/forgetting with physical acts of burial. Central to these meanings may be processes through which attachment to place was defined and links to past events were embedded in particular locations within the settlement.

INTRODUCTION

While burial is often assumed to be an action particularly related to the disposal of the human dead, it is not only human bodies that can be buried, and not all bodies need end as a simple burial in the ground. Instead burial can be a much more complex process, involving a series of actions, agents, objects, and contexts. Through a consideration of things that may be

DOI: 10.5876/9781607323295.c002

buried, the ways in which burial can take place and sometimes the way in which material is not buried, we shed some light on the extent to which burial in the late Neolithic of the Near East can be considered as a set of interrelated practices. The treatment and burial of human remains certainly relate to ways in which the dead may have been remembered and commemorated (and forgotten and transformed), but they should be understood within a wider set of behaviors through which material culture might be used in the maintenance of cultural memory.

This chapter focuses on northern Mesopotamia; most of the examples are drawn from the first half of the sixth millennium calibrated (cal.) BCE,[1] a period generally referred to as the Halaf. There is a deliberate concentration on material from the site of Domuztepe in southeaste Turkey (Figure 2.1). The richness of this material and our familiarity with it allow us to look at related practices within a more specific time frame and from a single geographical location. However, many of the patterns we identify were typical of a much wider geographical area, and elements can be recognized throughout the seventh and sixth millennia cal. BCE. Although the specific cultural practices would have diverged in different contexts, we believe that they drew on similar motivations and related understandings of the world.

Although archaeological practice has almost always given human remains a distinctive status, the recognition that acts of deposition, including burial, belong within a wider set of behaviors has a long history. Even in 1972, Schiffer argued that "all remains in a site are refuse when uncovered in archaeological context," including elements deriving from ritual activities (Schiffer 1972:163). A series of studies carried out within British prehistory has drawn on the notion of structured deposition (Richards and Thomas 1984), emphasizing the range of practices through which even the deposition of mundane material might impose meaning on places. Thus, refuse from feasting might be intentionally incorporated into a meaningful landscape (McOmish 1996), anchoring particular activities to a particular place. This is not to deny that burial of culturally generated material may also have utilitarian motivation, and this applies to the burial of human remains as well as more general refuse.

Processes and meaning of deposition ought to be a concern of Near Eastern archaeology, simply because so many sites take the form of classic tells and tepes that are produced through successive phases of deposition. However, we agree with the recent statement that "the social meanings of stratigraphy-making tend not to be critically probed or extensively discussed" (McAnany and Hodder 2009:2). The burial of culture material, especially burial practices that incorporate human remains, is an act embedded in a location and situated

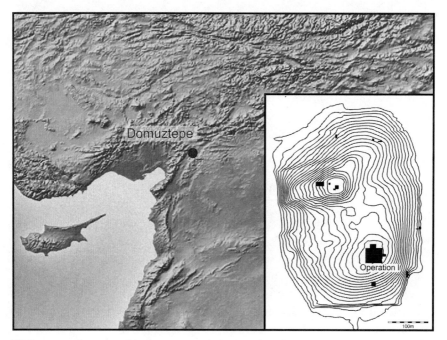

FIGURE 2.1. *Location of Domuztepe, with site plan (inset).*

within a wider practice that is constantly covering (and at times uncovering) phases of human activity (Chapman 1997; Steadman 2005). Most of the burials discussed here do not simply concern the excavation of a hole and its subsequent infilling. Instead, burial is a means of incorporating material from the present into other cultural remains from the past. Even the act of digging a pit disturbs earlier deposits. Burial practices of all sorts therefore intersect with other cultural practices, many of which have similar ambiguity between utilitarian and symbolic elements and often relate to issues of time, the past, locality and identity (Campbell 2012).

The link between human burials and wider patterns of depositional activity has been highlighted elsewhere. Shell mounds in the San Francisco Bay area have been seen as deliberate cultural features, where debris from large-scale feasting was used to create prominent middens, whose significance was then enhanced by the burial of both humans and sacred birds (Luby and Gruber 1999). Cheryl Claassen has recently observed similar patterns of human and dog burials associated with Archaic freshwater shell mounds in the Ohio River valley (Claassen 2010). Torres Strait Islanders produced large-scale bone and shell mounds, the refuse from ceremonial feasting accumulated over long time periods providing a relationship with both the recent and distant past. Associated human and dog teeth do not seem to relate to food remains, but may represent "a form of referencing that helped connect this deposit to various families and households" (McNiven 2013:573). Associations between the burial of feasting refuse and human remains can also been seen in the southern Levant during the Pre-Pottery Neolithic B period at Kfar HaHoresh (Goring-Morris and Horwitz 2007; Horwitz and Goring-Morris 2004).

THE DISPOSAL OF HUMAN REMAINS IN LATE NEOLITHIC NORTHERN MESOPOTAMIA

There is a wide variety of funerary practices known from the seventh and early sixth millennia cal. BCE in northern Mesopotamia (Akkermans 1989; Campbell 1992; Campbell 2007–8; Hole 1989; Pollock 2011). Simple inhumations do occur, usually crouched and often accompanied by a limited range of grave goods. Some of these occur within settlements, but unlike the earlier Neolithic, they are not usually beneath the floors of houses and were often in open areas within the settlement. Recent excavations at Tell el-Kerkh (Tsuneki 2010; Tsuneki 2011) and Tell Sabi Abyad (Akkermans 2008) have demonstrated the presence of sizable cemeteries during the late Ceramic Neolithic in this region, and the burials on the abandoned mound of Yarim Tepe I (Merpert and Munchaev 1973:108) suggest that they may be an under-recognized feature of the Halaf period as well.

However, there is a wide range of other funerary practices attested from both the Halaf and in the preceding millennium. Individual interments are most common, but group burials are also known, with bodies in a range of positions. Inhumation dominates but cremation also occurs. In some instances, bodies are fully or partially disarticulated, and there are examples of the burial of detached skulls. Grave goods may or may not accompany human remains. Burials may occur within settlements, in abandoned areas of settlements, and outside settlements. Human remains were not always buried; for example, they have been found in architectural contexts at Bouqras (Merrett and Meiklejohn 2007) and Tell Sabi Abyad (Verhoeven 2000). The frequent occurrence of fragmentary human remains documented at Fıstıklı Höyük (Pollock 2011:50) and Sabi Abyad (Aten 1996) may result from the disturbance of earlier burials (Aten 1996:118), but we agree with Susan Pollock (2011:50–51) that they often derive from activities carried out on the dead body prior to, or as an alternative to, burial. Two recent discussions of Halaf burial practices have suggested that this diversity may actually be a key characteristic (Campbell 2007–8; Pollock 2011). Pollock (2011:47) has drawn attention to the potential for improvisation within individual acts of burial and the idea that "ritual specialists might use the opportunities for creative performance to deliberately enhance the distinctiveness of their own practice in comparison to those of other communities, thereby reinforcing their own authority."

In this wider cultural setting, it is, therefore, not surprising that Domuztepe also shows a diversity of funerary practice. The most striking example is the funerary activity that took place in and around the so-called Death Pit, and that shows several different treatments of human remains associated with a single context. This complex burial deposit was created over a short timeframe, around 5575 cal. BCE. Portions of a minimum of thirty-five disarticulated individuals were buried in the pit itself, in phases 5a and 6 (Gauld et al. 2012). This was, however, not a simple burial in the sense of being related primarily to the disposal of the bodies. The remains had been highly processed, with extensive, deliberate disarticulation and fragmentation taking place prior to deposition. Patterned blows to the skull, thermal alteration, and human tooth marks suggest that these activities involved killing or sacrifice and some form of cannibalism (Kansa et al. 2009a). Undoubtedly this processing was an important focus through which identities and relationships might be strengthened or severed. It is possible to construct a range of interpretations for the disarticulation and mixing of body parts, ranging from a transformation of the individual dead into more generalized ancestors, to a deliberate destruction of identities, possibly even of a social group.

The Death Pit, however, was more complex than a simple hole in the ground for the disposal of human remains (Figure 2.2). Its earliest phase consists of a complex subdeposit that included large quantities of animal bones (phase 1). The inclusion of cattle bones, in particular, suggests feasting (see below) and points to the importance of the wider rituals through which the Death Pit gained its meaning. The Death Pit also incorporated large quantities of artifacts, particularly in phases 5a and 5b. These included sherds, lithics, stamp seals, and bone tools, which do not seem to be conventional grave goods (Campbell and Healey 2011; Fletcher and Campbell forthcoming). It is far from clear that these items are simply coincidental, incorporated into the Death Pit along with a more general soil matrix. The whole of the Death Pit was finally covered by a thick layer of ash, transported from a fire that took place elsewhere (phase 7), again attesting to the importance of a diverse range of rituals behind the "funerary" deposit itself. Intentional burial of the human dead is certainly part of the story of the Death Pit, but it was only one part.

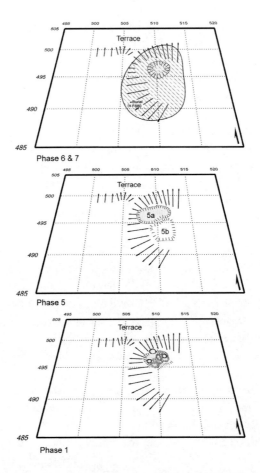

Phase 6 & 7

Phase 5

Phase 1

Phase 1: A scoop was made into the southern face of a terrace. Three or four shallow pits were dug into the base of resulting hollow and each filled with large quantities of articulating animal bones, stones, and pot sherds (shaded).
Phase 2: More material was placed over the pits in the bottom of the larger hollow.
Phase 3: The hollow was then flooded and allowed to dry out, leaving a thick deposit of silt. This may have happened twice.
Phase 4: A small pit was probably cut into the silt lenses and filled with animal bones.
Phase 5a: In the northern part of the Death Pit, animal and human bones, especially the latter, were tightly compacted within a largely pisé-like matrix (shaded). The top of this hard-packed deposit was modeled to create a shallow raised hollow.
Phase 5b: At the same time in the southern part of the Death Pit, more material was deposited, possibly to maintain a level with the hollow created by Phase 5a. This deposit contained abundant animal bones but few human remains.
Phase 6: Further bones, roughly equal proportions of humans and animals, were placed in the base of the raised hollow (shaded).
Phase 7: The entire area of the Death Pit was covered by a thick layer of ash, which probably lay over an area of 10–15m in diameter (hatched). Either at the same time as the ash was deposited or very shortly before the body of a child was placed on the southern edge of the Death Pit.

FIGURE 2.2. *Summary of the main phases in the Death Pit, Domuztepe.*

After the primary material was deposited in the Death Pit, it remained a focus of later activity. In part, this is visible in the human remains that were deposited around it, either laid on the surface or buried in shallow pits. These included one inhumation of an adult female laid on its back with tightly flexed legs, and two skulls as well as fragments of skulls, finger bones, and pieces of jaw. However, there was also a pig skull and other nonhuman bones along with a series of ash-filled pits. Other deliberately deposited remains may have been present that we failed to distinguish during excavation from the wider background of artifacts and ecofacts included in the site matrix.

These post–Death Pit deposits emphasize that burial can be a matter of degree. As well as material that was simply placed on the surface and remained visible, some material was probably only covered by a thin layer of soil rather than being deeply buried. The location of the inhumation, in particular, seems to have remained visible with the body perhaps only super-ficially obscured. The disturbed soil would have been obvious and the grave may have been detectable by other senses; smell in particular may have been significant as the body decomposed (Croucher and Campbell 2009). The site would also have required active monitoring to stop it being disturbed by animals. The shallow covering of soil over the corpse may have been because burial was not intended to be the end of interaction between the living and the dead. Four small pits were subsequently dug in the region of the legs. One of them allowed a femur to be removed and replaced after having been rotated through 180 degrees.

The deposition of fragmentary remains suggests that the remainder of the original whole must have been retained or deposited elsewhere. This may have created important links to other locations (possibly even other Death Pits) or social groups on site (cf. Chapman 2000). While the fragments of human bodies may be most striking, the fragmented nonhuman remains and artifacts may have been equally important, either in defining specific relationships or as indicators of more complex ritual actions that may not have been focused primarily on funerary or ancestral activities at all.

The creation of the Death Pit certainly transformed the use of space in its vicinity. It was marked by two large posts, and subsequently this part of the site changed from being a zone of domestic buildings to one in which there is little evidence of activity for perhaps seventy to eighty years. In changing the nature of the place in which it was situated and even the resonances of movement around the settlement, memories would have been created that had a powerful reconfiguring influence on the living population (Atakuman Eissenstat 2004; Campbell 2007–8). This, however, was not simply the product of the activities associated with the death of people. It was an association created by a much wider set of events, rituals, objects, and artifacts.

Beyond the Death Pit, there are a number of other contexts in which human remains occur at Domuztepe. There is one possible cluster of inhumations in pits. However, this had been truncated by a later cut, and only two inhumations were preserved to any extent. Both were crouched with heads to the east, and neither was accompanied by grave goods. Another crouched inhumation of a female adult was also found within the Red Terrace (see "The Ditch in the Red Terrace"), although this does not seem to have been in a cut; instead, it was placed on the surface of the terrace and covered by a thin layer of red soil. Another poorly preserved burial of a subadult was found within an earlier phase of the terrace and, elsewhere, a damaged infant burial was excavated under the base of a wall. It seems clear that individual burial of humans within the settlement was an exception. Individual fragments of human bone also regularly occur in more general deposits. The rarity of formal graves at the site strongly suggests that these remains do not simply derive from disturbed burials. These fragmentary remains include occasional complete or near complete skulls and fragments of skulls and jaw bones, as well as other body sections. Occasionally, there are indications of possible curation of human remains. In two cases associated with the Death Pit, fragments of human bone were found within pots, although those pots had ultimately been buried themselves.

These fragmentary remains may have provided links between the living community and buried deposits such as the Death Pit. Parts of bodies may have been buried while other parts were retained either for later disposal or for curation among the living. Equally, the appearance of these fragments in what was excavated as "general deposits" may suggest that that term is misleading. The term is used here to refer to a wide range of deposits that represent primary or secondary refuse, wall collapse, and erosion products. While these might seem to be the routine, meaningless material of site formation, accumulating through random processes, the occurrence of fragmented human remains should alert us to the possibility that these deposits may have carried particular significance and meaning. Site formation was itself a cultural practice.

BURIAL OF DOGS

Dog remains in association with buried human bones are often assumed to have belonged to the buried people, but this assumption is simplistic (Morey 2006) and the dog remains at Domuztepe are a case in point. The majority of the domestic dog specimens identified at Domuztepe come from the Death Pit, where they make up just under 2 percent of the faunal assemblage. Here, dog remains come from all parts of the skeleton, the most complete of which included one almost-complete skull and a complete humerus. Five mandibles and two maxillae also came from the pit and its environs, as well as four paws and a tail from one animal, which probably came from a pelt (Kansa et al. 2009a). The Death Pit contained partial remains of at least six dogs, and evidence for butchery or processing was rare (Bichener in prep).

The initial deposition of dog remains was of the dog pelt, placed into one of the shallow hollows made in the base of the larger pit during phase 1 of the Death Pit (Kansa et al. 2009a). The pelt itself was probably originally wrapped around something, which is no longer preserved. There are several possible interpretations: it could have represented specifically "dog remains," in the sense of fragmented parts of a dead dog; it could have been a specific piece of material culture, such as clothing; alternatively, it could also have served to bestow a doglike identity on the entity around which it was wrapped. In several respects this is rather similar to the use of fragmentary human remains to manipulate identities and create new meanings and links between different events.

Dog remains occur in a different form in phase 5a of the Death Pit. Significantly, this is the phase with the greatest concentration of fragmentary human remains. It also contained the majority of the dog bones from the Death Pit, and indeed the majority of dog bones from the site as a whole. There were three dog crania (Figure 2.3), a humerus, and four mandibles. After the sealing of the Death Pit, individual dog bones were placed around its periphery in a way that parallels the distribution of human bone fragments in the same area. Here, dogs are represented by isolated elements: mandibles, limb, and foot bones (Kansa et al. 2009a).

Elsewhere on the site, dog remains are very rare. Together with the coincidence of human and dog remains, this suggests that dogs were not common food animals. This is also suggested by fragmentation patterns more comparable to human bones than those of domestic ungulates (Kansa et al. 2009a). A similar observation has been made at contemporary sites, such as Tell Sabi Abyad (Russell 2010).

Humans and dogs in the Death Pit tend to be represented by the same body parts, chiefly the head and limbs. Even the methods of dispatch (blow to the side of the head) and butchery (beheading and mandible removal) were strikingly similar (Kansa et al. 2009a). Body part selection may be significant. The head carries the most recognizable features of a person or animal and may

FIGURE 2.3. *Dog cranium from phase 5a of the Death Pit, Domuztepe.*

have been selected to either represent individual identity or a specific aspect of a dividual identity (Croucher 2010; Fowler 2004; Strathern 1988). Perhaps the dog pelt was important in a similar way, retaining some aspect of identity or acting with a specific agency.

The placement of dogs in the Death Pit may also carry significance. Dogs are mainly placed among the human remains, perhaps suggesting a protective aspect. The dog elements later placed above and around the Death Pit could also be seen as guarding the remains within the pit or, conversely, protecting those still living from danger from the buried material. Certainly the area of the Death Pit subsequently remained distinct from domestic activities, which may suggest that, despite being in the heart of the settlement, burial alone was not sufficient to achieve a distance between the living and the buried.

There is a rich literature attesting to recurrent concepts of dogs guarding boundary zones. Dogs are seen guarding the boundary between the living and the dead, such as the Greek Cerberus or the Vedic Shyma and Sabala (White 1989). Dogs as protective agents appear in mythologies of the ancient world, including the Mesopotamian goddess of healing, Gula (Edrey 2008), the healing dogs of the Greek Asclepius (Day 1984), and the dogs used in purification and healing rituals by the Hittites (Collins 2002). Dogs could also be associated with more general liminal spaces, such as the animals offered to Hecate in Classical Greece (Bevan 1986) or the model dogs placed under thresholds in later Babylonian houses (West 1995). While we cannot claim that a similar role is demonstrated at Domuztepe, these parallels point to the potential variety and richness in the interpretation of buried deposits. While all the objects in a particular context may have been buried, they may have been attributed to distinct types of symbolism and agency.

BURIAL OF FEASTING REMAINS AND OTHER PROCESSED ANIMAL BONES

Most deposits of animal bones at Domuztepe are consistent with food refuse. Although many of these bones come from midden deposits or from secondary contexts where disposal appears to have been informal, some contexts suggest much more structure in disposal of faunal remains. There has been extensive discussion of the important role that feasting played in prehistoric societies (e.g., Dietler and Hayden 2001; Helwing 2003; Twiss 2008), and where structured deposition has been discussed in other contexts, the remains of food animals often have been found along with human remains. However, teasing out a specific pattern of behavior is more complex.

It is difficult to distinguish the refuse from ritual activities involving food from debris from daily or mundane meals, particularly because the distinction between ritual and mundane is almost always unclear. Every meal involves ritual behaviors and symbolic actions, often referenced and magnified in more formal situations. The challenge lies in distinguishing the symbolic elements of consumption in the archaeological record from the more generalized background of refuse disposal. Thus, and obviously, we must consider not only the food remains but also the nature of the deposit itself. Various criteria mark a deposit as distinctive, where location, context, and modification add symbolic or ritual significance (e.g., Hayden 2001; Helwing 2003). We explore four types of deposit at Domuztepe in order to gain a better understanding of the interplay between food, repeated behaviors, and community participatory events and the way in which they may be represented in the disposal of food remains.

Quotidian Deposits

Faunal remains from mundane, domestic contexts form the basis of our understanding of the quotidian subsistence economy at Domuztepe.[2] We have defined Domuztepe's quotidian faunal assemblage through the analysis of tens of thousands of specimens, most of which are from primary or secondary refuse deposits from across the site (Kansa et al. 2009b). The quotidian assemblage is dominated by the traditional suite of Near Eastern domesticates: sheep, goats, pigs, cattle, and, to a considerably lesser extent, dogs (Table 2.1). Ovicaprids (i.e., sheep and goats) dominate the assemblages, and a focus on older sheep suggests nonintensive wool production (Kansa et al. 2009b:909–10). Pigs constitute approximately 25 percent of the assemblage, and cattle remains vary between 21 percent and 28 percent of identified specimens. Fragmentation of the bones of food taxa suggests full carcass processing, and the presence of all body parts indicates onsite butchery (Kansa et al. 2009b). These data from quotidian deposits establish a baseline of the day-to-day exploitation of animals at Domuztepe against which we compare faunal remains from three extraordinary deposits below. The three deposits demonstrate a diversity of feasting behaviors at Domuztepe. Rather than conforming to a single well-defined "feasting signature," it is the ways that they differ from the quotidian deposits that make them significant.

The Ditch in the Red Terrace

The Red Terrace (Figure 2.4) is a striking feature running east-west across the southern part of Domuztepe, and probably only one of several long, linear boundaries that structured activity within the settlement. It has been excavated over a length of 50 m, although its full length may have been closer to 100 m. In excavation, it was marked by a distinctive strip of red soil, 10–15 m wide, although its exact width was altered at several points during its lifetime (an estimated 500–600 years). It was probably maintained through a series of regular refurbishments, perhaps through annual ceremonies carried out by large numbers of people. The Red Terrace acted as a boundary between activity zones. At times, it marked a limit to groups of domestic structures, while at others it demarcated more open areas. It was also the site of distinctive activities, some involving water-related processes such as clay levigation (Campbell 2012:316) and others probably connected to feasting. In particular, we would highlight the repeated occurrence of large ovens throughout the life of the Red Terrace, sometimes occurring in small groups suggesting cooking at a scale considerably beyond the individual household.

There was a secondary feature running for ca. 25 m on the same east-west alignment along the center of the Red Terrace. This was made up of a series of shallow intercutting pits, repeatedly dug along the same alignment. The composite of all these individual shallow pits is what we have loosely termed the "Ditch." While the terrace as a whole had few finds, the density of archaeological material in these pits points to the deliberate, recurrent disposal of refuse in this area. The practice of repeated small-scale actions aggregating to

TABLE 2.1 Species distribution by context

Taxon	Common Name	Quotidian NISP	Quotidian %	Death Pit NISP	Death Pit %	Ditch NISP	Ditch %	Op III NISP	Op III %
Bos taurus	Cattle	1278	21.2	732	36.7	387	10.5	150	42.6
Ovis aries, Capra hircus	Sheep, Goat	2684	44.5	850	42.6	1485	40.3	115	32.7
Ovis aries	Sheep	210	3.5	68	3.4	385	10.4	6	1.7
Capra hircus	Goat	186	3.1	70	3.5	526	14.3	13	3.7
Sus scrofa	Pig	1529	25.3	204	10.2	833	22.6	63	17.9
Canis familiaris	Dog	16	0.3	34	1.7	0	0.0	0	0.0
Bos taurus cf. *primigenius*	Wild cattle	1	< 0.1	3	0.2	1	< 0.1	0	0.0
Ovis orientalis, Capra aegagrus	Wild sheep, wild goat	1	< 0.1	0	0.0	0	0.0	0	0.0
Ovis orientalis	Wild sheep	3	0.1	0	0.0	2	0.1	0	0.0
Capra aegagrus	Wild goat	0	0.0	1	0.1	1	< 0.1	0	0.0
Gazella sp.	Gazelle	7	0.1	0	0.0	10	0.3	0	0.0
Cervus elaphus	Red deer	5	0.1	1	0.1	0	0.0	2	0.6
Dama dama	Fallow deer	5	0.1	0	0.0	3	0.1	0	0.0
Cervus, Dama	Red deer, fallow deer	29	0.5	5	0.3	32	0.9	0	0.0
Capreolus capreolus	Roe deer	3	0.1	1	0.1	0	0.0	0	0.0
Sus scrofa	Wild boar	11	0.2	0	0.0	1	< 0.1	0	0.0

continued on next page

Table 2.1—continued

Taxon	Common Name	Quotidian NISP	Quotidian %	Death Pit NISP	Death Pit %	Ditch NISP	Ditch %	Op III NISP	Op III %
Equus asinus, Equus hemionus	Wild ass, onager	1	<0.1	0	0.0	1	<0.1	0	0.0
Equus sp.	Equid	1	<0.1	1	0.1	3	0.1	0	0.0
Canis sp.	Canid	5	0.1	5	0.3	2	0.1	1	0.3
Canis sp., *Canis lupus*	Dog, wolf	3	0.1	0	0.0	0	0.0	0	0.0
Canis aureus	Jackal	0	0.0	1	0.1	0	0.0	0	0.0
Martes cf *martes*	Pine marten	1	<0.1	0	0.0	0	0.0	0	0.0
Ursus arctos	Brown bear	5	0.1	2	0.1	3	0.1	0	0.0
Vulpes vulpes	Fox	11	0.2	0	0.0	1	<0.1	0	0.0
Panthera pardus	Leopard	1	<0.1	0	0.0	0	0.0	0	0.0
Lepus spp.	Hare	5	0.1	1	0.1	9	0.2	0	0.0
Castor fiber	Eurasian beaver	1	<0.1	0	0.0	0	0.0	0	0.0
Rodentia	Rodent	6	0.1	2	0.1	0	0.0	1	0.3
Testudines	Tortoise/turtle	4	0.1	0	0.0	0	0.0	0	0.0
Aves	Bird	11	0.2	10	0.5	2	0.1	1	0.3
Anatinae	Duck	4	0.1	0	0.0	0	0.0	0	0.0
Fish	Fish	8	0.1	4	0.2	2	0.1	0	0.0
Total		6035	100	1995	100	3689	100	352	100.0

FIGURE 2.4. *Looking east along the Red Terrace, Domuztepe. The Ditch lies between the stone lines in the center of the photograph.*

a large-scale archaeological deposit is very similar to the formation of the rest of the Red Terrace. Although most of the individual pits could not be fully distinguished in excavation, we suspect that the Ditch was the product of hundreds of individual acts of digging and deposition.

Much of the refuse in the Ditch is composed of animal bones, which plausibly relate to feasting events. These discrete assemblages seem to have been quickly sealed, with little evidence of gnawing, weathering, or trampling. Although analysis is ongoing, there are some patterns that span the entire Ditch and differ in statistically significant ways from both the quotidian refuse and the other two feasting contexts. These patterns include an increase in the quantity of ovicaprids (65 percent) as compared to all contexts, and a slight decrease in the amount of pig (22.6 percent) relative to the quotidian contexts. What is most striking, however, is the comparative dearth of cattle (10.5 percent of the assemblage) and the lack of dog remains as compared both to the other feasting deposits and to the quotidian deposits. This pattern suggests the participants deliberately chose not to include these animals for the category of events that produced the fill of the Ditch.

Ovicaprid remains are characterized by an overrepresentation of butchery waste (skull and foot bones) and a dearth of the high meat package areas (upper portions of forelimbs and whole hind limbs; Table 2.2). There is a surprising overrepresentation of complete (or nearly complete) lower portion of forelimb bones (radii and ulnae), relative to humeri, femurs, and tibias. The abundance of complete proximal radii and ulnae, and the frequency with which one element can be matched with another, may suggest they were deposited while still bound by soft tissue. These data suggest that the contents of the Ditch may be refuse from meal preparation, and the meaty parts were taken elsewhere.

The Ditch and Red Terrace ovens together seem to represent the remains of repeated episodes of community feast preparation. The butchery refuse from this food preparation was not simply discarded. Instead, it seems to have been incorporated into a special zone within the Red Terrace itself. This could be interpreted in different ways, which need not be mutually exclusive. It may parallel the disposal of the distinctive pottery in the same context, which may have been to control socially powerful materials (Campbell 2010:154). The incorporation of feasting refuse in the Red Terrace may have tied the feasting to a particular location, embedding community memories in a particular place. Or it may have been linked to other meanings of the Red Terrace, perhaps symbolically offering food to a location that may have been deeply linked to the settlement's past (Campbell 2012). The use of the shallow scoops along

TABLE 2.2 Domuztepe element distribution by taxa

Sheep/Goat

Skeletal Element	Ditch	Ditch	Death Pit	Death Pit	Op III	Op III
	R	L	R	L	R	L
Scapula	41	35	22	24	3	5
Humerus	34	43	30	20	3	3
Radius	84	90	26	21	2	4
Ulna	52	55	18	12	1	1
Metacarpal	27	26	19	15	2	2
Femur	12	10	16	10	1	1
Tibia	20	12	29	22	0	1
Astragalus	77	77	10	7	1	2
Calcaneus	61	58	9	9	0	5
Metatarsal	40	44	9	15	2	3
Ph. 1	148	—	29		3	
Ph. 2	64	—	17		4	
Ph. 3	12	—	7		1	

Cattle

Skeletal Element	Ditch	Ditch	Death Pit	Death Pit	Op III	Op III
	R	L	R	L	R	L
Scapula	11	2	5	3	2	3
Humerus	5	6	12	12	8	4
Radius	12	6	9	12	5	3
Ulna	8	3	10	5	0	0
Metacarpal	8	8	9	10	3	2
Femur	3	4	11	7	5	5
Tibia	7	3	14	14	3	4
Astragalus	7	10	11	9	0	2
Calcaneus	8	8	6	4	0	1
Metatarsal	4	4	6	10	5	4
Ph. 1	33	—	55	—	5	
Ph. 2	26	—	49	—	4	
Ph. 3	24	—	42	—	4	

continued on next page

TABLE 2.2—*continued*

Pig

Skeletal Element	Ditch	Ditch	Death Pit	Death Pit	Op III	Op III
	R	L	R	L	R	L
Scapula	16	17	4	4	4	1
Humerus	16	17	3	3	1	1
Radius	8	8	5	6	0	0
Ulna	10	19	5	4	0	0
Metacarpal	16	18	4	1	1	0
Femur	3	5	0	3	0	1
Tibia	10	8	4	6		
Astragalus	8	7	1	1	3	0
Calcaneus	11	8	3	3	1	0
Metatarsal	8	16	1	3	1	2
Ph. 1	51	—	10	—	5	—
Ph. 2	26	—	6	—	2	—
Ph. 3	13	—	4	—	1	—

the line of the Ditch for the disposal of this type of material lasted for at least 50–100 years. The food preparation and feasting must have been highly structured, made up of ritualized steps that explicitly referenced the many times the same actions had been carried out in the past.

OPERATION III

A second extraordinary deposit comes from the northern part of the site, in Operation III, dating to ca. 5650–5500 cal. BCE. The relevant deposits are at the base of developed soil horizons, so contextual information is poorly preserved. A dense spread of animal bones lay on a discontinuous surface marked by patches of small pebbles, extending over an area of 2.5 × 1.5 m. These faunal remains are plausibly the remains of feasting episodes, but we do not know the context in which the feasts took place. Several episodes of dumping of refuse seem to be represented, which strikes a parallel with the Ditch in that these deposits are the products of repeated actions. However, on this occasion, no pits or scoops were dug in which to bury the refuse.

The faunal remains from Operation III show a high occurrence of cattle. Almost half (42.6 percent) of the 352 identified bones come from cattle, and these come from prime-age animals (see Table 2.1). The meaty parts of cattle carcasses (forelimb, hind limb, and back) are overrepresented at the expense of head and foot bones, relating the deposit to consumption rather than to preparation. The cattle bones show a high number of articulations (10 percent, as opposed to 2 percent in the quotidian areas), suggesting quick deposition that was not left open to scavengers. In contrast to the cattle, ovicaprid and pig bones from Operation III reflect a more normal signature, with few articulations (2 percent for ovicaprids and none for pigs) and all body parts present. We would suggest that the cattle remains, in this case, were the distinctive contents and were repeatedly added to a midden that was already accumulating, and each time quickly covered over.

The Death Pit

The Death Pit has already been discussed with reference to both human and dog remains. However, there were also processed bones from a minimum of 11 cattle, 21 sheep and goats, and 8 pigs. In essence, evidence of food animals from the Death Pit points to an event potentially involving hundreds of people who butchered, processed, and consumed extremely large amounts of meat over a short timeframe (Kansa et al. 2009a).

Remains from the primary domestic animals occur in all phases of the Death Pit; however, while animal remains are abundant in all phases, they are only strongly associated with human remains in phase 5a and phase 6 (Figure 2.2). Spatial analyses have suggested some clustering with cattle bones more common in the eastern half, pig bones in the Southeast, sheep/goat bones in the North and West, and, as mentioned above, dog bones concentrated in the area where most of the human bones were found. We consider that the phases represent spatially or temporally distinct deposits (Kansa et al. 2009a:table 3b). These patterns may relate to deliberate placement of feasting remains, basket-dumping episodes, or the temporal sequences of activities occurring outside the Death Pit.

The bones (both animal and human) in the Death Pit display evidence for cut marks, fragmentation, and body part representation consistent with the preparation and discard of food debris (Gauld et al. 2012). However, the Death Pit contains a higher relative proportion of cattle and dogs, as well as three times fewer pigs than have been recovered from all non–Death Pit contexts. The cattle bone assemblage reflects culling of a living herd—prime-age females and their young, as well as one male (Kansa et al. 2009a). The same pattern was observed on wild cattle bones from a similar feasting assemblage at Kfar HaHoresh (Horwitz and Goring-Morris 2004). Regardless of the motivation for its creation, the animal contents of the Death Pit reflect an enormous expense of cattle, whose milk and breeding would be sorely missed. The sheep and goats show a similarly narrow range of ages and a preponderance of females (Kansa et al. 2009a). Articulating elements, which suggest primary deposition, occur for 5 percent of both cattle and sheep/goat specimens, but do not occur at all for pigs. The pig bones found in the Death Pit may thus reflect background "noise" rather than intentional deposition. Their remarkably low occurrence in a site where pork consumption was extremely common points to their intentional exclusion from the Death Pit feasting event(s).

The animal remains in the Death Pit differ in several ways from those recovered from the Ditch and Operation III. They are part of a much more complex set of deposits that were not produced by repeated action. The scale of the feasting was probably much larger. The food refuse is also much more deeply buried. The Ditch deposits were only placed in shallow scoops and must have been disturbed each time a new scoop was dug in the same location, while the deposits in Operation III may have been simply covered over. The depth of burial and degree of separation from the everyday world may suggest different ways in which discard could be managed. The position of the bones in the Death Pit may also suggest a more complex rationale. Many of the animal bones were placed beneath the human remains, suggesting that the deposition of the food refuse in some way prepared the spot for the deposition of the human remains, possibly by drawing on their role in large-scale community feasting. This may be supported by other evidence for the preparation of the Death Pit; it was twice inundated with water immediately before the human bones were deposited (Campbell 2007–8:127).

That structured deposition at Domuztepe seems to be intimately associated with feasting should come as no great surprise, but it does give us important leverage in understanding acts of burial as part of social processes rather than simply as archaeological deposits. At times these may have involved very large numbers of people. Faunal evidence indicates that some of these activities occurred at specific times of the year (Kansa et al. 2009b). We can trace this pattern across different scales, ranging from large, spectacular one-off events such as the Death Pit, through regular, repeated practices that had an important connection to the large-scale structure of the settlement, as in the Ditch, down to less archaeologically visible scales. We should probably see

STUART CAMPBELL, SARAH WHITCHER KANSA, RACHEL BICHENER, AND HANNAH LAU this pattern extending all the way to everyday acts of consumption. Feasting was a key context in which social relations and interactions would be defined and redefined—and it produced material remains that required careful disposal due to the power and meaning derived from their creation. It is obvious, but still worth noting, that feasting is notable partly because it readily leaves archaeological remains but it may be taken as a proxy for community actions that otherwise leave little trace. Other activities, such as dancing or storytelling, might also be considered but are less visible.

BURIAL OF OBJECTS

At both Domuztepe and at other contemporary sites, objects could be buried on their own in ways that are reminiscent of the treatment of human remains. For example, there is a series of finely made small stone pots, often with short spouts, which seem to have been deposited individually in pits shortly before the final abandonment of Domuztepe, ca. 5450 cal. BCE (Campbell 2013). These are isolated finds, and only one has an association with other material remains. In that example, however, three human deciduous teeth were found in the fill of the vessel (Figure 2.5). This find strongly suggests a possible link between the stone pots and people, perhaps marking a particular stage in the development of an individual. Burial in this case might be linked not to death but to the living. Or, put another way, it might be linked to the loss or discard of a dividual aspect of a human identity during the life cycle of a person (Croucher 2012:9–12; Fowler 2004).

The incorporation of artifacts, sometimes fragmentary and possibly originating in refuse or midden material, alongside human remains in the Death Pit has already been noted. These do not seem to have been grave goods in any meaningful sense; they seem to have been objects that, if they were deliberately included in the burial, may have brought their own sets of meanings. Any refuse incorporated in the Death Pit was only selected because the Death Pit was a suitable place of disposal. The refuse may have been created in processes associated with other material in the pit (e.g., feasting). The context may have allowed for the disposal of dangerous material that needed to be contained in some way. Or the refuse may have been necessary to prepare the pit for the remainder of the deposits. It is unlikely that the soil and the apparently broken, mundane artifacts used to construct parts of the Death Pit were randomly selected. They may have come from specific places that brought into being important processes of enchainment, linking different places and contexts together through the associations that were created (Chapman 2000).

FIGURE 2.5. *Stone bowl (dt3517) with three milk teeth found (two pictured) in its fill,*
Domuztepe.

Although we tend to prioritize the human remains and consider them the
primary feature of the Death Pit, less obvious aspects of the material buried in
it may have carried equal importance.

One of the most striking examples of the burial of objects comes from a
contemporary site. An exceptional vessel/figurine was found in a pit in the
Halaf levels of Yarim Tepe II in north Iraq, broken and associated with

STUART CAMPBELL, SARAH WHITCHER KANSA, RACHEL BICHENER, AND HANNAH LAU burning (Merpert and Munchaev 1987). It had been treated in a way that is analogous to human funerary treatment, which sometimes also has elements of burial, fragmentation, and burning (Campbell 2008). The removable head was not found with the rest of the pot, a practice that may parallel the special treatment occasionally given to human skulls. It is probable that this vessel/figurine represented a specific mythical or supernatural being and, therefore, possible that its burial was considered the burial of an "individual." However, nonanthropomorphic objects could be treated in a similar way, including a second vessel/figurine of a pig from Yarim Tepe II.

Some objects may have acquired specific power and agency (Campbell 2010). At Domuztepe, a series of fragmentary pottery vessels from the Ditch were painted with representations of houses, usually in combination with trees and other figurative motifs (Figure 2.6). These designs contrast markedly with the usual geometric patterns on Halaf pottery. The decoration probably carried particular symbolic meanings, perhaps relating to social narratives and mythologies. It is undoubtedly significant that these fragmentary vessels were associated with the remains of food preparation, and they probably had a role in the ritual practices. These were objects with powerful meanings derived from both their design and their use. They needed to be disposed of in particular ways, perhaps to control powers that they were endowed with or perhaps incorporating their associations into the place in which they were buried.

BURIAL OF ARCHITECTURE AND SOIL

Architecture is often rebuilt and modified over long periods and, at Domuztepe, we have speculated that buildings were sometimes dismantled and destroyed. This may suggest a structured pattern in which buildings were deliberately forgotten or obscured. Indeed, settlement mounds like tells or tepes might be thought of as settlement systems that constantly obscure their earlier phases by burying them but also convert them into a very visible signal of the continuity between the distant past and the present. Elsewhere the maintenance of architecture played an important role in signaling lineages (Hodder and Pels 2011; McAnany and Hodder 2009). At Domuztepe, houses tend to be relatively short-lived and their incorporation into the matrix of the site fairly rapid, but there are other structures where processes related to burial had a much longer-term role in managing links between the present and the past.

An example of what might be termed continual burial comes not from a building but from the Red Terrace, discussed in a different context above. It

FIGURE 2.6. *Painted vessel with the unusual building motif that is frequently found in the Ditch assemblage (digitally restored).*

is surprising that the terrace started to be formed at the beginning of the Halaf (ca. 6100 cal. BCE), while we can date its final stages to around 5500 cal. BCE. The processes that maintained the terrace lasted up to six hundred years. Although the depth of deposits that make up the Red Terrace is almost 2 m, it is not a single structure. Instead, it is the product of repeated actions that were maintained over a long time period. The terrace was repeatedly scraped clean and refurbished through the deposition of small quantities of red soil brought from beyond the settlement, probably from soil that had washed off the low hills to the west of the site (Gearey et al. 2011). This constantly obscured previous modifications of the terrace and, over time, buried early phases deep under the surface.

This process of refurbishment and renewal occurred regularly, possibly annually. It seems to be part of a larger process through which meaning was re-created, validated, and reinforced. Crucially, it included mechanisms of burial and deposition that could obscure as well as clarify and remodel. Earlier configurations were covered over, and the layout of walls and ovens reestablished in different locations. Earlier phases rarely seem to have been destroyed. Instead, they were buried and incorporated into the steadily accumulating monument. Undoubtedly, this process of change and renewal was an important focal point in the production of memory as well as creating a constant element of ritual practice, against which the rhythm of daily life might be set (Campbell 2012). The process does not seem to have been centrally connected to funerary activities. Two burials within the Red Terrace have already been mentioned, and the Death Pit was ultimately cut into its southern edge, so it could in some way be augmented by the burial of the dead. However, these deposits seem secondary and were only added to the main monument after several hundred years of previous existence.

An even more unexpected example of the power and importance of burial at Domuztepe came to light in 2011 (Campbell and Healey 2012). One of the features cut into the later stages of the Red Terrace was a deep shaft, circular in plan and approximately 1.1 m in diameter, with an original depth of more than 9 m. The bottom of the shaft penetrated the water table. The shaft could have, therefore, functioned as a well. However, it seems only to have been in use for a very short period, perhaps to draw water out for a specific purpose. Even more surprising is that the deposits that had been excavated from the bottom 3.5 m of the shaft appear to have been carefully replaced. The artifactual assemblage within this deepest fill belonged entirely to the earlier Ceramic Neolithic. There was no contamination of the distinctly different material that would have dated to the time at which the shaft was dug. Strata from which such an assemblage could have derived were ca. 6 m below the surface, so an alternative source of an uncontaminated early Ceramic Neolithic assemblage is very unlikely. This strongly suggests that the population who first excavated this "well" shaft into the early Ceramic Neolithic levels recognized the material as something different and set it aside until the shaft was finished; they then buried it where it had come from, almost as though they did not want to disturb their ancestors. Excavation may have had the power to access but also to disturb what was buried, while burial may have had the power to reinstate and control.

DISCUSSION AND CONCLUSION

Although this analysis draws heavily on the evidence from Domuztepe, contemporary sites suggest similar patterns. While these are often less explicit—due to issues of preservation, excavation or publication—we suggest that burial is an action with widespread cultural significance. This significance is unlikely to be restricted to the Halaf. For example, parallels with Kfar HaHoresh in the Pre-Pottery Neolithic B period have already been cited, and there are many echoes of related practices at Çatalhöyük (Hodder and Pels 2011; Meskell et al. 2008; Russell at al. 2009).

Burial, therefore, needs to be reclaimed from being a simple funerary behavior. Burial was a process that could be applied to a wide range of material. Bearing in mind the nuances of context and the interred material, it may be useful to consider burial as a type of transformation that could be applied to culturally significant objects. The transformation might achieve different outcomes, but it was a way of taking socially charged material and changing its relationship with the world. Burial might hide and obscure, aiding in processes of forgetting. It might incorporate material into a place, promoting remembrance and augmenting spatial meanings. It might utilize the properties of a location to control the material that had been buried and to separate the material from the everyday world, perhaps as part of processes through which liminality was defined and maintained. Practical elements would certainly have been a factor too; burial of decomposing material, whether human or animal, is also a hygienic procedure. These different types of transformation were probably not exclusive and are certainly not exhaustive.

It is certainly true that the human body was the focus of attention and special treatment. However, this did not always result in the final burial of a body, and the focus was not unique to the human body. Animals such as dogs could apparently be treated in ways that were very similar to the treatment of humans, including the occasional selection for burial. This may suggest either that dogs could be seen as aspects of the identity of people, living or dead, or were ascribed agency or social personae in themselves (Dwyer and Minnegal 2005; Jones 2009). The selection of some objects, such as the female vessel/figurine at Yarim Tepe I, for burial may also suggest that objects either had agency in their own right or through representation of other beings. Other buried material may have had different cultural associations and power. There is a repeated suggestion that debris associated with the preparation or consumption of food as part of feasting events was given special attention. Placing the debris in the ground may have created a "durable trace of their memory" (Thomas 1999:72), but it could have buried more abstract elements of human social events. Metaphorical links between eating, dying, and memory (Hamilakis 1998) may be extended into parallel processes of burial. These links may be seen in the wider context of societies living in locations where burial of previous settlements was an important element of life.

Burial was probably used to achieve several different aims. In general, it might be thought of as something connected to embedding meaning in places, to practices of remembering and forgetting, as well as investing social capital in specific locations. In part, this is a way of creating and managing the past as part of the present, lived world. This might be particularly relevant when it is associated with fragmentation of bodies and objects, with only parts of the whole being buried, perhaps as a way of enchaining the buried (the past) with the present.

Other meanings might also be attached to the practice of burial. Burial as an action creates a boundary between the buried object and the living world, placing the buried object in a different context hidden from everyday life. Unlike some transformations, burial can be reversed. In some cases at Domuztepe, later excavation allowed subsequent access to the buried object and might have been a way in which that different context could be contacted—perhaps even a way of interacting with the past. Burial can also act as a mechanism through which potent, potentially dangerous material can be contained and controlled. Indeed this interpretation can be applied to decaying rubbish as well as more obviously ritual material (cf. Hill 1996:20–22). However, many of the processes through which artifacts and refuse become socially charged is through their role in a ritual context, whether that is achieved through feasting, ceremonies around death, or other processes.

It is perhaps also useful to consider burial more generally as an action that can sustain many metaphors. Burial is something that naturally occurs in several stages. A pit is dug, objects are placed in it, it is refilled, and perhaps its location marked before it gradually becomes incorporated into the matrix of the site. This cycle permits a rhythm of execution, as well as creating a frame that has both a beginning and an end. Each stage has the potential to be dramatic and filled with symbolism. Pollock's (2011) recent analysis of Halaf burial practices has drawn on Frederik Barth's (1987) ethnographic analysis of ritual practices among the Baktaman to emphasize the role of ritual specialists as performers, borrowing and improvising in response to the occasion and their audience rather than following static and homogenous scripts. The act of burial offers attractions to the ritual practitioner as something that draws a diversity of potential symbolism together with a staged process that could help provide structure to a performance, as well as leave a permanent link between place and memory.

While this discussion may have established burial as a process applicable to a range of material, it is useful to bring the discussion back to human remains. Human remains were probably never a simple, unified category in the way that we are familiar with in our contemporary lives. Some bodies were buried shortly after death, with no apparent processing of the body and no later disturbance. However, this was far from a standard practice during the Halaf. Bodies could be broken up and mixed together. They could probably also be consumed, at least in particular circumstances (Kansa et al. 2009a). We suspect that they had complex identities that could sometimes be unpacked by treatment after death. Some of these aspects of identity may also have been shared by other things, both animals and objects, particularly those generated through powerful cultural processes. So human remains in an archaeological context should not always be thought of as a human body belonging to a specific, self-contained individual. Instead, perhaps they should be considered as part of a culturally created entity—something not inherently different or distinct from other types of socially powerful material. Burial is then something that could be used on some occasions for specific reasons, within a set of creative ritual practices. It was used with intentionality, to transform, to control, to make links to place, to structure ways of remembering or forgetting as well as to fulfill dramatic needs of ritual. It may have gained its meaning and power through its use in multiple contexts. In fact, there may be relatively few instances in which burial was used simply to dispose of human remains. More commonly, it may have been used as an action on a set of culturally significant items that sometimes included human remains.

Reclaiming burial from being a simple shorthand for funerary practice and placing it as a much wider cultural practice does not diminish the importance of the burial of human remains in the prehistoric Near East. Instead, it highlights the extent to which burial is not simply a grave cut or an archaeological feature. It is part of a much richer set of cultural practices that relate to past cosmologies, ritual practices, and ways in which people interacted with their worlds. For archaeologists, of course, burial is a particularly significant act, because it is that action that has often ensured preservation in the archaeological record. Indeed, burial and subsequent excavation also offer modern archaeologists a role in the continued processes of memory and the creation of new links from the present to the past.

NOTES

1. Calibration is required to convert radiocarbon (14C) dates to calendar years.
2. It should be emphasized that we are drawing on a Domuztepe-specific definition of "mundane" practices. Domuztepe exhibits just one example of the continuum of subsistence strategies employed by Neolithic people during the Halaf.

REFERENCES

Akkermans, Peter M. M. G. 1989. "Halaf Mortuary Practices: A Survey." In *To the Euphrates and Beyond: Archaeological studies in Honour of Maurits N. van Loon*, edited by Odette M. C. Haex, Hans H. Curvers, and Peter M. M. G. Akkermans, 75–88. Rotterdam: A. A. Balkema.

Akkermans, Peter M. M. G. 2008. "Burying the Dead in Late Neolithic Syria." In *Proceedings of the 5th International Congress on the Archaeology of the Ancient Near East, Madrid, April 3–8 2006*, edited by Joaquín Córdoba, Miquel Molist, Carmen Pérez, Isabel Rubio, and Sergio Martínez, 621–45. Vol. 3. Madrid: Centro Superior de Estudios sobre el Oriente Próximo y Egipto.

Atakuman Eissenstat, Çiğdem. 2004. *Ritualization of Settlement: Conditioning Factors of Spatial Congruity and Temporal Continuity during the Late Neolithic of Southeastern Anatolia*, PhD thesis, University of California, Los Angeles.

Aten, Nico. 1996. "Note on the Human Skeletal Remains." In *Tell Sabi Abyad: The Late Neolithic Settlement*, edited by Peter M. M. G. Akkermans, 114–18. Leiden: Nederlands Instituut voor het Nabije Oosten.

Barth, Fredrik. 1987. *Cosmologies in the Making: A Generative Approach to Cultural Variation in Inner New Guinea*. Cambridge: Cambridge University Press. http://dx.doi.org/10.1017/CBO9780511607707.

Bevan, Elinor. 1986. *Representations of Animals in Sanctuaries of Artemis and Other Olympian Deities*. Oxford: Archaeopress.

Bichener, Rachel E. in prep. *The Practical and Symbolic Role of the Domestic Dog in the Later Neolithic of the Near East*. PhD thesis, Department of Archaeology, University of Manchester.

Campbell, Bronwen. 2013. "Stone Bowls of the Halaf Period: Function, Style and Breakage at Domuztepe." In *Interpreting the Late Neolithic of Upper Mesopotamia*, edited by Olivier Nieuwenhuyse, Reinhard Bernbeck, Peter M. M. G. Akkermans, and J. Rogasch, 241–49. Turnhout: Brepols.

Campbell, Stuart. 1992. *Culture, Chronology and Change in the Later Neolithic of North Mesopotamia*. Unpublished PhD thesis, Department of Archaeology, University of Edinburgh, Edinburgh.

Campbell, Stuart. 2007–8. "The Dead and the Living in Late Neolithic Mesopotamia." In *Sepolti tra i vivi. Evidenza ed interpretazione di contesti funerari in abitato. Atti del Convegno Internazionale (Università degli Studi di Roma "La Sapienza" 26–29 Aprile 2006)*, edited by Gilda Bartoloni and M. Gilda Benedettini, 125–40. Rome: Università degli studi di Roma "La Sapienza."

Campbell, Stuart. 2008. "Feasting and Dancing: Gendered Representation and Pottery in Later Mesopotamian Prehistory." In *Gender through Time in the Ancient Near East*, edited by Diane Bolger, 53–76. Lanham, MD: AltaMira Press.

Campbell, Stuart. 2010. "Understanding Symbols: Putting Meaning into the Painted Pottery of Prehistoric Northern Mesopotamia." In *The Development of Pre-State Societies in the Ancient Near East: Studies in Honour of Edgar Peltenburg*, edited by Diane Bolger and Louise Elder, 147–55. Oxford: Oxbow Books.

Campbell, Stuart. 2012. "Rhythms of the Past: Time and Memory at Late Neolithic Domuztepe." In *Broadening Horizons 3*, edited by Ferran Borrell, Mònica Bouso, Anna Gómez Bach, Carles Tornero, and Oriol Vicente, 305–24. Barcelona: Servei de Publicacions de la Universitat Autònoma de Barcelona.

Campbell, Stuart, and Elizabeth Healey. 2011. "Stones of the Living and Bones of the Dead? Contextualising the Lithics in the Death Pit at Domuztepe." In *The State of the Stone: Terminologies, Continuities and Contexts in Near Eastern Neolithic Lithics*, edited by Elizabeth Healey, Stuart Campbell, and Osamu Maeda, 327–42. Berlin: Ex Oriente.

Campbell, Stuart, and Elizabeth Healey. 2012. "A 'Well' and an Early Ceramic Neolithic Assemblage from Domuztepe." *Neo-Lithics* 2/11:19–25.

Chapman, John. 1997. "The Origins of Tells in Eastern Hungary." In *Neolithic Landscapes*, edited by Peter Topping, 139–64. Oxford: Oxbow Books.

Chapman, John. 2000. *Fragmentation in Archaeology: People, Places and Broken Objects in the Prehistory of South Eastern Europe*. London: Routledge.

Claassen, Cheryl. 2010. *Feasting with Shellfish in the Southern Ohio Valley: Archaic Sacred Sites and Rituals*. Knoxville: University of Tennessee Press.

Collins, Billie Jean. 2002. "Animals in Hittite Literature." In *A History of the Animal World in the Ancient Near East*, edited by Billie Jean Collins, 237–50. Leiden: Brill.

Croucher, Karina. 2010. "Bodies in Pieces in the Neolithic Near East." In *Body Parts and Bodies Whole*, edited by Katharina Rebay-Salisbury, Marie Louise Stig Sorensen, and Jessica Hughes, 6–19. Oxford: Oxbow Books.

Croucher, Karina. 2012. *Death and Dying in the Neolithic Near East*. Oxford: Oxford University Press.

Croucher, Karina, and Stuart Campbell. 2009. "Dying for a change? Bringing new senses to Near Eastern Neolithic mortuary practice." In *Que(e)rying Archaeology: The Proceedings of the 30th Annual Chacmool Conference, Calgary*, edited by Susan Tereny, Natasha Lyons, and Janse-Smekal Kelly, 95–105. Calgary: Archaeological Association of the University of Calgary.

Day, Leslie P. 1984. "Dog Burials in the Greek World." *American Journal of Archaeology* 88 (1): 21–32. http://dx.doi.org/10.2307/504595.

Dietler, Michael, and Brian Hayden. 2001. *Feasts: Archaeological and Ethnographic Perspectives on Food, Politics, and Power*. Washington: Smithsonian Institution Press.

Dwyer, Peter D., and Monica Minnegal. 2005. "Person, Place or Pig: Animal Attachments and Human Transactions in New Guinea." In *Animals in Person: Cultural Perspectives on Human-Animal Intimacy*, edited by John Knight, 37–60. Oxford: Berg.

Edrey, Meir. 2008. "The Dog Burials at Achaemenid Ashkelon Revisited." *Tel Aviv* 35 (2): 267–82.

Fletcher, Alexandra, and Stuart Campbell. Forthcoming. "It's ritual, isn't it? Mortuary and Feasting Practices at Domuztepe." In *Commensality: From Everyday Food to Feast*, edited by Susanne Kerner, Cynthia Chou, and Morten Warmind. Berg: Oxford.

Fowler, Christopher. 2004. *The Archaeology of Personhood: An Anthropological Approach*. London: Routledge.

Gauld, Suellen C., James S. Oliver, Sarah Whitcher Kansa, and Elizabeth Carter. 2012. "On the Tail End of Variation in Late Neolithic Burial Practices: Halaf Feasting and Cannibalism at Domuztepe, Southeastern Anatolia." In *Bioarchaeology and Behavior: The People of the Ancient Near East*, edited by Megan Perry, 8–34. Gainesville: University Press of Florida. http://dx.doi.org/10.5744/florida/9780813042299.003.0002.

Gearey, Benjamin R., Alexandra Fletcher, William G. Fletcher, Stuart Campbell, Ian Boomer, David Keen, Jane Reed, and Emma Tetlow. 2011. "From Site to Landscape: Assessing the Value of Geoarchaeological Data in Understanding the Archaeological Record of Domuztepe, South-East Turkey." *American Journal of Archaeology* 155 (3): 465–82.

Goring-Morris, Nigel, and Liora K. Horwitz. 2007. "Funerals and Feasts during the Pre-Pottery Neolithic B of the Near East." *Antiquity* 81 (3): 902–19.

Hamilakis, Yannis. 1998. "Eating the Dead: Mortuary Feasting and the Politics of Memory in the Aegean Bronze Age Societies." In *Cemetery and Society in the Bronze Age Aegean*, edited by Keith Branigan, 115–32. Sheffield: Sheffield Academic Press.

Hayden, Brian. 2001. "Fabulous Feasts: A Prolegomenon to the Importance of Feasting." In *Feasts: Archaeological and Ethnographic Perspectives on Food, Politics and Power*, edited by Michael Dietler and Brian Hayden, 23–64. Washington, D.C.: Smithsonian Press.

Helwing, Barbara. 2003. "Feasts as a Social Dynamic in Prehistoric Western Asia: Three Case Studies from Syria and Anatolia." *Paléorient* 29 (2): 63–85. http://dx.doi.org/10.3406/paleo.2003.4765.

Hill, Jeremy D. 1996. "The Identification of Ritual Deposits of Animals Bones: A General Perspective from a Specific Study of 'Special Animal Deposits' from the Southern English Iron Age." In *Ritual Treatment of Human and Animal Remains*, edited by Sue Anderson and Katherine Boyle, 17–32. Oxford: Oxbow Books.

Hodder, Ian, and Peter Pels. 2011. "History Houses: A New Interpretation of Architectural Elaboration at Çatalhöyük." In *Religion in the Emergence of Civilization: Çatalhöyük as a Case Study*, edited by Ian Hodder, 163–86. Cambridge: Cambridge University Press.

Hole, Frank. 1989. "Patterns of Burial in the Fifth Millennium." In *Upon This Foundation: The Ubaid Reconsidered*, edited by Elizabeth Henrickson and Ingolf Thuesen, 149–80. Copenhagen: Carsten Niebuhr Institute.

Horwitz, Liora K., and Nigel Goring-Morris. 2004. "Animals and Ritual during the Levantine PPNB: A Case Study from the Site of Kfar Hahoresh, Israel." *Anthropozoologica* 39 (1): 165–78.

Jones, Paula L. 2009. "Considering Living-Beings in the Aceramic Neolithic of Cyprus." *Journal of Mediterranean Archaeology* 22 (1): 75–99. http://dx.doi.org/10 .1558/jmea.v22i1.75.

Kansa, Sarah Whitcher, Suellen C. Gauld, Stuart Campbell, and Elizabeth Carter. 2009a. "Whose Bones Are Those? Preliminary Comparative Analysis of Fragmented Human and Animal Bones in the "Death Pit" at Domuztepe, a Late Neolithic Settlement in Southeastern Turkey." *Anthropozoologica* 44 (1): 159–72. http://dx.doi.org/10.5252/az2009n1a7.

Kansa, Sarah Whitcher, Amanda Kennedy, Stuart Campbell, and Elizabeth Carter. 2009b. "Resource Exploitation at Late Neolithic Domuztepe: Faunal and Botanical Evidence." *Current Anthropology* 50 (6): 897–914. http://dx.doi.org /10.1086/605910.

Luby, Edward M., and Mark F. Gruber. 1999. "The Dead Must Be Fed: Symbolic Meanings of the Shellmounds of the San Francisco Bay Area." *Cambridge Archaeological Journal* 9 (1): 95–108. http://dx.doi.org/10.1017/S0959774300015225.

McAnany, Patricia A., and Ian Hodder. 2009. "Thinking about Stratigraphic Sequence in Social Terms." *Archaeological Dialogues* 16 (1): 1–11. http://dx.doi.org /10.1017/S1380203809002748.

McNiven, Ian J. 2012. "Ritualized Middening Practices." *Journal of Archaeological Method and Theory* 20 (4): 552–87.

McOmish, David. 1996. "East Chisenbury: Ritual and Rubbish at the British Bronze Age–Iron Age Transition." *Antiquity* 70:68–76.

Merpert, Nikolai I., and Rauf M. Munchaev. 1973. "Early Agricultural Settlement in the Sinjar Plain, Northern Iraq." *Iraq* 35:97–113.

Merpert, Nikolai I., and Rauf M. Munchaev. 1987. "The Earliest Levels at Yarim Tepe I and Yarim Tepe II in Northern Iraq." *Iraq* 49:1–37.

Merrett, Deborah C., and Christopher Meiklejohn. 2007. "Is House 12 at Bouqras a Charnel House?" In *Faces from the Past: Diachronic Patterns in the Biology of Human Populations from the Eastern Mediterranean*, edited by Marina Faerman, Liora K. Horwitz, Tzipi Kahana, and Uri Zilberman, 127–39. Oxford: British Archaeological Reports.

Meskell, Lynn, Carolyn Nakamura, Rachel King, and Shahina Farid. 2008. "Figured Lifeworlds and Depositional Practices at Çatalhöyük." *Cambridge Archaeological Journal* 18 (2): 139–61. http://dx.doi.org/10.1017/S095977430800022X.

Morey, Darcy F. 2006. "Burying Key Evidence: The Social Bond between Dogs and People." *Journal of Archaeological Science* 33 (2): 158–75. http://dx.doi.org/10.1016/j.jas.2005.07.009.

Pollock, Susan. 2011. "Making a Difference: Mortuary Practices in Halaf Times." In *Breathing New Life into the Evidence of Death: Contemporary Approaches to Bioarchaeology*, edited by Aubrey Baadsgaard, Alexis T. Boutin, and Jane E. Buikstra, 29–54. Santa Fe: School for Advanced Research Press.

Richards, Colin, and Julian Thomas. 1984. "Ritual Activity and Structured Deposition in Later Neolithic Wessex." In *Neolithic Studies: A Review of Some Current Research*, edited by Richard Bradley and Julie Gardiner, 189–218. Oxford: British Archaeological Reports.

Russell, Anna. 2010. *Retracing the Steppes: A Zooarchaeological Analysis of Changing Subsistence Patterns in the Late Neolithic at Tell Sabi Abyad, Northern Syria, c. 6900–5900 BC*. Leiden: Leiden University.

Russell, Nerissa, Louise Martin, and Katheryn C. Twiss. 2009. "Building Memories: Commemorative Deposits at Çatalhöyük." *Anthropozoologica* 44 (1): 103–25. http://dx.doi.org/10.5252/az2009n1a5.

Schiffer, Michael B. 1972. "Archaeological Context and Systemic Context." *American Antiquity* 37 (2): 156–65. http://dx.doi.org/10.2307/278203.

Steadman, Sharon. 2005. "Reliquaries on the Landscape: Mounds as Matrices of Human Cognition." In *Archaeologies of the Middle East: Critical Perspectives*, edited by Susan Pollock and Reinhard Bernbeck, 286–307. Oxford: Blackwell.

Strathern, Marilyn. 1988. *The Gender of the Gift: Problems with Women and Problems with Society in Melanesia*. Berkeley: University of California Press. http://dx.doi.org/10.1525/california/9780520064232.001.0001.

Thomas, Julian. 1999. *Understanding the Neolithic*. London: Routledge.

Tsuneki, Akira. 2010. "A Newly Discovered Neolithic Cemetery at Tell el-Kerkh, Northwest Syria." In *Proceedings of the 6th International Congress on the Archaeology of the Ancient Near East, May 5th–10th 2008, "Sapienza"—Università di Roma*, edited by Paolo Matthiae, Frances Pinnock, Lorenzo Nigro, and Nicholò Marchetti, 697–713. Wiesbaden: Harrassowitz Verlag.

Tsuneki, Akira. 2011. *Life and Death in the Kerkh Neolithic Cemetery*. Tsukuba: University of Tsukuba.

Twiss, Katheryn C. 2008. "Transformations in an Early Agricultural Society: Feasting in the Southern Levantine Pre-Pottery Neolithic." *Journal of Anthropological Archaeology* 27 (4): 418–42. http://dx.doi.org/10.1016/j.jaa.2008.06.002.

Verhoeven, Marc. 2000. "Death, Fire and Abandonment: Ritual Practice at Later Neolithic Tell Sabi Abyad, Syria." *Archaeological Dialogues* 7 (1): 46–83. http://dx.doi.org/10.1017/S1380203800001598.

West, David R. 1995. *Some Cults of Greek Goddesses and Female Daemons of Oriental Origin*. Kevelaer: Butzon and Bercker.

White, David G. 1989. "Dogs Die." *History of Religions* 28 (4): 283–303. http://dx.doi.org/10.1086/463162.

3

*Strange People and
Exotic Things*

Constructing Akkadian
Identity at Kish, Iraq

WILLIAM J. PESTLE,
CHRISTINA TORRES-ROUFF,
AND BLAIR DAVERMAN

ABSTRACT

Issues of ethnicity have long vexed archaeologists studying Mesopotamian societies of the late third millennium BCE. Scholars working in the region have frequently debated the existence and distinctiveness of Sumerian and Akkadian ethnic groups, as well as the nature of their potential interrelationship. Through an analysis of both biological evidence (nonmetric traits) and mortuary treatment data gleaned from the burials of the A "Cemetery" at the site of Kish, Iraq, the present work explores possible ways in which an Akkadian ethnic identity may have been conceived of and commemorated during the time of Akkadian imperial ascendancy (ca. 2350–2150 BCE). In keeping with recent discussions of ethnic ascription and self-identification—which have stressed the flexible, situational, and politicized nature of ethnogenesis and ethnic identification—here we attempt to situate the discussion within what must have been a fraught and fluid time for the inhabitants of Kish. Despite data suggesting some biological differences between individuals buried in the A "Cemetery," the relative homogeneity of burial treatment seen in graves representing both the late Early Dynastic III and Akkadian periods cries out for interpretation. This pattern may speak to a lack of distinct Akkadian ethnic identity (at least in the time and place under study) or possibly to an attempt by those making the later Akkadian Period burials to play down the remembrance of possible Sumerian-Akkadian ethnic differences. The latter explanation would be tantalizing evidence of the strategic politics of identity on the part of Akkadians living at Kish in a time of political flux.

DOI: 10.5876/9781607323295.c003

DEDICATION

In a volume that seeks to understand ways that humans remember and commemorate the dead, we would be remiss if we did not begin by remembering and commemorating our friend and colleague Donny George Youkhanna. We remember him fondly and dedicate this chapter to his memory.

INTRODUCTION

Commemoration of the deceased often forms a central element of intentional burial (although see, for example, Conklin [2001], where mortuary treatment is designed to promote forgetting the dead). Through diverse aspects of burial treatment and ceremony, a community not only expresses emotions that accompany the death of one of its members, but also remembers and/or communicates real or imagined aspects both of the deceased individual's character and accomplishments as well as of their group identity. As the representation of group identity is intrinsically political, such commemoration rapidly takes on connotations of domination, conformity, assimilation, or resistance. Here we follow Sian Jones (1997:84) in considering ethnicity as a "culturally ascribed identity . . . based on the expression of a real or assumed shared culture and common descent (usually through the objectification of cultural, linguistic, religious, historical and/or physical characteristics)." As such, few aspects of group identity are as awash with the potential for manipulation as ethnicity.

In this chapter, we critically explore the ways in which group identity, specifically a distinct Akkadian ethnicity (if such an identity existed), was (or was not) communicated and commemorated in the burials of the ancient Mesopotamian city of Kish's A "Cemetery."[1] These residential burials were dug down from the floors of buildings or houses overlying the remnants of a structure known as the "A Palace" in the eastern precinct of the city of Kish. As the cultural, ethnic, and historical contexts of these burials is somewhat ambiguous, rather than providing a single interpretation for these acts of commemoration, we apply a bioarchaeological lens to present several possible rationales for the mortuary communication, or lack thereof, of Akkadian ethnicity. Bioarchaeology, which combines biological and cultural lines of evidence to reconstruct life (and death) in the past (Buikstra and Beck 2006), is ideally suited to the study of a phenomenon like ethnicity, which so clearly crosses the nature-nurture divide. The analysis of both biological (skeletal and dental nonmetric) and cultural (mortuary treatment) data yields, in the present case, more fine-grained and nuanced understandings of ethnic identity politics than might otherwise be attained.

ETHNICITY IN ARCHAEOLOGY

The study of ancient ethnicity—in the guise of race, language family, or cultural group—has been of central interest to archaeologists since early in the discipline (Jones 1997). With the work of Frederik Barth (1969), anthropological sensibilities regarding the nature of ethnicity changed, ushering in archaeological research that acknowledged the dynamic and politicized nature of ethnogenesis—the maintenance, and disappearance, of ethnic identity (Jones 1997:64). As presently understood in archaeology, "ethnicity is best seen as a process of identification and differentiation, rather than as an inherent attribute of individuals or groups," and far from being immutable, it, "can be altered by manipulation of the appropriate symbols" (Emberling 1997:306). As such, ethnicity is but one of a suite of *potentially* reversible identities or social personae that a person can assume and occupy, and, like many others, its assumption combines elements of self-identification and identification by others (Barth 1969). The politics of ethnic identification are crosscut and complicated, particularly in complex/plural societies, by the myriad other social identities (gender, class, age, race, occupation, religion) that an individual can simultaneously and situationally occupy (Meskell 2007:25; Okamura 1981).

While generalized statements about the behavior of people in complex societies vis-à-vis their ethnicity are prone to error (e.g., a subordinated ethnic group always does *x*), a few postulates about the rationale guiding such decisions are useful to consider. It is crucial to recognize that (1) ethnicity is the product of decisions made by active agents who function within existing structures, but who also construct, reinforce, or dismantle identity through daily practice, and (2) these agents' decisions are guided, at least in part, by attempts to maximize social, political, or economic standing (Eifert, Miguel, and Posner 2010; Emberling 1997:310; Jones 1997:87–92), oftentimes against identifications imposed by or embedded in prevailing social structures (Nagel 1994). Therefore, ethnicity is not a primordial identity into which people can neatly be fit. Instead, it is intrinsically and intensely dynamic, negotiated, and politicized. Depending on circumstances, a person or group may choose to emphasize or deemphasize (part of) their ethnicity to gain advantages or to make a statement. As such, the detection and decipherment of ethnicity in prehistoric societies can provide a window into the very dynamics that governed them.

Given the complexity of contemporary ethnic identity politics, the difficulty in identifying and studying ethnicity in the past is evident. Nonetheless, in his review of the archaeology of ethnicity, Geoff Emberling (1997:311) enumerates a four-step process by which archaeologists might identify "material markers of ethnicity." Paraphrased somewhat, this process entails (1) identification of a potential group through distinct material culture/practice or historical reference, (2) delineation of group boundaries through outgroup comparison, (3) confirmation that distinct material culture or practice is a marker of ethnicity (and not another social identity) through contextualized study, and (4) confirmation of ethnic difference through other categories of evidence. Emberling observes that not all types of material culture are equally useful in the study of ethnicity (Emberling 1997:325). He singles out several landmark studies (e.g., Beck 1995) establishing that mortuary ritual, in particular, can serve as a powerful, useful, and archaeologically visible marker of ethnicity. More recent mortuary analyses (e.g., Chesson 2001a; Chesson 2001b; Joyce 2001) have reinforced this notion, finding that for the living members of a community (be that community defined by common ethnicity, religion, or political identity), the practice of burial and mortuary treatment is one of the ways local community was created and maintained (Scott 2011:75). In burial treatment—the way in which kin and community commemorated the deceased—we might find crystallized evidence of this dynamic self-ascribed identity.

We proceed here by setting the stage regarding what is known from historical and archaeological sources of Mesopotamia's ethnic landscape in the late third millennium BCE. Following this, we discuss potential mortuary representations of ethnicity in A "Cemetery" burials.

ETHNICITY IN LATE THIRD MILLENNIUM BCE MESOPOTAMIA

As mentioned above, since at least the late 1930s, there has been an active, and occasionally heated, debate about (a) the existence, in the late third and early second millennia BCE, of distinct Sumerian and Akkadian ethnicities; (b) the distinctiveness (or lack thereof) of these two (ethnic?) groups in various behaviors, material culture, and political institutions; and (c) the tone and tenor of their relationship. The seminal work (Jacobsen 1939a) on this topic was effective in laying to rest the racial overtones in these analyses, and, appropriate to its historical context, playing down the significance (and certainly any notion of inherent animosity) of the Semitic/non-Semitic divide. The presence of both Semitic (Akkadian) and Sumerian names on the rolls of the Kings of Kish (Goetze 1961) attests to a far more complex and nuanced relationship.

Today, there is general agreement that, in antiquity, Sumer and Akkad were toponyms, that is, place-names, with Sumer referring to southern Mesopotamia's city-states and Akkad to the more northern regions. There is also agreement that Sumerian and Akkadian refer to distinct languages; while Sumerian has no known linguistic associations, Akkadian is classified as a Semitic language (Kraus 1970). What is far more controversial is whether or not these terms also had emic meaning as ethnonyms (group names), with some scholars (e.g., Bahrani 2006; Emberling 1997; Kraus 1970) arguing that there were no such ethnic groups and others (e.g., Gelb 1960; Goetze 1961; Kamp and Yoffee 1980; McMahon 2006; Nissen 1993; Sassmannshausen 2005; Tricoli 2005; Wilcke 1975) contending the opposite, to a greater or lesser degree. While archaeologists might imagine that the availability of texts would aid in resolving this issue, Assyriologists have, as yet, been unable to reach consensus regarding the appropriateness of these terms as bona fide designations of ancient ethnicity.

It is into this somewhat contentious arena that we offer the present work. It is our hope that through an analysis of mortuary treatment at Kish's A "Cemetery," a burial place that was in use when Sargon, an Akkadian, first assumed suzerainty, we will shed some light on the nature of possible ethnic difference in ancient Mesopotamia. While Sargon's ascension is predated by the presence of Akkadians/Akkadian speakers in Kish, that moment may well have marked a time of flux in the city, and a time in which pressures for or against Akkadian self-identification, if such a thing existed, could have been particularly potent.

THE CITY OF KISH

The ruins of Kish are located on the floodplains of an ancient channel of the Euphrates River, 15 km northeast of the modern city of al-Hillah, Iraq (Figure 3.1). Occupied from the Proto-Literate Period through the dawn of the Islamic Age, Kish's heyday came during the Early Dynastic Period (2900–2350 BCE), when the city's rulers, the Kings of Kish made famous in the Sumerian King List, held sway over a large swath of the Mesopotamian Plain (Smith 2003). Here, we focus on burials from a period at the end of this regional preeminence, when power in and over Mesopotamia shifted away from Kish.

From 1923 to 1933, the joint Oxford University–Field Museum Expedition to Mesopotamia (JOFME) carried out an extensive program of excavation in and around the boundaries of ancient Kish (Langdon 1924; Mackay 1925, 1929; Watelin 1930, 1934). All told, the JOFME unearthed evidence of 5,000 years of occupation on nearly twenty mounds across the site's 24 square kilometers (2,400 ha). Among the traces of this occupation were substantial palaces and ziggurats from the Early Dynastic Period, a large Neo-Babylonian

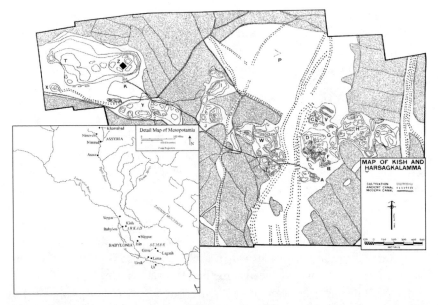

FIGURE 3.1. *Map of Mesopotamia showing location of Kish and plan of the city (Courtesy Jill Seagard, Field Museum of Natural History).*

temple, and over 700 burials from the Early Dynastic through Achaemenid Periods. Pursuant to the terms of the British Mandate's excavation permits, the resulting collections were divided between the Iraq Museum, the Ashmolean Museum at Oxford University, and the Field Museum of Natural History in Chicago.

Unfortunately, due to the poor quality of much of the excavation and field documentation, the untimely deaths of a number of the principal excavators, and the division of the collections among institutions, a full reckoning of the site and its significance has never been produced (Pestle et al. 2006). A second generation of Kish scholars did substantial work to advance our understanding of Kish (Gibson 1972; Lloyd 1969; Moorey 1978; Rathbun 1975), and since 2004 a multidisciplinary team has been moving toward a recontextualization of the site's material remains. Working from collections and archival records curated at the Field Museum of Natural History and Ashmolean Museum, this team (of which the authors are but a small part) has sought to critically assess the lifeways of the ancient inhabitants of Kish from a variety of theoretical and practical perspectives. Here, we present one portion of a larger bioarchaeological reassessment of the site's burials (Pestle,

Torres-Rouff, and Daverman in press), focusing on over 150 graves from the A "Cemetery."

THE A "CEMETERY"

ARCHAEOLOGY

The low tell of Mound A is located in the eastern half of the site of Kish, directly south of the larger and well-known Ingharra complex (Figure 3.1). From 1923 to 1925, Ernest Mackay—the most capable of the JOFME's field directors—excavated Mound A, revealing an intriguing stratigraphic sequence of life at the end of the Early Dynastic (ED from hereon) and beginning of the subsequent Akkadian periods (Mackay 1925, 1929). Discounting scattered EDI (2950–2750 BCE) pottery from the northwest corner of the mound (Moorey 1970:89–90), the earliest evidence of activity is a substantial plano-convex brick palace (the A "Palace") that appears to have been built in stages during the EDIII period (2600–2350 BCE) (Mackay 1929; Moorey 1970, 1978). It seems that the "A Palace," which featured elegant friezes depicting offerings and captives borne to the city's king, was destroyed and abandoned late in EDIII, after which a series of modest domestic structures was erected in its place (Gibson 1972; Mackay 1929; Moorey 1970, 1978). These later structures, largely made of bricks remaining from the palace, appear to have been erected soon after the palace's destruction (Moorey 1970:92). It is from within these buildings that the A "Cemetery" burials were made, with the orientation of the burials, and the lack of any superposition of walls over grave cuts, attesting to their contemporaneity (Mackay 1925; Moorey 1970, 1978). Despite the implications of the title A "Cemetery," the intramural nature of burial shows that Mound A was not a formalized place used only for disposal of the dead.

While there has been some disagreement since the excavation about the chronology of the A "Cemetery" burials (Breniquet 1984; Moorey 1970, 1978; Whelan 1978), general consensus holds that with the exception of five late (Neo-Babylonian or later) burials (nos. 0, 41, 44, 111, and 114), the remaining 150 graves date to a relatively restricted period of time (contra Hrouda and Karstens 1967). In the most thorough treatments of the A graves, Roger Moorey argues convincingly that the cemetery was only in use for "two or three generations" (Moorey 1978:74), or "no more than a century or so" (Moorey 1970:104). This conclusion, which is based on the overwhelming stylistic homogeneity of the material culture (in particular, the pottery) found in the A graves rather than any form of absolute chronometric dating, quickly gained the support of

McGuire Gibson (1972), although some (e.g., Whelan 1978) have questioned Moorey's interpretation.

HISTORICAL CONTEXT

As described above, the archaeological sequence on Mound A begins with the construction, remodeling/renovation, and occupation of the "A Palace," followed by its destruction and, ultimately, the construction of private homes and placement of burials on the Mound. These events appear to have transpired over the course of a few centuries spanning the EDIII and Akkadian Periods (ca. 2350–2150 BCE) (Gibson 1972:80; Moorey 1970:93–94; 1978).

While it can be dangerous to associate archaeological phenomena with known events, for Kish's A "Cemetery," there is enough historical and textual evidence for this time period to advance some, admittedly tenuous, associations. The historical sources in question (the Sumerian King List and others) must be viewed somewhat skeptically given that they may postdate (significantly) the events that they describe and that they are (even more than most) intrinsically politicized representations of said events (Brisch 2013; Liverani 1993). Thus, while the following historical reconstruction is speculative, and may prove to be inaccurate in small or large part, what is obvious is that the use life of the A "Cemetery" covers a period of pronounced and significant change in the site and the region's political, if not ethnic, constitution.

Working from the Sumerian King List, which becomes more secure by the end of the Early Dynastic Period (Brisch 2013:117), and archaeological evidence, it would appear that the late Early Dynastic (EDII/EDIII in particular) marks the zenith of Kish's political sway (Steinkeller 1993:107–8). The prominence of Kish in this period has been confirmed archaeologically by Gibson's surface survey, which found that Kish reached its apogee as the dominant regional city in EDIII (Gibson 1972:48). This period of Kish's prominence can presumptively be associated with the reign of King Ur-Zababa and his predecessors (Jacobsen 1939b:107–8, 160).

The rule of Ur-Zababa, according to Sargonic inscriptions, "ended in a catastrophe which left Kish ruined and partly deserted" (Jacobsen 1939b:178). It is generally agreed (e.g., Astour 2002:72–73; Jacobsen 1939b:178–79) that this catastrophe was perpetrated by Lugalzagesi of Uruk: "Kish was smitten with weapons; its kingship to Uruk was carried. In Uruk Lugal-zage-si became king and reigned 25 years" (Jacobsen 1939b:111). The storming and destruction by fire of the "A Palace," as well as some lesser damage seen on the adjacent Ingharra ziggurats (Moorey 1966:43–44), can putatively be associated with the actions of Lugalzagesi or events surrounding his sacking of Kish. As such, the period preceding the use of Mound A as a residential and burial space was one of great flux; in those years Kish first attained, and then lost to Uruk, great regional power. Temporally, at least some of the burials on Mound A may come from the period of Lugalzagesi's rule over Kish, especially given the rapid chronology provided by Moorey (1978) for the erosion of the destroyed palace's walls.

Prior to his defeat by Lugalzagesi, Ur-Zababa had in his royal retinue—serving in the role of cup-bearer or perhaps governor of a vassal state (Hamblin 2006:73–74; Jacobsen 1939b:111, 178)—one Sargon, an Akkadian. With the defeat of his king, Sargon took to the field against Lugalzagesi, ultimately defeating him in battle and driving him from the northern Mesopotamian plain, going so far as to take control of his lands in the Sumerian south (Hamblin 2006:74).[2] Sargon's exploits and ascendancy are commemorated in contemporary royal inscriptions (Frayne 1993:13):

> Sargon, king of Akkad ... king of the world ... was victorious over Uruk in battle, conquered fifty governors [of Lugalzagesi] with the [divine] mace of the god Ilaba, as well as the city of Uruk, and destroyed [Uruk's] walls. Further, he captured Lugalzagesi, king of Uruk, in battle [and] led him off to the gate of the god Enlil in a neck stock.

The rise of Sargon, sometime before 2330 BCE, marks the beginning of one of the world's first empires, the Akkadian, named after the place, language, people (?), and the city of Agade, (founded by Sargon and presently unidentified) of the northern Mesopotamian plain. According to the Sumerian King List, Sargon and his successors reigned and for the following 200-plus years his successors held sway before power again shifted South to Uruk (Jacobsen 1939b:115). The restoration and resettlement of Kish was one of Sargon's first acts as king (Hirsch 1963:36). If, as seems likely, the destruction of the "A Palace" took place near the end of Ur-Zababa's or the beginning of Lugalzagesi's reigns, the houses built atop Mound A and a substantial portion of the A "Cemetery" burials ought to be associated with the time of Sargon's restoration of Kish.

RESEARCH QUESTION

Irrespective of historical particularities, the A "Cemetery"'s period of use was one of substantial political flux. Over the course of decades, the city, led by local rulers, held sway over a substantial portion of (at least) northern

Mesopotamia; was later damaged or destroyed, losing power to the Sumerian south; was subsequently restored; and reclaimed at least some of its previous power and prestige. Using a bioarchaeological approach that incorporates the study of human skeletal remains in their immediate, mortuary context, as well as their broader cultural milieu, we explore whether the city's changing political fate, which brought it under the sway of three potentially ethnically distinct leaders/regimes in the course of a century, are manifest in changes in either the biological makeup of those buried in the A "Cemetery" or in their mortuary treatment. Our investigation of these questions, it is hoped, will help shed light on the rather contentious issue of Mesopotamian ethnicity, specifically the long-standing debate about the possible distinctiveness of Sumerian and Akkadian ethnicities.

METHODS AND MATERIALS

To evaluate these questions, we employed two distinct lines of investigation beyond those that normally constitute a basic osteological assessment: analysis of mortuary treatments, in particular grave goods, and biodistance analyses of human skeletal remains. The guiding principles for both lines of inquiry are provided here.

Each set of remains was assessed for numerous morphological, pathological/traumatic, metric, and discrete epigenetic features following guidelines and standards established in *Standards for Data Collection from Human Skeletal Remains* (Buikstra and Ubelaker 1994) with additional data collection criteria derived from Buzon et al. (2005) as well as with modifications appropriate to our research questions. While the larger reanalysis of the Kish skeletal material had a broad focus, two specific aspects of that study are of particular relevance to the present work: (1) demographic assessments and (2) biodistance (biological relatedness) analysis.

Adult individuals from Mound A were examined for known sexually dimorphic cranial and pelvic traits;[3] in cases in which both cranial and pelvic bones could be assessed, pelvic traits were considered more reliable indicators. For most analyses, sex was classified along a five-point scale (Female–Probable Female–Indeterminate–Probable Male–Male), although for certain iterations, these five categories were condensed into three (Female-Indeterminate-Male). For subadults (individuals under eighteen at the time of their death), chronological age was estimated by observing the state of dental eruption and the degree of epiphyseal fusion as well as through the measurement of long bone diaphyses. For adults, age was determined through evaluation of the degeneration of the pubic symphysis and the degree of cranial suture closure (Buikstra and Ubelaker 1994). Individuals who could be aged by any of these means were grouped into the following broad age categories defined for our analysis: neonate (NE, conception to 6 months), infant I (I1, 6 months–6 years), infant II (I2, 6–12 years), juvenile (JU, 12–18 years), young adult (YA, 18–35 years), middle adult (MA, 35–50 years), old adult (OA, 50+ years). When the specific age of adult individuals could not be clearly determined, they were placed into a generic adult category (A, 18+ years). Poor preservation meant that demographic information for many individuals could not be determined with any degree of certainty.

With the demographic profile of the A "Cemetery" burials established, we focused on determining the degree of biological affinity (relatedness) between these individuals and people buried in other areas of the city, as well as between subsets of the A "Cemetery" burials. We scored crania and dentition for nonmetric traits (Tables 3.1 and 3.2): discrete morphological features that can be readily observed and scored (on either a presence/absence basis or using a graded scale) during macroscopic analysis of skeletal remains. Such traits include extrasutural bones (ossicles), abnormal bony or dental projections, and variation in the number or positions of foramina (holes for blood vessels or nerves) (Buikstra and Ubelaker 1994:85). Observation and scoring of nonmetric traits were made with reference to drawings, photographs, and, for dental nonmetric traits, with a series of standardized casts distributed by Arizona State University (Turner, Nichol, and Scott 1991). These traits show considerable variation in expression and a high degree of heritability. They have been employed in biodistance and evolutionary studies in biological anthropology with great efficacy since at least the late 1950s (Berry and Berry 1967; Cheverud and Buikstra 1981a, b, 1982; Richtsmeier and McGrath 1986; Saunders 1989; Self and Leamy 1978; Sjøvold 1973, 1977).

The present work deals only with the seventy-five traits found on the cranium and dentition due to a dearth of postcrania. Cranial nonmetric trait definitions and scores were based on Buikstra and Ubelaker (1994) and Berry and Berry (1967), while dental nonmetrics followed Turner, Nichol, and Scott (1991). A full list of traits can be found in Tables 3.1 and 3.2. Positive occurrences of each trait, as well as absences and instances in which observations could not be made, were all recorded. Bilateral traits were scored for maximum degree of expression, a practice that maximizes sample size (Sutter and Cortez 2005), and graded (nondichotomous) data were made dichotomous about the overall sample mean after data collection was complete and in advance of statistical analysis. Following data collection, individuals were grouped by burial

TABLE 3.1 Evaluated cranial nonmetric traits

Trait	Bone/Suture/Landmark Examined for Trait
Metopic suture	Frontal
Supraorbital notch	Frontal
Supraorbital foramen	Frontal
Accessory supraorbital foramen	Frontal
Frontal grooves	Frontal
Fronto-temporal articulation	Junction of frontal and temporal
Maxillary torus	Maxilla
Multiple infraorbital foramina	Maxilla
Accessory lesser palatine foramen	Palatine
Palatine torus	Palatine
Infraorbital suture	Zygomatic
Multiple zygomatico-facial foramina	Zygomatic
Os japonicum	Zygomatic
Marginal tubercule	Zygomatic
Parietal foramen	Parietal
Divided parietal	Parietal
Typanic dihiscence	Temporal
Auditory exostosis	Temporal
Suprameatal pit or spine	Temporal
Flexure of superior sagittal sulcus	Occipital
Highest nuchal line	Occipital
Paracondylar process	Occipital
Bridging of jugular foramen	Occipital
Pharyngeal tubercule	Occipital
Inca bone	Occipital
Condylar canal	Occipital
Double condylar facet	Occipital
Precondylar tubercle	Occipital
Divided hypoglossal canal	Occipital
Foramen ovale incomplete	Sphenoid
Foramen spinosum incomplete	Sphenoid

continued on next page

TABLE 3.1—*continued*

Trait	Bone/Suture/Landmark Examined for Trait
Rocker mandible	Mandible
Mental foramen	Mandible
Mandibular torus	Mandible
Mylohyoid bridge	Mandible
Bregmatic bone	Bregma
Coronal ossicle	Coronal suture
Epipteric bone	"Junction of frontal, parietal, temporal, and sphenoid"
Asterionic bone	"Junction of occipital, parietal, and temporal"
Apical bone	Lambda
Lambdoid ossicle	Lambdoid suture
Ossicle in occipito-mastoid suture	Occipito-Mastoid suture
Ossicle at parietal notch	Parietal notch
Sagittal ossicle	Sagittal suture

mound and sex. Biodistances (estimates of biological relatedness) between the resulting groups were calculated using C.A.B. Smith's Mean Measure of Divergence (MMD) following Torstein Sjøvold (1977). This statistical technique calculates the degree of similarity or dissimilarity between a priori groups (here, burial mound and sexes) using the relative frequency of expression of the various nonmetric traits observed in each group.

Biodistance studies of this sort are uncommon in Mesopotamian archaeology, likely a result of issues surrounding preservation and conservation of human remains from the region. However, some scholars working in the larger region have carried out studies that integrate biodistance studies into considerations of ethnicity and relatedness (Buzon 2006; Pilloud and Larsen 2011; Ullinger et al. 2005). Jaime Ullinger and colleagues (2005) used dental nonmetric traits to explore whether changes in material culture in the Levant were associated with population changes as well. In another vein, Marin Pilloud and Clark Spencer Larsen (Pilloud and Larsen 2011) considered relatedness within the Çatalhöyük population by integrating biological affinity with spatial patterning at the site, revealing that biology did not dictate burial location and may suggest a fluid conception of kinship. Our work aims to contribute to these discussions of biological relatedness that move beyond large-scale migrations to consider the effects of this biological diversity at a local scale.

TABLE 3.2 Evaluated dental nonmetric traits

Trait	Tooth/Teeth Examined for Trait
Winging	Maxillary central incisors
Tuberculum dentale	Maxillary central incisors
Peg-shaped lateral incisor	Maxillary lateral incisors
Labial convexity	Maxillary incisors
Shoveling	Maxillary incisors
Double-shoveling	Maxillary incisors
Canine mesial ridge	Maxillary canines
Canine distal accessory ridge	Maxillary canines
Distosagittal ridge	Maxillary first premolar
Enamel extension	Maxillary premolars and molars
Upper premolar root number	Maxillary premolars
Carabelli trait	Maxillary first molar
Upper molar root number	Maxillary first molar
Upper molar root number	Maxillary second molar
Peg-shaped third molar	Maxillary third molar
Metacone expression	Maxillary molars
Hypocone expression	Maxillary molars
Cusp 5	Maxillary molars
Parastyle	Maxillary molars
Distoarticular ridge	Mandibular canines
Lower canine root number	Mandibular canines
Tomes' root	Mandibular first premolar
Anterior fovea	Mandibular first molars
Deflecting wrinkle	Mandibular first molars
Lower molar root number	Mandibular first molars
Lower molar root number	Mandibular second and third molars
Protostylid	Mandibular molars
Lower molar groove pattern	Mandibular molars
Cusp 5	Mandibular molars
Cusp 6	Mandibular molars
Cusp 7	Mandibular molars

Each biodistance comparison between the groups in question was computed twice, once using the full suite of traits observed in the remains (all trait analysis) and a second time using only traits exhibiting statistically significant contingency χ^2 values (p < 0.1) between a priori groupings. At present, there is some disagreement about the appropriateness of each of these approaches, with some scholars (e.g., Shimadza and Corruccini 2005) suggesting that all observed traits must be used to make the analysis statistically rigorous, and others (e.g., Rothhammer et al. 1984; Sutter and Cortez 2005) arguing that MMD *requires* that traits vary significantly between the groups being analyzed. This latter step undoubtedly has the effect of amplifying existing differences between samples and thus increasing the chances of finding statistically significant differences between them (Sutter and Mertz 2004:135); however, as this debate remains unresolved, we present both sets of data. In addition to the raw MMD values, we also calculated standard deviations and standardized MMD distances, which were then used to generate Multidimensional Scaling plots that represent the similarities and dissimilarities between the groups under analysis in two-dimensional space.

The analysis of the mortuary treatment of the Mound A individuals is based on Mackay's (1925, 1929) notes and publications, Moorey's (1970, 1978) recontextualization of the material, and Karen Wilson's ongoing efforts as part of the Kish Project. Due to the quality of excavation and documentation, there are inevitable limitations to these sources, some of which are nearly a century old. The recent reassembly of excavation records previously divided between the Field Museum and the Ashmolean at Oxford has gone a long way in filling gaps in our knowledge of the state of the Mound A graves. In particular, Mackay's carefully annotated field cards have survived, and the content and structure of many graves have been reconstructed (Moorey 1978).

As mentioned above, five graves significantly postdate the third millennium BCE, and as such are not considered here. The remaining 150 graves (which contain as many as 162 individuals due to occasional multiple interments) belong to the initial phase of the cemetery's use-life. Of particular interest here is a subset (nine in total) of Mound A graves that, based on grave goods, are agreed to be Akkadian in date; whereas the other 141 date to EDIII (Gibson 1972:79–80; Moorey 1970:94–95). The Akkadian-period graves are A2, A6, A14, A38, A52, A92, A102, A104, and A106. In particular, we are interested in examining and comparing these two temporal subsets of graves for evidence of continuity or discontinuity in burial treatment and grave good provisioning. In doing so, we are guided by Hans Nissen (Nissen 1993:91), who wrote, "No one would ever talk in terms of total discontinuity or a complete break between the Early Dynastic and the Akkadian periods . . . rather, the question is, whether at the beginning of the Akkad period new elements arose to a degree which would force us to talk about relative discontinuity rather than continuity."

Using this combination of skeletal data and archival information on mortuary treatment, in concert with contemporary readings of memory and commemoration, we hope to contribute to a more nuanced understanding of death and commemoration at Kish.

RESULTS

As in our discussion of methods, we present separately here the results of the two distinct lines of inquiry, dealing first with the results of our biodistance studies and second with the patterned variation in mortuary treatment and grave good provisioning.

BIODISTANCE

Unfortunately, due to the small sample size (n = 9) of well-preserved skeletal remains from the late Akkadian burials from Mound A, we were prevented from comparing their biological makeup with the larger Early Dynastic sample. As such, our first iteration of the biodistance analysis grouped individuals by mound. The 61 Mound A individuals for whom we possessed skeletal remains were compared with the remains of 399 individuals interred in the Ingharra complex and 16 individuals from the later (Neo-Babylonian) Mound W. Table 3.3 presents the results of this iteration, which included 476 individuals and 66 traits. While no significant differences were found between the individuals from these three mounds with all 66 traits taken into account, there is some suggestion (in the form of positive standardized MMD values) that biological differences may have existed between the individuals from Mound A and the Ingharra complex. This hint at biological difference is strengthened when the same analysis is performed using only those traits that vary significantly between the groups in question (12/66 traits; Table 3.4). Using these traits alone, we found a statistically significant degree of biological variation between each of the mound populations. These results, and in particular the extremely high degree of observed difference between the Mound A and Ingharra populations, can be considered robust given that (a) these results were presaged by the all trait analysis above, (b) their extremely high standardized MMD values (anything over 2 is statistically significant at p = 0.05;

TABLE 3.3 Standardized MMD values and significances, all traits by mound/area

	Mound A	Ingharra	Mound W
Mound A	—	1.13	-1.6
Ingharra	Not Sig.	—	-1.57
Mound W	Not Sig.	Not Sig.	—

TABLE 3.4 Standardized MMD values and significances, significantly varying traits only by mound/area

	Mound A	Ingharra	Mound W
Mound A	—	6.8	2.28
Ingharra	Sig.	—	3.4
Mound W	Sig.	Sig.	—

"Traits: supraorbital foramen, accessory supraorbital foramen, tympanic dihisenence, multiple infraorbital foramen, highest nuchal line, fronto-temporal articulation, supermeatal pit or spine, condylar canal, cusp 5 (M^1–M^3), lower canine root number, hypocone expression (M^1–M^3), and Carabelli's trait (M^1)"

a value of nearly 7 is astronomical), and (c) a relatively large number of traits (12) were still included in this iteration. The meaning of these differences is, however, somewhat contingent, as they could result from temporal difference in the city's biological makeup, given that Ingharra burials are predominantly from the Early Dynastic, A "Cemetery" burials date to the Early Dynastic/Akkadian transition, and those from Mound W are late (Neo-Babylonian or Achaemenid).[4]

However, when sex is taken into account, another possible cause for the observed differences becomes evident. Grouping individuals by mound and sex attributions creates a pool of 181 individuals, for which 58 traits could be observed, from Ingharra and the A "Cemetery." Mound W individuals were excluded given the small sample size for sexed individuals. The results of the all trait analysis are presented in Table 3.5. With all 58 traits considered, there were no statistically significant differences between the four groups. That being said, the positive standardized MMD value found for the comparison of the males from the A "Cemetery," and the Ingharra females hints at some degree of underlying biological difference. When this same analysis was performed using only the traits that exhibited statistically significant variation among the four groups (9/58 traits), the trends hinted at above leap to the fore. These results are presented in Table 3.6. While no statistically significant biological differences were found between the females from the A "Cemetery" and members

TABLE 3.5 Standardized MMD values and significances, all traits by mound/area and sex

	A Females	A Males	Ingharra Females	Ingharra Males
A females	—	-0.53	-1.33	-1.65
A males	Not Sig.	—	1.01	-0.15
Ingharra females	Not Sig.	Not Sig.	—	-0.32
Ingharra males	Not Sig.	Not Sig.	Not Sig.	—

TABLE 3.6 Standardized MMD values and significances, significantly varying traits only by mound/area and sex

	A Females	A Males	Ingharra Females	Ingharra Males
A females	—	2.43	0.97	1.29
A males	Sig.	—	4.66	2.94
Ingharra females	Not Sig.	Sig.	—	0.11
Ingharra males	Not Sig.	Sig.	Not Sig.	—

"Traits: accessory supraorbital foramen, infraorbital suture, rocker mandible, supermeatal pit or spine, condylar canal, labial convexity, deflecting wrinkle, hypocone expression, and upper molar root number (M^2)"

of either sex from Ingharra, the males from the A "Cemetery" were found to be significantly distinct from each of the other groups. In other words, while the males and females from Ingharra and the females from the A "Cemetery" were all drawn from the same breeding population, it would appear that the males from the A "Cemetery" were different. Viewing these results after multidimensional scaling (Figure 3.2), whereby the observed MMD values are represented in two-dimensional space, the degree to which the A "Cemetery" males differ from all of the other individuals under analysis is evident. Based on these analyses, it would appear that the A "Cemetery" males are decidedly and significantly biologically distinct from the other individuals buried at Kish.

Given Mound A's particular history and the shifting political context of the time it was in use, these findings offer a tantalizing hint of the populational changes that may have been affiliated with the onset of the Akkadian Period. Whether these differences are, as suggested below, a consequence of the influx of "exotic" males into the city, the strength of the observed difference at this time of flux is nonetheless intriguing.

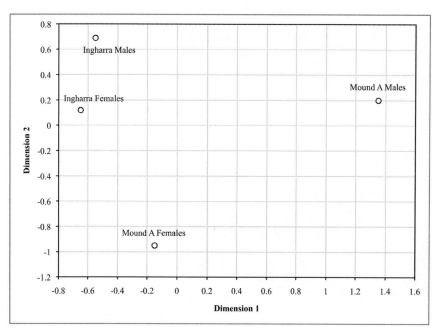

FIGURE 3.2. *Two-dimensional Multidimensional Scaling of positive standardized Mean Measure of Divergence results.*

MORTUARY TREATMENT

In terms of their mortuary treatment, the A "Cemetery" burials are remarkably similar. Most of the grave cuts were simple and rectangular in shape, although they were dug to widely varying depths, from 20 cm to over 4 m (Mackay 1929:131). While three of the grave cuts (13, 15, and 115) showed evidence of brick flooring or mud plastering (Mackay 1925:10; 1929:130), the remaining cuts were unembellished. The bodies of the deceased were not placed in any sort of coffins, although a further three graves (63, 91, and 121) do have evidence of reed or rush matting either placed underneath or wrapped around the body (Mackay 1929:130). With the notable exception of the lone preserved infant among the A "Cemetery" burials (A36), individuals were most commonly placed on their side in a semiflexed position (Mackay 1925; 1929). Legs were generally somewhat contracted, with knees pulled toward the chest while the hands were drawn toward the face (as in Figure 3.3) or placed under the head (Mackay 1925:12–13; 1929:129–30). It appears that neither the body's orientation nor the side on which it was placed followed any set protocol.

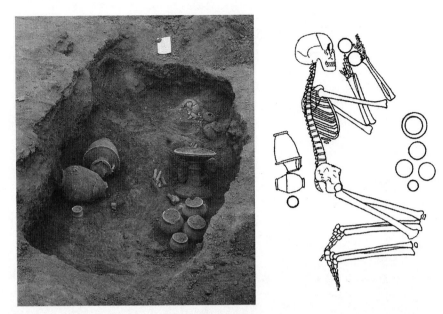

FIGURE 3.3. *Typical A "Cemetery" grave (A5) (Photograph courtesy Field Museum of Natural History [ID# a_oxford_166], line drawing after Mackay 1925).*

These patterns are familiar from contemporary graves at nearby sites such as Fara (Heinrich 1931), Ur (Woolley 1934), and Abu Salabikh (Postgate 1980).

Typical burials contained single individuals interred with a suite of goods. Children, as well as men and women of all ages, were represented. Children, including one infant, were buried in eighteen of the graves. Despite the overwhelming preponderance of single burials, three sets of paired burials, all adults, were also found (A16, A34, and A56). The excavation notes discuss that two of these paired graves (A16 and A34) included a male and a female, while only one of the two individuals in A56 could be sexed (male). These sex determinations (Buxton 1924; Buxton and Rice 1931; Mackay 1925, 1929), based on both the occasional study of osteological remains and the assignation of sex to the bearers of particular gendered objects, are not completely reliable. We can only partially corroborate this assessment with bioarchaeological data, as the curated collection currently includes only the fragmented remains of one individual of indeterminate sex (FM192783) and one male (FM192803) from A16 and another individual of indeterminate sex (FM192759) from A56.

While just under 40 percent of the A "Cemetery" graves had been looted (or were reaccessed after primary burials for removal and secondary reinterment), the remaining grave furnishings were still impressive in number and quality. A multitude of objects was the rule for most graves; only four individuals (< 3 percent) were interred with no goods at all. Pottery was a standard element in the mortuary assemblage, appearing in 92 percent (138/150) of the burials. Ceramic vessels, which varied in shape and number (A106, e.g., was interred with 21 pots in 8 distinct styles), were a standard grave good (as in Figure 3.3). While no other material was as ubiquitous as ceramics, people were frequently interred with items of personal adornment, including beads (89/150, 59.3 percent), cosmetic shells (66/150, 44.0 percent), rings (19/150, 12.7 percent), earrings (50/131, 38.2 percent), pins (73/150, 48.7 percent), and bracelets (17/150, 11.3 percent). Also frequently present were certain goods that may have expressed the characteristics, habits, or identities of the deceased, such as cylinder seals (63/150, 42.0 percent), weapons (including axes [14/150, 9.3 percent] and daggers/knives [30/150, 20.0 percent]), tools (including adzes and needles [6/150, 4.0 percent], spindle whorls [5/150, 3.3 percent], awls [2/150, 1.3 percent], and instruments [clappers, 10/150, 6.7 percent]). This appraisal of the mortuary assemblage indicates (unsurprisingly) the presence of a somewhat standardized corpus of mortuary treatments and grave accompaniments that guided the treatment of the deceased at Mound A. This standardization did not, however, preclude a certain degree of individualization/variability, which, we have argued elsewhere (Torres-Rouff, Pestle, and Daverman 2012), may reflect commemoration of aspects of individual identity as well as that of the mourners.

Breaking down the Mound A graves into those from the Early Dynastic (n = 141) and Akkadian (n = 9) periods, there is general continuity in mortuary treatment and provisioning, with some minor differences that might be markers of ethnic difference (although we present these here simply as interesting details given that the small sample size from the Akkadian Period may weaken or invalidate this argument). First, none of the "Akkadian" burials are noted as consisting of anything other than a simple rectangular grave cut directly into the soil, thereby conforming to the broad structural pattern (135/141) observed in the Early Dynastic graves. While we lack data on the position and orientation of some of the "Akkadian" burials (A2, A6, A14, and A38), there is fairly little of note that differentiates the other five Akkadian period burials from the rest of the individuals buried on Mound A. A52, for instance, is one of at least four individuals (of both periods) whose head was placed atop the stem of a ceramic brazier in the manner of a (rather uncomfortable) pillow. Furthermore, A104 was one of at least six individuals from the total sample who had one hand positioned in front of his face while the other was at the side of his body. Neither of these slight differences in mortuary treatment is exclusive to the Akkadian period burials and, as such, they are unlikely to have served as ethnic markers. It therefore seems that the broad strokes of burial treatment were unchanged in an archaeologically visible way during the Akkadian period.

In terms of grave contents, while the subset of nine burials has been determined to be *temporally* Akkadian (as judged by attributes of artifact style, attributes that are present in demonstrably later assemblages at sites in the Diyala and at Ur), if they are *culturally* or *ethnically* Akkadian, it is only subtly expressed. Taken as a whole, and judged against the 141 Early Dynastic III burials, these nine burials are almost wholly undifferentiated in the provisioning of different artifact types. As we discuss in more detail elsewhere, a theme of general mortuary standardization is also found when the mortuary assemblages of females and males from Mound A are compared (Torres-Rouff, Pestle, and Daverman 2012:207–8), while more marked differences are found between individuals of different social statuses (Pestle, Torres-Rouff, and Daverman in press).

Examining the relative frequency with which 24 different classes of artifact (e.g., ceramics, beads, knives, amulets, etc.) were present in these two temporal subsets of Mound A graves, only one artifact type, clappers (Figure 3.4), showed a statistically significant difference in relative frequency (Fisher's exact test, p = 0.01). While 33.3 percent (3/9) of the Akkadian grave assemblages included examples of these metallic instruments, only 5.0 percent (7/141) of the Early Dynastic graves were so provided. Possible meanings of this difference are discussed below, but it must be noted that this one significant difference is quite aberrant, as the relative frequency of provisioning of the other twenty-three artifact classes is quite similar, if not nearly identical. For instance, 100 percent (9/9) of Akkadian graves featured ceramics versus 91.5 percent (129/141) of Early Dynastic graves (Fisher's exact test, p = 1.0); 44.4 percent (4/9) of the Akkadian and 44.0 percent (62/141) of the Early Dynastic graves included cosmetic shell (Fisher's exact test, p = 1.0); 11.1 percent (1/9) of the Akkadian and 12.8 percent (18/141) of the Early Dynastic graves included rings (Fisher's exact test, p = 1.0); and so on.

Switching focus from the simple presence/absence of various artifact classes to a more fine-grained examination of stylistic variation *within* said classes, there is evidence of subtle variation between the objects in each subset of graves, but an overriding theme of continuity in mortuary treatment is still present. In terms of specific differences, all nine of the Akkadian period burials featured a particular variety of footed ceramic jar (Mackay's type

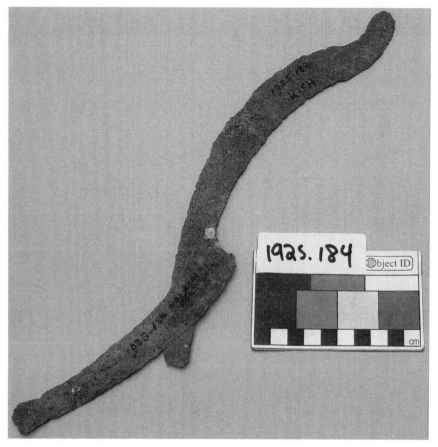

FIGURE 3.4 *Pair of copper-alloy clappers (As.1924-184) (Photograph by author [WJP]).*

C) featuring a "broad, collar-like rim, pronounced shoulder and raised foot" (Moorey 1970:95), like that in Figure 3.5, which is found in Akkadian contexts at both Nippur (McCown, Haines, and Hansen 1967) and Ur (Nissen 1966). Grave A52 also contained another type of ceramic vessel, a mother-goddess jar (Mackay type A), with "high foot, tall neck, pronounced outer-ledge rim and richly decorated handle," (Moorey 1970:94–95), which is stylistically similar to an Akkadian vessel from the Diyala Region (Delougaz, Hill, and Lloyd 1967). Finally, graves A52, A102, and A104 also each contained copper-alloy straight pins (Figure 3.6) with a pierced shank, a stylistic type associated with Akkadian occupation levels at Ur (Nissen 1966). In all three of these cases, while the specific style of the artifact is distinct and even characteristic of

FIGURE 3.5 *Akkadian-style Mackay type A vessel from grave A106 (Photograph courtesy of Field Museum of Natural History [AN 156225]).*

later graves, other quite similar variants of these artifact types are ubiquitous in Early Dynastic graves. All told, 46.8 percent (66/141) of the Early Dynastic burials included examples of Mackay's type A ceramics (mother-goddess jars), 56.7 percent (80/141) had specimens of Mackay's type C (footed jars), and 48.9 percent (69/141) had pins of one variety or another. The distinctive objects from the nine Akkadian graves are thus variations on a theme—they are ultimately objects found throughout the Mound A graves.

As such, several minor differences in treatment of the body, types of artifacts provided, and the style of the provided artifacts may have differentiated these Akkadian graves from those of the Early Dynastic period. However, there are no classes/types of artifacts or burial treatments that are found widely in one temporal subset of the graves and not at all in the other. Differences are indeed present, but they are extremely understated. In fact, we contend that any nine graves selected from the sample of 150 third millennium BCE A "Cemetery"

FIGURE 3.6 *Akkadian-style copper-alloy straight pins with pierced shank from grave A104 (As. 1925.172) (Photograph by author [WJP]).*

burials would likely produce variation or differences of the observed magnitude, if not greater. Returning to where we began this discussion, there is a startling homogeneity to the A "Cemetery" burials both within and between the periods of the cemetery's use-life.

DISCUSSION

Several intriguing possibilities regarding the commemoration and remembrance (or lack thereof) of ethnicity in the A "Cemetery" burials come to the fore when we reconcile the rather disparate results of our analyses. While we explicitly reject any conflation of our biodistance results with notions of "racial" difference in this portion of the Kish population (Bahrani 2006), our data suggest that the males from the A "Cemetery" had a different population history or descent, either in their immediate or distant pasts, than that of Mound

A's females, or for that matter from the males and females from the adjacent Ingharra complex. Indeed, this difference in descent is one of the named characteristics suggested by Jones (1997) in her definition of ethnic groups.

Results of this sort are consistent with, for example, a pattern of male exogamy and matrilocality, in which men were marrying local women and moving into (and eventually dying and being buried in) their wives' village/city. That being said, the historical context of the cemetery and its placement atop the ruins of the "A Palace" suggest a different conclusion. Perhaps the observed biological differences are best explained if we interpret Mound A males as the remnants of an invading or conquering force involved, directly or indirectly, with Sargon's actions against Kish under Lugalzagesi and/or his restoration of the city after its conquest by Sumerian forces. While such interpretations are obviously speculative, they do match with the available biological and historical data. Based on artifact styles, it is clear that some portion of the burials represents the period of Akkadian/Sargonic rule.

Therefore, the biodistance, historical, and temporal data point to the presence of Akkadians or of an Akkadian-ness (perhaps as a distinct ethnicity, see McMahon 2006:59) in at least some of the A "Cemetery" burials. However, in the mortuary treatment—the ways in which these individuals were remembered and commemorated—we see little, if any, significant difference. What can be made of such similarity and uniformity in mortuary treatment and grave good provisioning in tandem with biological differences and historical upheaval? Here we explore several possibilities.

First, it is possible, in this case at least, that the lack of proof is indeed proof of absence. Perhaps we are not seeing ethnicity represented in differential mortuary treatment because there were simply no ethnic differences between the individuals of the A "Cemetery" that needed to be remembered or represented. While we have demonstrable biological differences within the Mound A burial population, perhaps these biologically distinct men are drawn from only a slightly different genetic stock and not a wholly distinct cultural or ethnic group. This interpretation would concord well with at least one side of the argument, discussed above, regarding the ethnic dynamics of the ancient Near East, and buttress the contention that distinct Akkadian and Sumerian ethnic groups did not exist in the third millennium BCE (Emberling 1997:315).

However, if some sort of underlying ethnic difference *was* present, the overall uniformity of the mortuary treatments might also suggest that this ethnic distinction did not carry sufficient (or the appropriate type of) social meaning for the living community at Mound A to commemorate in death. Perhaps they even sought to minimize its social role. As stated above, ethnicity is but one in a suite of identities that can be remembered via commemorative acts or ceremonies, and while we have found some evidence for differences in the treatment of various age-grades, statuses, and possibly sexes among the individuals buried in the A "Cemetery" (Torres-Rouff, Pestle, and Daverman 2012), it is clear that a politicized Akkadian-ness was not a preeminent factor in determining the commemorative aspects of burial treatments. We see subtle differences in burial treatment; however, none of these differences are a pronounced sign denoting "Akkadians" to the modern eye.

It must be noted, however, that just because we cannot clearly differentiate ethnically derived differences in burial treatment, ethnicity per se may still have been marked in life and death at Kish. Indeed, we do see some slight differences in burial treatments: differences that the living community at Kish may have seen and understood much more clearly. For instance, we note but cannot ascribe ethnic meaning to the provisioning of clappers, which were found in 33.0 percent of the Akkadian period graves versus 5.0 percent of the Early Dynastic burials. Perhaps their inclusion was biographical or individual, and the individuals interred with them were dancers or musicians. Regardless, they may have carried social weight and communicated social meaning to the living people who placed them in the grave. In this instance, our etic understanding of the ethnic code may be missing significant emic aspects of the cultural ascription of ethnicity. Moreover, the loss of organic goods due to differential preservation may have seriously handicapped our ability to "see" ethnicity in these burials. In many societies, perishable materials like clothing serve to differentiate peoples whose durable goods (e.g., cooking and serving ware) might otherwise exhibit substantial similarities (Díaz-Andreu et al. 2005; Jones 1997; Rodman 1992). Interestingly, at the A "Cemetery" we do have an abundance of pins recovered from burial assemblages. Given that these pins, which likely held the once-present clothing together, are strikingly similar, it suggests the possibility that the clothing worn by the people buried at A "Cemetery" was similar in structure if not necessarily in decorative elements. Ultimately, it is these decorative features, these elements of style, that likely served to convey ethnicity (e.g., Wiessner 1983) and as such are lost to us.

The relative silence of the commemoration of ethnic expression in these burials leads us to refer back to the more politically conscious understanding of ethnic ascription and commemoration advanced by Emberling (1997) and Jones (1997), among others. As David Lowenthal (1985:210) cogently argues, "memories are not ready-made reflections of the past, but eclectic, selective reconstructions." Building on this point, we ask whether the apparent lack of commemoration of ethnic difference, in an instance with demonstrable differences in descent, is a strategy by which the burying community sought some sort of advantage. Is this particular manner of remembering (or forgetting) aspects of past or present identity an example of the tendency of people to "remember or forget the past according to the needs of the present" (Van Dyke and Alcock 2003:3)? It would appear that by commemorating deceased individuals in the same manner, the members of the living community of Mound A may have been attempting to advance a message of similarity or cohesion. In other words, by following these common local standards of mortuary treatment, those burying the dead at Kish were forging bonds and nurturing traditions (Chesson 2001a:110). While differences between subsets of A "Cemetery" individuals were present, the identity that was being commemorated was one that stressed cohesion.

The use of homogenizing mortuary treatments to mask biological or ethnic difference may have been part of a strategy intended to gain or maintain political or economic advantages in a time of great flux, or simply a way of coping with changing circumstances (much like displaced refugees described by, for instance, Parkin 1999). It is important to recall that during the period considered here Kish had undergone substantial changes in leadership in a relatively short period of time. The city had been sacked and restored, perhaps even in the lifetime of some of the people buried in Mound A. It is possible that for the contemporary "local" inhabitants of Kish, the commemoration of some sort of Akkadian ethnic identity by a group of recently arrived, possibly "foreign" military men, would have been jarring. Indeed, depending on who was doing the burying of these individuals (other Akkadians residents at Kish or the local "host" community), the precise intent that may have guided these homogenizing mortuary treatments may have differed. Were these "foreigners" attempting to assimilate or local residents pushing local values and mortuary customs? Either way, the muting of difference through homogenizing burial treatments on the part of the burying community could have served to defuse possible tension or have served as a means of forgetting. In a time at which expressions of Akkadian-ness may have carried problematic social or political weight, a commemorative message that says, in effect, "we are all the same" might go some way toward obviating potential issues.

CONCLUSION

In the A "Cemetery" burials from Kish, we are presented with an intriguing mixture of biological difference and a general cultural homogeneity. In the temporal and historical context of this cemetery, these somewhat disparate lines of evidence lend themselves to at least two broad understandings of the nature and dynamics of ethnicity and its commemoration in third millennium BCE Mesopotamia. As some authors have suggested, it is possible that Sumerian and Akkadian ought not be understood in ethnic terms. These linguistic differences instead may have been a form of social boundary construction between ethnically similar groups (e.g., Barth 1969), something that may be reflected in our analyses of the mortuary context as well.

Perhaps more intriguingly, while it is likely that there were ethnic differences present in that time and place, it was to the advantage of at least some members of the living community to downplay differences in how the dead were remembered and their identities commemorated. The small hints we have of Akkadian-ness in the pots and pins found with some individuals suggests that there was some awareness of these cultural differences and that this homogenization was not an intentional whitewashing of all differences. By adopting an understanding of ethnicity that allows for dynamic and politically engaged self-ascription, we can see the commemorative act of burial at Kish as part of a strategy employed to mask biological, and perhaps ethnic, differences. Ultimately, it seems that the actions of remembering and commemorating the dead at Mound A spoke to the cohesion of Kish society, possibly as a part of, or even in spite of, political turmoil.

ACKNOWLEDGMENTS

Funding for the Kish Project came from NEH Grant PI-500014-04, the Field Museum of Natural History, Colorado College, and the Associated Colleges of the Midwest. We would also like to thank Alexis Boutin, Nina Cummings, Mark Hubbe, Benjamin Porter, Jill Seagard, Karen Wilson, and the staffs of the Field, Ashmolean, and British Natural History Museums.

NOTES

1. In this chapter and elsewhere, we have adopted the convention of calling the collectivity of burials from Mound A the A "Cemetery" (with cemetery in quotes) to avoid the impression that this was a cemetery in the contemporary sense of the word. These burials were residential, and the use of the word "Cemetery" would carry inaccurate connotations if the reader were to assume otherwise.

2. Alternative versions of this succession have Sargon rebelling against a weakened Ur-Zababa and making league with Lugalzagesi for a time before later turning on him (Hamblin 2006).

3. Cranial traits used in adult sex assessment: prominence of the mental eminence, glabella, nuchal lines, and mastoid processes; shape and thickness of the supraorbital margins. Pelvic traits: shape of the subpubic concavity, subpubic angle, ischiopubic ramus ridge, greater sciatic notch, preauricular sulcus, and ventral arc (Buikstra and Ubelaker 1994).

4. Dating of burials in Mounds A and W was relatively straightforward and based on stylistic grounds, whereas burials in Ingharra were dated both by artifact association and stratigraphic positioning (see Pestle, Torres-Rouff, and Daverman in press for a more detailed discussion of the dating of these burials).

REFERENCES

Astour, Michael C. 2002. "A Reconstruction of the History of Ebla (Part 2)." In *Eblaitica: Essays on the Ebla Archives and Eblaite Language*, edited by Cyrus H. Gordon and Gary A. Rendsburg, 57–195. Winona Lake, IL: Eisenbrauns.

Bahrani, Zainab. 2006. "Race and Ethnicity in Mesopotamian Antiquity." *World Archaeology* 38 (1): 48–59. http://dx.doi.org/10.1080/00438240500509843.

Barth, Fredrik. 1969. "Introduction." In *Ethnic Groups and Boundaries: The Social Organization of Culture Difference*, edited by Fredrik Barth, 1–38. Boston: Little, Brown.

Beck, Lane A. 1995. "Regional Cults and Ethnic Boundaries in 'Southern Hopewell.'" In *Regional Approaches to Mortuary Analysis*, edited by Lane A. Beck, 167–87. New York: Plenum. http://dx.doi.org/10.1007/978-1-4899-1310-4_8.

Berry, A. Caroline, and R. J. Berry. 1967. "Epigenetic Variation in the Human Cranium." *Journal of Anatomy* 101 (2): 361–79.

Breniquet, Catherine. 1984. "Le cimetiere A de Kish: Essai d'interpretation." *Iraq* 46 (1): 19–28.

Brisch, Nicole. 2013. "History and Chronology." In *The Sumerian World*, edited by Harriet Crawford, 111–27. London: Routledge.

Buikstra, Jane E., and Lane A. Beck. 2006. *Bioarchaeology: The Contextual Analysis of Human Remains*. New York: Elsevier.

Buikstra, Jane E., and Douglas H. Ubelaker. 1994. *Standards for Data Collection from Human Skeletal Remains*. Fayetteville: Arkansas Archeological Survey.

Buxton, L. H. Dudley. 1924. "On the Human Remains Excavated at Kish." In *Excavations at Kish*, edited by S. Langdon. Vol. 1. Paris: Paul Geuthner.

Buxton, L. H. Dudley, and D. Talbot Rice. 1931. "Report on the Human Remains Found at Kish." *Journal of the Royal Anthropological Institute of Great Britain and Ireland* 61:57–119. http://dx.doi.org/10.2307/2843826.

Buzon, Michele R., Jacqueline T. Eng, Patricia M. Lambert, and Phillip L. Walker. 2005. "Bioarchaeological Methods." In *Handbook of Archaeological Methods*, edited by Herbert D. Maschner and Christopher Chippendale, 871–918. Lanham, MD: AltaMira Press.

Buzon, Michele R. 2006. "Biological and Ethnic Identity in New Kingdom Nubia: A Case Study from Tombos." *Current Anthropology* 47:683–95. http://dx.doi.org/10 .1086/506288.

Chesson, Meredith S. 2001a. "Embodied Memories of Place and People: Death and Society in an Early Urban Community." In *Social Memory, Identity, and Death: Anthropological Perspectives on Mortuary Rituals*, edited by Meredith S. Chesson, 100–113. Arlington, VA: Archaeology Division of the American Anthropological Association. http://dx.doi.org/10.1525/ap3a.2001.10.1.100.

Chesson, Meredith S. 2001b. "Social Memory, Identity, and Death: An Introduction." In *Social Memory, Identity, and Death: Anthropological Perspectives on Mortuary Rituals*, edited by Meredith S. Chesson, 1–10. Arlington, VA: Archaeology Division of the American Anthropological Association. http://dx.doi.org/10.1525/ap3a.2001.10.1.1.

Cheverud, James M., and Jane E. Buikstra. 1981a. "Quantitative Genetics of Skeletal Nonmetric Traits in the Rhesus Macaques on Cayo Santiago. I. Single Trait Heritabilities." *American Journal of Physical Anthropology* 54 (1): 43–49. http://dx.doi .org/10.1002/ajpa.1330540106.

Cheverud, James M., and Jane E. Buikstra. 1981b. "Quantitative Genetics of Skeletal Nonmetric Traits in the Rhesus Macaques on Cayo Santiago. II. Phenotypic, Genetic, and Environmental Correlations between Traits." *American Journal of Physical Anthropology* 54 (1): 51–58. http://dx.doi.org/10.1002/ajpa.1330540107.

Cheverud, James M., and Jane E. Buikstra. 1982. "Quantitative Genetics of Skeletal Nonmetric Traits in the Rhesus Macaques of Cayo Santiago. III. Relative Heritability of Skeletal Nonmetric and Metric Traits." *American Journal of Physical Anthropology* 59 (2): 151–55. http://dx.doi.org/10.1002/ajpa.1330590205.

Conklin, Beth A. 2001. *Consuming Grief: Compassionate Cannibalism in an Amazonian Society*. Austin: University of Texas Press.

Delougaz, Pinhas, Harold D. Hill, and Seton Lloyd. 1967. *Private Houses and Graves in the Diyala Region*. Chicago: University of Chicago.

Díaz-Andreu, Margarita, Sam Lucy, Stasa Babic, and David N. Edwards, eds. 2005. *The Archaeology of Identity: Approaches to Gender, Age, Status, Ethnicity, and Religion*. London: Routledge.

Eifert, Benn, Edward Miguel, and Daniel N. Posner. 2010. "Political Competition and Ethnic Identification in Africa." *American Journal of Political Science* 54 (2): 494–510. http://dx.doi.org/10.1111/j.1540-5907.2010.00443.x.

Emberling, Geoff. 1997. "Ethnicity in Complex Societies: Archaeological Perspectives." *Journal of Archaeological Research* 5 (4): 295–344. http://dx.doi.org/10.1007/BF02229256.

Frayne, Douglas. 1993. *Royal Inscriptions of Mesopotamia, Early Periods.* Vol. 2: *Sargonic and Gutian Period (2334–2113 B.C.).* Toronto: University of Toronto Press.

Gelb, Irvin J. 1960. "Sumerians and Akkadians in their Ethno-Linguistic Relationships." *Genava* 8:258–72.

Gibson, McGuire. 1972. *The City and Area of Kish.* Coconut Grove, FL: Field Research Projects.

Goetze, Albrecht. 1961. "Early Kings of Kish." *Journal of Cuneiform Studies* 15 (3): 105–11. http://dx.doi.org/10.2307/1359020.

Hamblin, William J. 2006. *Warfare in the Ancient Near East to c.1600 BC.* New York: Routledge.

Heinrich, Ernst. 1931. *Fara: Ergebnisse der Ausgrabungen der Deutschen Orient-Gesellschaft in Fara und Abu Hatab 1902/03.* Berlin: Staatlich Museen zu Berlin.

Hirsch, Hans. 1963. "Die Inschriften der Könige von Agade." *Archiv für Orientforschung* 20:1–82.

Hrouda, Barthel, and Karsten Karstens. 1967. "Zur inneren Chronologie des Friedhofes 'A' in Ingharra/Chursagkalama bei Kis." *Zeitschrift für Assyriologie* 58:256–67.

Jacobsen, Thorkild. 1939a. "The Assumed Conflict between Sumerians and Semites in Early Mesopotamian History." *Journal of the American Oriental Society* 59 (4): 485–95. http://dx.doi.org/10.2307/594482.

Jacobsen, Thorkild. 1939b. *The Sumerian King List.* Chicago: University of Chicago Press.

Jones, Sian. 1997. *The Archaeology of Ethnicity.* London: Routledge.

Joyce, Rosemary. 2001. "Burying the Dead at Tlatilco: Social Memory, Social Identities." In *Social Memory, Identity, and Death: Anthropological Perspectives on Mortuary Rituals,* edited by Meredith S. Chesson, 12–26. Arlington, VA: Archaeology Division of the American Anthropological Association. http://dx.doi.org/10.1525/ap3a.2001.10.1.12.

Kamp, Kathryn A., and Norman Yoffee. 1980. "Ethnicity in Ancient Western Asia during the Early Second Millennium B.C.: Archaeological Assessments and Ethnoarchaeological Prospectives." *Bulletin of the American Schools of Oriental Research* 237: 85–104. http://dx.doi.org/10.2307/1356508.

Kraus, Fritz R. 1970. *Sumerer und Akkader: Ein Problem der altmesopotamischen Geschichte.* Amsterdam: North Holland Publishing.

Langdon, Stephen. 1924. *Excavations at Kish I (1923–1924)*. Paris: Paul Geuthner.

Liverani, Mario. 1993. "Model and Actualization: The Kings of Akkad in the Historical Tradition." In *Akkad the First World Empire: Structure, Ideology, Traditions*, edited by Mario Liverani, 41–68. Padua: Sargon.

Lloyd, Seton. 1969. "Back to Ingharra: Some Further Thoughts on the Excavations at East Kish." *Iraq* 31 (1): 40–48. http://dx.doi.org/10.2307/4199864.

Lowenthal, David. 1985. *The Past is a Foreign Country*. Cambridge: Cambridge University Press.

Mackay, Ernest. 1925. *Report on the Excavation of the "A" Cemetery at Kish, Mesopotamia*. Chicago: Field Museum of Natural History.

Mackay, Ernest. 1929. *A Sumerian Palace and the "A" Cemetery at Kish, Mesopotamia*. Chicago: Field Museum of Natural History.

McCown, Donald E., Richard C. Haines, and Donald P. Hansen. 1967. *Nippur I: Temple of Enlil, Scribal Quarter, and Soundings*. Chicago: University of Chicago Press.

McMahon, Augusta. 2006. *Nippur V. The Early Dynastic to Akkadian Transition: The Area WF Sounding at Nippur*. Chicago: University of Chicago Press.

Meskell, Lynn. 2007. "Archaeologies of identity." In *The Archaeology of Identities*, edited by Timothy Insoll, 23–43. New York: Routledge.

Moorey, P.R.S. 1966. "A Re-Consideration of the Excavations on Tell Ingharra (East Kish), 1923–33." *Iraq* 28:18–51.

Moorey, P.R.S. 1970. "Cemetery A at Kish: Grave Groups and Chronology." *Iraq* 32(2):86–128. http://dx.doi.org/10.2307/4199897.

Moorey, P.R.S. 1978. *Kish Excavations, 1923–1933*. Oxford: Clarendon Press.

Nagel, Joane. 1994. "Constructing Ethnicity: Creating and Recreating Ethnic Identity and Culture." *Social Problems* 41 (1): 152–76. http://dx.doi.org/10.2307/3096847.

Nissen, Hans J. 1966. *Zur Datierung des Königsfriedhofes von Ur*. Bonn: Rudolf Habelt Verlag.

Nissen, Hans J. 1993. "Settlement Patterns and Material Culture of the Akkadian Period: Continuity and Discontinuity." In *Akkad the First World Empire: Structure, Ideology, Traditions*, edited by Mario Liverani, 91–106. Padua: Sargon.

Okamura, Jonathan Y. 1981. "Situational Ethnicity." *Ethnic and Racial Studies* 4 (4): 452–65. http://dx.doi.org/10.1080/01419870.1981.9993351.

Parkin, David J. 1999. "Mementoes as Transitional Objects in Human Displacement." *Journal of Material Culture* 4 (3): 303–20.

Pestle, William J., Christina Torres-Rouff, and Blair M. Daverman. In press. "Life and Death at Kish: Re-Analysis of the Human Skeletal Remains." In *Kish Reconsidered*, edited by Karen Wilson. Chicago: University of Chicago Press.

Pestle, William J., Karen Wilson, Stephen Nash, and Sarah Coleman. 2006. "Reconciling the Past: A Catalogue of Scattered Collections." In *Archäologie und Computer, Kulturelles Erbe und Neue Technologien*, 1–11. Vienna: Stadtarchäologie Wien.

Pilloud, Marin A., and Clark Spencer Larsen. 2011. "'Official' and 'practical' kin: Inferring social and community structure from dental phenotype at Neolithic Çatalhöyük, Turkey." *American Journal of Physical Anthropology* 145 (4): 519–30. http://dx.doi.org/10.1002/ajpa.21520.

Postgate, J. Nicholas. 1980. "Early Dynastic Burial Customs at Abu Salabikh." *Sumer* 36:65–82.

Rathbun, Ted. 1975. *A Study of the Physical Characteristics of the Ancient Inhabitants of Kish, Iraq*. Coconut Grove, FL: Field Research Projects.

Richtsmeier, Joan T., and Janet W. McGrath. 1986. "Quantitative Genetics of Cranial Nonmetric Traits in Randombred Mice: Heritability and Etiology." *American Journal of Physical Anthropology* 69 (1): 51–58. http://dx.doi.org/10.1002/ajpa.1330690107.

Rodman, Amy Oakland. 1992. "Textiles and Ethnicity: Tiwanaku in San Pedro de Atacama, Chile." *Latin American Antiquity* 3 (4): 316–40. http://dx.doi.org/10.2307/971952.

Rothhammer, Francisco, Silvia Quevedo, José A. Cocilovo, and Elena Llop. 1984. "Microevolution in Prehistoric Andean Populations: Chronologic Nonmetrical Cranial Variation in Northern Chile." *American Journal of Physical Anthropology* 65 (2): 157–62. http://dx.doi.org/10.1002/ajpa.1330650207.

Sassmannshausen, Leonhard. 2005. "'Sumerians' and 'Akkadians' in the Akkadian Period." In *Ethnicity in Ancient Mesopotamia: Papers Read at the 48th Rencontre Assyriologique Internationale, Leiden, 1–4 July 2002*, edited by W. H. Van Soldt, R. Kalvelagen, and D. Katz, 333–39. Leiden: Nederlands Instituut voor Het Nabije Oosten.

Saunders, Shelley R. 1989. "Nonmetric Skeletal Variation." In *Reconstruction of Life from the Skeleton*, edited by M. Y. İşcan and K. A. R. Kennedy, 95–108. New York: Liss.

Scott, Rachel E. 2011. "Religious Identity and Mortuary Practice: The Significance of Christian Burial in Early Medieval Ireland." In *Breathing New Life into the Evidence of Death: New Approaches to Bioarchaeology*, edited by Aubrey Baadsgaard, Alexis T. Boutin, and Jane E. Buikstra, 55–77. Santa Fe: School for Advanced Research Press.

Self, Steven G., and Larry Leamy. 1978. "Heritability of Quasi-Continuous Skeletal Traits in a Randombred Population of House Mice." *Genetics* 88 (1): 109–20.

Shimadza, Izumi, and Robert Corruccini. 2005. "Comment on: The Nature of Moche Human Sacrifice." *Current Anthropology* 46 (4): 540–41.

Sjøvold, Torstein. 1973. "The Occurrence of Minor Non-metrical Variants in the Skeleton and Their Quantitative Treatment for Population Comparisons." *Homo* 24:204–33.

Sjøvold, Torstein. 1977. "Non-Metrical Divergence between Skeletal Populations: The Theoretical Foundation and Biological Importance of C. A. B. Smith's Mean Measure of Divergence." *Ossa: International Journal of Skeletal Research* 4 (Suppl. 1): 1–133.

Smith, Adam T. 2003. *The Political Landscape: Constellations of Authority in Early Complex Polities.* Berkeley: University of California Press.

Steinkeller, Piotr. 1993. "Early Political Development in Mesopotamia and the Origins of the Sargonic Empire." In *Akkad the First World Empire: Structure, Ideology, Traditions*, edited by Mario Liverani, 107–30. Padua: Sargon.

Sutter, Richard C., and Rosa J. Cortez. 2005. "The Nature of Moche Human Sacrifice: A Bio-Archaeological Perspective." *Current Anthropology* 46 (4): 521–49. http://dx.doi.org/10.1086/431527.

Sutter, Richard C., and Lisa Mertz. 2004. "Nonmetric Cranial Trait Variation and Prehistoric Biocultural Change in the Azapa Valley, Chile." *American Journal of Physical Anthropology* 123 (2): 130–45. http://dx.doi.org/10.1002/ajpa.10311.

Torres-Rouff, Christina, William J. Pestle, and Blair M. Daverman. 2012. "Commemorating Bodies and Lives at Kish's 'A Cemetery': (Re)presenting Social Memory." *Journal of Social Archaeology* 12 (2): 193–219. http://dx.doi.org/10.1177/1469605312439972.

Tricoli, Sara. 2005. "Sargon the Semite: Preliminary Reflections on a Comparative Study of Sargon of Akkad and His Dynasty." In *Ethnicity in Ancient Mesopotamia: Papers Read at the 48th Rencontre Assyriologique Internationale, Leiden, 1–4 July 2002*, edited by W. H. Van Soldt, R. Kalvelagen, and D. Katz, 372–92. Leiden: Nederlands Instituut voor Het Nabije Oosten.

Turner, Christy G., C. R. Nichol, and George Richard Scott. 1991. "Scoring Procedures for Key Morphological Traits of the Permanent Dentition: The Arizona State University Dental Anthropology System." In *Advances in Dental Anthropology*, edited by Mark A. Kelley, and Clark Spencer Larsen, 13–31. New York: Wiley-Liss.

Ullinger, Jaime M., Susan Guise Sheridan, Diane E. Hawkey, Christy G. Turner, and Robert Cooley. 2005. "Bioarchaeological Analysis of Cultural Transition in the Southern Levant using Dental Nonmetric Traits." *American Journal of Physical Anthropology* 128 (2): 466–76. http://dx.doi.org/10.1002/ajpa.20074.

Van Dyke, Ruth M., and Susan E. Alcock. 2003. "Archaeologies of Memory: An Introduction." In *Archaeologies of Memory*, edited by Ruth M. Van Dyke and Susan E. Alcock, 1–14. Malden, MA: Blackwell. http://dx.doi.org/10.1002/9780470774304.ch1.

Watelin, Louis Charles. 1930. *Excavations at Kish III (1925–1927)*. Paris: Paul Geuthner.

Watelin, Louis Charles. 1934. *Excavations at Kish IV (1925–1930)*. Paris: Paul Geuthner.

Whelan, Estelle. 1978. "Dating the A Cemetery at Kish: A Reconsideration." *Journal of Field Archaeology* 5 (1): 79–96.

Wiessner, Polly. 1983. "Style and Social Interaction in Kalahari San Projectile Points." *American Antiquity* 48 (2): 253–76. http://dx.doi.org/10.2307/280450.

Wilcke, Claus. 1975. "Politsche Opposition nach sumerischen Quellen: der Konflikt zwischen Königtum und Ratsversammulung. Literaturwerke als politische Tendenzschriften." In *La Voix de L'opposition en Mésopotamie*, edited by A. Finet, 37–65. Brussels: Institut des Haut Etudes de Belgique.

Woolley, C. Leonard. 1934. *The Royal Cemetery. Ur Excavations 2*. Oxford: British Museum and Museum of the University of Pennsylvania.

4

Commemorating Disability
in Early Dilmun

*Ancient and Contemporary
Tales from the Peter B.
Cornwall Collection*

ALEXIS T. BOUTIN AND
BENJAMIN W. PORTER

ABSTRACT

In late 1940 and early 1941, Peter B. Cornwall, then
a graduate student at Harvard University, conducted
an expedition to Bahrain and Saudi Arabia's Eastern
Province. During his travels, he surveyed several sites
and, in some instances, excavated burials containing
human remains and associated artifacts. In addition
to the challenges that most doctoral students face
when pursuing a degree, Cornwall had to contend
with deafness, which had left him able to speak, but
not hear, from a young age. Impressively, the portions of his data that he published aided in relocating
ancient Dilmun, a polity that ran along the western
shore of the Arabian Gulf during the Bronze and Iron
Ages. In 1945, Cornwall deposited his collection in the
Phoebe A. Hearst Museum of Anthropology at the
University of California, Berkeley. However, systematic study of the collection's human remains, artifacts,
and excavation notes has been limited. The Dilmun
Bioarchaeology Project was formed in 2008 by the
authors and their collaborators at the University of
California, Berkeley, and Sonoma State University
to study the collection. One of the most exceptional
skeletons belongs to a young woman, who lived and
died during the Early Dilmun period (ca. 2050–1800
BCE). A malformed upper right arm, "knock-knees,"
and unusually short stature would have differenti-
ated her visibly from the surrounding population and
somewhat modified her mobility. Yet she was buried
with more numerous and elaborate grave goods than
her contemporaries, raising the possibility that her loss
was especially profound. The authors investigate the
sociocultural meanings of disability, tacking between

DOI: 10.5876/9781607323295.c004

the experiences of a twentieth-century archaeologist and the ancient woman whose remains he brought to light.

INTRODUCTION

In 1941, Peter B. Cornwall, a young, deaf Harvard graduate student and early explorer of the Arabian Gulf, excavated the skeleton of a young woman,[1] Hearst museum catalog number 12-10146, who lived during the Early Dilmun period (ca. 2050–1800 BCE) on what is today the island nation of Bahrain. This young woman's right arm was unusual in appearance and function, and her walking had been irregular during life. Despite her unusual bodily form, her tomb was marked by a large number of objects, an indication that she was a highly valued person in Dilmun society. In this chapter, we place these two persons with disabilities alongside one another to consider how they managed their corporeal conditions during life and how their societies commemorated them in death.[2]

Interdisciplinary research on disability provides several insights with which archaeologists can consider this classificatory phenomenon in past contexts (Barnes and Mercer 2010; Davis 1997; Johnstone 2001; Siebers 2008). Perhaps the most important lesson is the critique of modern medical definitions of disabilities: these are made in contrast to an ideal normative body that functions with full ambulatory, cognitive, and sensorial capacities within a built environment that is recursively designed to accommodate such ideal bodies. Cross-cultural and historical studies of disability alternatively reveal that what constitutes "disabled" in any one setting consists of arbitrarily assigned stigmas that are embedded in cultural ideologies (Edwards 1997; Goffman 1963; Stiker 2000). This recognition of disability's contingent nature requires archaeologists to identify its constitution within particular historical settings using whatever material evidence and written sources are available (Hubert 2000). Because bioarchaeology and mortuary archaeology place the human body at the center of inquiry, they create opportunities for collaboration between the fields to reconstruct alternative notions of disability.

Despite this natural marriage, archaeological research on disability has seen limited attention, with a theme issue of *Archaeological Review from Cambridge* (Finlay 1999) representing a notable exception. It is significant that four of its five research articles either make use of or are founded upon the contextual analysis of human skeletal remains. Here and elsewhere, Charlotte Roberts's scholarship (e.g., Roberts 1999, 2000, 2011) on disability in past populations is seminal. Her comprehensive investigations of leprosy and tuberculosis, among other pathological conditions, are mindful of the interpretive limitations inherent to the skeletal record, from the restriction of many diseases to the body's soft tissues, to the representativeness of cemetery populations. For these reasons, she emphasizes the necessity of pairing secondary evidence (clinical, historical, ethnographic, etc.) with osteological data to reconstruct social perceptions, identities, and experiences of disability in the past. Nevertheless, extreme caution is required when making such interpretations: every suggestion of functional restrictions, discomfort and pain, care and dependence "may have been an accurate picture but, equally, may not have been" (Roberts 2000:53). A promising model for a bioarchaeology of care has been proposed recently (Tilley and Oxenham 2011), in spite of earlier warnings that such interpretations are potentially ethnocentric and stretch the boundaries of archaeological inference too far (Dettwyler 1991; cf. Roberts 2000).

Past societies lacked medical technologies that ameliorated challenging conditions for those persons possessing nonnormative bodies. One can conjecture, therefore, that the spectrum of human bodily forms and capacities potentially varied more across a population than they do currently. People who experienced and survived traumatic injuries, or were born with congenital defects, could have been more frequent and visible as they lived their lives in the fullest capacities possible given their particular corporeal circumstances. Tony Waldron (2007) points out that evidence for disability from human skeletal remains is far scarcer than historical, iconographic, and clinical data would lead us to expect. Based on the little evidence that does exist, scholars have used the survival of persons with disabilities through and beyond childhood as a proxy for levels of empathy, compassion, and care in a given family (Hawkey 1998), community (Molleson 1999; Stirland 1997), and/or species (Trinkaus and Zimmerman 1982).

The acknowledgment that past societies thought about ability and the human bodily form in distinct ways also presents an opportunity to reflect on disability in contemporary archaeological practice. Much like the investigation of gender in past societies raised archaeologists' awareness of the structural hurdles women face in the discipline (Moser 2007; Nelson, Nelson, and Wylie 1994), so too might awareness increase of the barriers that persons with disabilities face in archaeological practice. Reified stereotypes of field and laboratory research present archaeology as a craft that requires the body's full capacity, especially mobility and use of the five senses to document and interpret evidence. Archaeologists "walk" the landscape, "dig" ancient buildings, and describe their evidence using vision and touch. Such capacities are embedded in undergraduate archaeological field schools and graduate school pedagogy. This disciplinary insistence on the able-bodied archaeologist is reinforced in popular representations of archaeological practice, whether it is field shots for cable television documentaries or the more sensational narratives of Indiana Jones and Lara Croft. Likewise, biographies (Trigger 1980 on Childe), memoirs (Woolley 1953) and disciplinary histories (Moorey 1991; Trigger 1989; Willey and Sabloff 1993) commemorate archaeologists as hero-scientists who combine physical and intellectual qualities to explore landscapes and make new scientific discoveries about the past.

This thinking about disability inspires us to perform an anachronistic exercise exploring the lives of two persons with disabilities who lived four millennia apart, drawing on evidence from the Dilmun Bioarchaeology Project (DBP) (for additional information, see Boutin et al. 2012; Porter and Boutin 2012). Cornwall's contributions to this understanding of Early Dilmun society are still being realized through the authors' work on the DBP. Contextual analyses of the Cornwall collection suggest that the human remains derive from twenty-four burial features in Bahrain dating from the third millennium BCE to the first millennium CE. Many burial features contained objects such as vessels, jewelry, weapons, and occasionally faunal remains. In almost all instances, photographs and drawings of the context for these materials are absent, making it impossible to reconstruct tomb architecture, body position, and the arrangement of mortuary offerings.

Cornwall (1944:111) reported recovering ten adult skeletons, all but one of whom he speculated were male, as well as a complete absence of remains belonging to "young children." Based on this understanding of the skeletal population, Cornwall (1944:121) inferred that "only adult warriors of the tribe" and "the sons and wives of the king or his chief men" were buried in mounds. In several instances, the DBP's findings have revised his assumptions about the assemblage's paleodemographic profile, not to mention prehistoric social organization and gender relations. Osteological analysis of the human remains has determined that the collection consists of a minimum of thirty-four individuals.[3] Twenty-four adults, as well as one adolescent, were sufficiently well preserved to permit sex estimation. Of these 25 individuals, 19 (76 percent) are males or probable males, while six are females or probable females (24 percent). Therefore, males outnumber females by 3 to 1 in the collection. Of the individuals for whom an age category was estimated, the vast majority (76.5 percent) are adults; middle adults (35–50 years) are the best represented. However, adolescents, children, infants, and one fetus are also present in smaller numbers. Research on the Cornwall collection continues with plans for the publication of a final report in the near future synthesizing the results of analysis and interpretation.

A DEAF MAN IN ARABIA: THE PETER B. CORNWALL EXPEDITION

Cornwall (b. 1913, d. 1972), at the time a graduate student in Harvard's Anthropology Department, was fascinated by the archaeology and history of Bahrain and eastern Saudi Arabia. Both areas had seen only limited investigation in previous decades (e.g., Mackay 1929) and called out for more scholarly attention. After seeking funds from various research institutions, Cornwall left for the Gulf in late 1940, where he spent several months first excavating tumulus fields in Bahrain and later surveying archaeological sites in eastern Saudi Arabia (Cornwall 1944, 1946a, 1946b; also see Porter and Boutin 2012:fig. 3 for a map of Cornwall's itinerary and table 1 for a list of surveyed sites). This was remarkable work for the time, since the concurrent world war frustrated most archaeological expeditions to the Middle East.

Cornwall's Gulf expedition was also notable because he was deaf. Sources report that Cornwall lost his ability to hear when he was a young man.[4] Cornwall did have the capacity to speak, and he could respond orally to handwritten questions, many of which were archived in the Hearst Museum's accession file. Despite his hearing loss, Cornwall's educational record demonstrates that he grew into a young scholar unafraid to meet life's challenges and deeply passionate about archaeology and the ancient world. His resume describes how he attended the exclusive Phillips Academy, graduating in 1932, began his undergraduate degree at Stanford, and later completed it at the University of Toronto. He then earned his master's degree in Christ Church College at Oxford University, and later his PhD in anthropology from Harvard. Private correspondence between his professors and grading assessments from his Oxford tutors describe Cornwall as a hardworking, inquisitive student, although they often note their inability to communicate with him in meetings. Cornwall's familial wealth no doubt permitted him to mitigate those aspects of his education in which hearing was needed. His father was a prominent real estate salesman and developer in the San Francisco Bay area. According to one letter, Cornwall paid students to write down lecture notes for him so he could study course materials in private.

Cornwall's wealth, however, did not completely lift barriers to an education in archaeology. He faced institutional discrimination in graduate school as he attempted to design his dissertation research around his interests in the Gulf. Several letters discuss Cornwall's deafness and question whether or not he held the ability to carry out his research. In a 1940 letter, Carleton Coon, an anthropologist and Cornwall's advisor at Harvard, wrote to Theodore McCown, a physical anthropologist and the Hearst Museum director at the time, notifying him that Cornwall would soon contact him seeking UC

Berkeley's financial support. The Cornwall family already had deep ties to the University of California, with Cornwall's grandfather serving as a trustee and his father having attended school there. Toward the beginning of the letter, Coon writes,

> Cornwall is 100% deaf, and we have to communicate with him by writing things on a pad. His own voice is normal . . . Living in a world of his own, with books instead of friends, he has developed a mania—that of an archaeological survey of the parts of Saudi Arabia controlled by the Standard Oil Company of California. As it stands, he has the permit, but insufficient funds.

Later in the letter, Coon reassures McCown that Cornwall is capable of carrying out his research:

> His deafness is a great disability. On the other hand, he has been deaf for the last 13 years, and has worked in Egypt and Greece, etc. and gone thru Oxford, without it hindering him. Here, he works all the time, gets A's despite the fact that he can't hear a word in lectures. Personally he is a very fine fellow; everyone is impressed by his personality and character, and his great courage. On the personal score, I should list him A#1. Scholastically, he is first rate as well, except that he lacks the connective tissue and viewpoints that can be acquired only through conversation, and not thru books. How he is as an archaeologist, I don't know.

Toward the end of the letter, Coon reveals that his department colleagues have decided not to back Cornwall's expedition.

> Naturally, the idea of sending a deaf man to Arabia did not meet instant approval here, even if the money aspect has not arisen. However, he is confident, and he will be with the oil people most of the time. Being turned down here was a considerable blow to him. He naturally wants to take the trip, and stated that he would rather let the University of California have it (*any recovered archaeological materials*) than any other institution [italics added].

Altogether, Coon's letter presented Cornwall and his project in a sympathetic light, anticipating the concerns that a nonintimate might raise upon learning of Cornwall's deafness. Nevertheless, McCown responded in a short note reporting that no matter how much he would like to support Cornwall, the museum's financial resources were limited. McCown did eventually change his mind, and the Hearst partly supported Cornwall's project.

Despite these initial setbacks in fund-raising, correspondence indicates that Cornwall raised the needed amounts from his father's associates and left for the Gulf in fall 1940. Cornwall's field notes, photographs, and travel correspondence reveal little about how he managed his deafness during fieldwork. His letters to the Hearst Museum convey a sense of excitement and optimism over his discoveries, as well as a bit of urgent secrecy that his news be kept quiet until he can return home to complete the analysis of his materials. In one field photograph (Figure 4.1), a man believed to be Cornwall poses with workmen in front of an excavated tumulus. One letter from Cornwall to McCown suggests that Cornwall may have recruited Robert MacDonald, who was said to have competency in Arabic, to join him on the expedition. While Cornwall's travel correspondence never mentions MacDonald by name, one can assume that MacDonald's participation would have eased many of Cornwall's difficult encounters. There is also reason to suspect that Cornwall worked and traveled with employees of Standard Oil, which was actively exploring eastern Arabia at this time for petroleum sources and had agreed in 1939 to provide Cornwall with logistical support. Based on all available evidence, then, it appears that Cornwall was successful in his fieldwork and travels despite initial speculation that his deafness would impede his research.

In spring 1941, Cornwall shipped the excavated materials back to the United States. The Hearst Museum eventually reached an agreement with Cornwall that it would pay for the cost of shipping in exchange for him depositing the materials in the museum after completing his analysis and publications. Cornwall studied these materials in a small laboratory he set up in his family's home in Ross, just north of San Francisco. The results of his work were published in his Harvard dissertation (Cornwall 1944) and a handful of journal articles that presented his excavations in Bahrain (Cornwall 1943), his conclusions about Dilmun's location and history (Cornwall 1946b), and his survey of sites on the Arabian mainland (Cornwall 1946a). By 1945, Cornwall had finished his research and later gave the human skeletal remains and objects to the Hearst Museum. It is clear from internal Hearst Museum communications, as well as from letters between museum staff and Cornwall, that the staff had some difficulties communicating with him from this point forward. Cornwall had promised to come to Berkeley to help unpack and catalog the materials, but despite repeated requests, he failed to carry out this obligation. The museum staff was also concerned about the lack of field documentation describing the location and condition of excavated evidence. A fact-finding visit to Cornwall's Ross home in 1945 presented an opportunity for the staff to ask him these questions directly. The handwritten questions on scraps of paper that were used to communicate with Cornwall remain in the museum's

FIGURE 4.1. *Peter Cornwall and his hired laborers posing for a photograph in front of an unspecified tumulus in Bahrain (Photo courtesy of the Phoebe A. Hearst Museum of Anthropology).*

accession file; however, Cornwall's responses were delivered orally, leaving no way of knowing his replies.

Cornwall last communicated with the Hearst Museum in 1952, informing them in a letter that he was moving to Rome, and leaving an address in the Monteverde neighborhood where he would reside. Although sources shed little light on the remaining years of his life, it seems clear that Cornwall did not pursue a career in archaeology much beyond his dissertation research. Persons who knew Cornwall in Rome during these later decades of his life (and wish to remain anonymous) report that he traveled extensively and collected antiquities and paintings. His death certificate indicates, and sources concur, that his final years were characterized by alcoholism. Cornwall died in 1972 at fifty-nine while in a coma due to complications from cirrhosis of the liver. Records show that his body was cremated in Italy and his ashes were repatriated to the United States soon afterward. They were eventually interred alongside the rest of his family at Cypress Cemetery in Colma, California.

Cornwall's experiences provide rare insight into how a young scholar with a perceived disability came of age in the discipline of archaeology during the first half of the twentieth century. At first glance, Cornwall stands in contrast to the able-bodied representations of hero-scientists that are common in contemporary popular culture and are implicitly replicated in the professional discipline. Yet Cornwall also held the qualities that marked so many archaeologists of his age—a genuine interest in the past, a tolerance for risk, a love for travel, and, not least, access to private funding sources to finance his research. These attributes must be remembered when representing Cornwall's life through the prism of his deafness.

LIVING AND DYING IN EARLY DILMUN

Cornwall's field research was an early step in the investigation of ancient Dilmun, a polity that extended along the western central Gulf coast, including what is today, from north to south, Kuwait, the al-Hasa Eastern Province of Saudi Arabia, Bahrain, and Qatar (Figure 4.2). Written sources originating from Dilmun are limited to a select corpus of texts that reveals little about its society and history (Potts 1990:217–31, 305–34). Complementing this scant record are Mesopotamian written sources, particularly economic documents and word lists that describe the key products, like dates, pearls, and textiles, for which Dilmun was known. Ultimately, archaeological research is the primary means by which Dilmun's history has been reconstructed (e.g., Bibby 1970; more recently, Højlund 2007:123–27; Laursen 2008; Potts 1990), with some areas being more available to excavation and survey (e.g., Bahrain and Kuwait) than others (e.g., Saudi Arabia) in the recent past. Qala'at al-Bahrain on the north edge of Bahrain Island is the best excavated and published site from which Dilmun's development can be observed (Højlund and Hellmuth Andersen 1994). Excavations here and elsewhere (e.g., Barbar, Failaka, Saar) have determined that Dilmun witnessed uneven levels of social complexity between the third and first millennia BCE, with three episodes of marked development during the Early (Qala'at al-Bahrain stratum IIa–IIb, ca. 2050–1800 BCE), Middle (Qala'at al-Bahrain stratum IIIa–IIIb, ca. 1500–1200 BCE), and Late (Qala'at al-Bahrain stratum IV, mid-first millennium BCE) Dilmun periods.

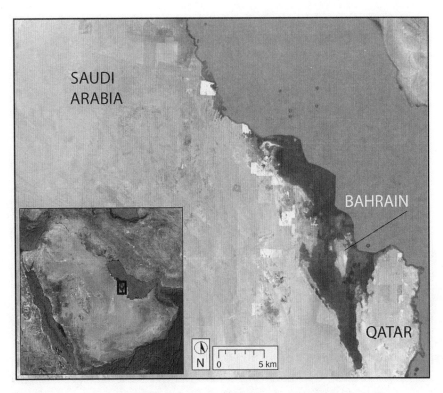

FIGURE 4.2. *A map of the central Gulf region, highlighting eastern Saudi Arabia, Bahrain, and Qatar (Image modified from Google Earth 2011; Image: US Geological Survey, 2011 GeoEye, 2011 Digital Globe; Data: SIO, NOAA, US Navy, NGA, GEBCO).*

Dilmun's first episode of development most concerns us here. The Early Dilmun period is characterized by the polity's increased commercial contacts with Mesopotamia, western Iran, the Oman Peninsula, and the Harappan societies of the Indus River valley. In Qala'at al-Bahrain's period IIA, these connections are manifest in the presence of local objects associated with foreign seals, weights, and ceramic vessels, particularly from Mesopotamia and the Indus River valley (see Potts 1990:192–231 for a description). In a later phase of Early Dilmun's development, public architecture increased in size at Barbar (Temple II) and Qala'at al-Bahrain (Period IIb–c). Starting in approximately 1800 BCE, Early Dilmun witnessed a steady, although not complete, abatement in settlement activity.

A key archive for reconstructing Early Dilmun society has been the extensive mortuary landscape of mounded tumuli, fields of which are still visible along the

Saudi Arabian coast, and on the western and northern sides of Bahrain Island. Excavations by Cornwall and several others following him over the decades (e.g., During Caspars 1980; Højlund 2007; Ibrahim 1982; Mughal 1983) have provided a rich understanding of Early Dilmun's mortuary practices as well as an osteological database from which the island's society can be studied. Most burial mounds consisted of a stone-lined chamber in which the deceased person was laid on his/her side with legs flexed and hands curled under the head in a sleeping position (e.g., Højlund 2007:fig. 258). Often included in the stone chamber with the body were one or two ceramic vessels that likely contained organic materials, and occasionally a sheep or goat, all materials designated for the deceased to bring into the afterlife (Højlund 2007; Kveiborg 2007). Encircling the chamber was a ring wall constructed several courses high. Dirt, sand, and gravel were then used to fill in this circular area, encasing the stone chamber. In most cases, the ring wall eventually collapsed and the dirt fill was allowed to erode, creating the cone shape that most tumuli currently exhibit. While most were modest in size, some tumuli can be characterized as monumental, possessing a more elaborate chamber design and a larger amount of materials constructed over the chamber. The amount of effort and resources needed to construct these so-called "royal" mounds suggest that Early Dilmun society possessed some degree of social differentiation (Højlund 2007:129–36).

Osteological analysis of persons interred in these tumuli has provided another window into Early Dilmun society. Unfortunately, the sizes of skeletal samples for this era—many of which derive from the salvage excavation of a small number of sites—are dwarfed by those from later periods. Accordingly, scholarship on health and demography during the Tylos period (ca. 350 BCE–250 CE) has been nuanced and extensive (e.g., Littleton 1998a, 2003, 2011), while research on Early Dilmun skeletal samples has either highlighted case studies in paleopathology (e.g., Frohlich, Ortner, and al-Khalifa 1989; Rashidi et al. 2001) or analyzed them in a comparative manner to show changes in subsistence and health over space and time (e.g., Littleton 2007; Littleton and Frohlich 1989, 1993).

One of the earliest synthetic analyses of Early Dilmun skeletal data was conducted by Bruno Frohlich (1986). This assemblage numbered over three hundred individuals, the majority of whom apparently derived from the tumulus field at Hamad Town (south of Aali), with the rest having been collected by various Danish expeditions to Bahrain. Among the demographic trends he noted were an unexpectedly low representation of subadults, which he attributed to poor preservation, and a sex ratio biased in favor of males. These trends were later verified by Judith Littleton (2007) in her more focused analysis of fifty-seven individuals from the Hamad Town assemblage. She also argued (Littleton 2007:187) for a "prosperous" economy based on comparatively low frequencies of nutritional deficiency and infectious disease.

The dentitions of these Early Dilmun people provide additional information about their diet, health, and behavior. Karen Højgaard (1980, 1986) studied the teeth recovered from twenty-two Early Dilmun tumuli near Aali, noting frequent caries and concomitant antemortem tooth loss (AMTL) beginning at a fairly early age. She also speculated (Højgaard 1986:66) that some AMTL may be attributed to therapeutic extraction. Littleton and Frohlich (1989, 1993) provided additional data to substantiate these observations and further speculate about their cause, based on the teeth of seventy-five skeletons from Saar and the Hamad Town assemblage. They characterized the frequency of caries as high, with lesions on 13.3 percent of all teeth (Littleton and Frohlich 1993:435), although John Lukacs (1995:154–55) points out that if better account had been taken of teeth lost antemortem, the true caries rate would have been 40–50 percent higher. The ubiquity of caries is almost certainly to blame for rampant AMTL, which began in adolescence, eventually affecting 84.6 percent of adults over thirty-five (Littleton and Frohlich 1989:67). The high caries and AMTL rates combine with several other factors—the early onset and locations of caries, mild attrition (especially of the molars), and slight calculus deposits—to suggest a nonfibrous, relatively nonabrasive diet high in fermentable carbohydrates and low in proteins and fats. Drawing on archaeological and textual evidence, Littleton and Frohlich (1989, 1993) envision a mixed economy for the Early Dilmun period: irrigation agriculture emphasizing date palm cultivation, with intercropping of vegetables and other fruits, would have been a primary food source; herding (of sheep and goats) and fishing would have provided a secondary food source; and grains, which may have been imported, would have played a minor dietary role.

EMBODYING NONNORMATIVITY: 12-10146

We now turn to one rather exceptional person, whose skeleton and grave goods Cornwall recovered from Tumulus B-5, part of a tumulus field several kilometers southeast of Qala'at al-Bahrain. This skeleton, 12-10146, is stored in the Hearst Museum's Paleopathology collection. Its cranial skeleton is mostly complete (at least three-quarters of the bones are present), while one-quarter to one-half of all postcranial bones are extant.

The skeleton is that of a probable female, based on pelvic and cranial morphology (Ascádi and Nemeskéri 1970; Buikstra and Ubelaker 1994; White,

Black, and Folkens 2012). Discriminant function analysis of the humerus and femur also suggests that the skeleton is female (France 1998). Analysis of ossification and fusion of the epiphyses (Scheuer and Black 2004) produces an age estimate of 18 to 23 years. This estimate is consistent with dental development (Liversidge and Molleson 2004), pubic symphysis morphology (Brooks and Suchey 1990; Suchey and Katz 1998), and cranial suture closure (Meindl and Lovejoy 1985). However, it should be noted that 18 to 23 years represents her physiological age, based on skeletal and dental maturation. According to bioarchaeological aging standards, this would identify her as a late adolescent or very young adult. A more nuanced and contextualized interpretation of social age (Perry 2005), however, would place her firmly in young adulthood, as in ancient Mesopotamia it was common for women to marry in their middle to late teens (Roth 1987).

Pathological Conditions

The most obvious and striking indicator of pathology is seen in 12-10146's right humerus, which is unusually short (maximum length 19.2 cm). It exhibits a varus deformity, such that the proximal epiphysis (i.e., the head of the humerus) is rotated posteromedially and inclined inferiorly relative to the bone's longitudinal axis (Figure 4.3). Because of the displacement of the head and absence of the anatomical neck, the tip of the greater tuberosity is the bone's most proximal point. The articular surface of the humeral head is irregularly shaped, with rounded contours that meet at a deep cavity in the center. No other abnormal pitting, porosity, or sclerotic bone is present.

The abnormal angulation and shortening of the humerus resulted in biomechanical alterations to the shoulder region (Figure 4.4), including a prominent curvature where the deltoid muscle inserts on the humeral shaft. The right glenoid fossa of the scapula (i.e., the complementary portion of the shoulder joint) has an area of erosion and sclerotic bone formation in the superior one-third of the articular surface. This abnormal bone growth probably resulted from the impingement of the humerus's greater and lesser tuberosities during abduction of the upper arm. The left humerus is unfortunately not extant, but the left glenoid fossa is completely normal in appearance, suggesting that the pathological condition was unilateral.

Humerus varus deformity (HVD) is caused by damage to the bone's epiphyseal growth plates. The development of the medial portion of the epiphyseal plate is retarded or arrested, while the undamaged lateral portion continues to grow normally. Consequently, the biomechanical influence of the rotator

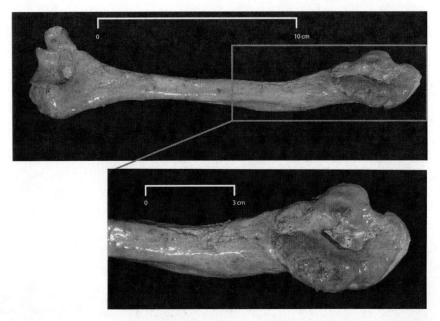

FIGURE 4.3. *Medial view of proximal end of 12-10146's right humerus (Photo: C. Morgan).*

cuff tendons causes a progressive varus rotation of the humeral head, while the premature and irregular fusion of the bone's proximal end (which is responsible for 80 percent of longitudinal growth) causes significant shortening (Ellefsen et al. 1994; Ogden, Weil, and Hempton 1976). However, this young woman's unusually short upper right arm was not the only nonnormative aspect of her body.

The femurs of 12-10146 exhibit femoral anteversion, known in modern vernacular as "knock-knees." This condition is related to bilateral coxa valga, in which the angle between the femur's neck and shaft is greatly increased (more than 135 degrees), so that the neck's orientation is nearly vertical (Castriota-Scanderbeg and Dallapiccola 2005; Haverkamp and Marti 2007). Indeed, the neck shaft angle of 12-10146's right femur (determined radiographically) is 141 degrees (Figure 4.5), which would have affected how she walked. Femoral anteversion forces people to "internally rotate their femurs and adduct their feet. This may cause compensatory torsion of the tibias resulting in foot eversion and valgus deformity with medially displaced patellae" (Johnson and Davies 2006: 97). Although no morphological abnormalities were present on 12-10146's tibias (to indicate twisting) or tarsals (to suggest that they were

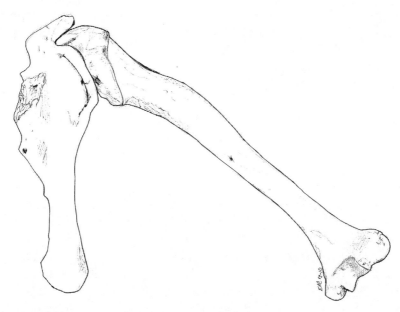

FIGURE 4.4. *Posterior view of articulation of right humerus with scapula at shoulder joint (Drawing: E. Carleton).*

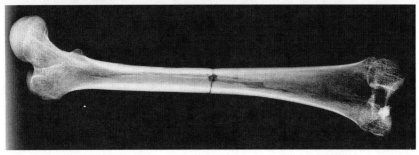

FIGURE 4.5. *Anterior photograph (top) amd anterior-posterior radiograph (bottom) of 12-10146's right femur (Photo: C. Morgan; radiograph courtesy of E. Gaensler).*

rotated outward), a smooth-edged, crescent-shaped concavity on the medial condyle of her left femur could have been caused by displacement of the patella.

Indices of 12-10146's stature and robusticity were compared to a metric database compiled from archaeological sites in Anatolia, Syria, Mesopotamia, and Iran, which date between the fourth and first millennia BCE (Boutin 2008:117–18 ff.). The maximum length of her femur (35.6 cm) is three standard deviations below the mean for ancient Near Eastern females. The ulna (broken postmortem, but with no gross pathologies) was at least 21.3 cm long, which would locate it roughly two standard deviations below the female mean for maximum length. The femur's length produced stature estimates ranging from 137.5 cm (4 ft. 6.1 in.)[5] to 144.3 cm (4 ft. 8.8 in.). This stature range is substantially lower than both the mean female stature from the ancient Near East (156.6 cm; 5 ft. 1.7 in.) and the average stature of a small sample (N = 15) of Early Dilmun females (158.6 cm; 5 ft. 2.4 in.) (Littleton 2007:182). Long bone circumference also can be used as a proxy for overall body size (Safont, Malgosa, and Subirà 2000). The midshaft circumference of 12-10146's femur (6.7 cm) is approximately 1.5 standard deviations below the mean for ancient Near Eastern females. Therefore, it seems that 12-10146 would have been noticeably shorter, as well as slightly built, compared to her female peers.

Compared to her Early Dilmun peers, 12-10146's dental health was quite good. The four anterior teeth that are present and complete are not carious and exhibit light attrition. Of the twelve posterior teeth that are present and mostly complete, attrition is only slightly heavier. One tooth (left M_1) has an extensive interproximal carious lesion that has destroyed much of the mesial crown. There is no evidence of abscessing or bone loss, and no teeth were lost antemortem. No linear enamel hypoplasias were observed on the anterior teeth, but three of the third molars and one second molar each exhibit one hypoplastic lesion. The lesion on the second molar was occasioned by some sort of systemic physiological stressor between six and seven years of age (after Goodman and Rose 1991). Fewer guidelines are available for estimating age-at-defect formation for third molars, but based on crown development patterns these hypoplastic events probably occurred in early adolescence and thus were distinct from those that affected the second molar.

DIFFERENTIAL DIAGNOSIS

Clinical research has recorded the joint occurrence of HVD and coxa valga in skeletal dysplasias, metabolic diseases, and other neuromuscular and genetic disorders (Ellefsen et al. 1994; Ogden, Weil, and Hempton 1976). Premature and irregular fusion of the epiphyses, which commonly manifests in the proximal humerus and distal femur, is one symptom of thalassemia (Currarino and Erlandson 1964). Indeed, this is the etiology that I. Hershkovitz et al. (1991) propose for a case of HVD from Prepottery Neolithic Israel/Palestine. The coxa valga and premature fusion of the medial humeral head of 12-10146 appear consistent with this diagnosis. However, other expected indicators of thalassemia, namely cranial and postcranial manifestations of marrow hyperplasia (Weatherall and Clegg 2001), are absent.

Vitamin D deficiency in childhood—otherwise known as rickets—can cause bowing and bending of long bones, and angulation and fractures at the growth plates (Brickley and Ives 2008). Rickets has been documented in Late Dilmun and Tylos period Bahrain (Littleton 1998b). However, the bone softening symptomatic of rickets would cause a reduced angle between the femoral neck and shaft (coxa vara), not the increased angle that 12-10146 exhibits (coxa valga).

Achondroplasia (classic dwarfism) presents shortened long bones, as well as angulation at the growth plates. However, 12-10146 does not exhibit other characteristic signs of achondroplasia, such as bulging of the skull vault, a constricted basicranium, flaring of the epiphyseal plates, and vertebral abnormalities (Resnick 1995). Her estimated stature (137.5–144.3 cm) also is taller than expected for either true achondroplasia or pseudoachondroplasia, in which a height of no more than 130 cm is expected (Ortner 2003:482). Certain of the spondyloepiphyseal dysplasias do feature HVD, coxa valga, and reduced stature (e.g., Strudwick type; Hall 2005:1). However, the characteristic changes to the vertebral bodies, short (or absent) femoral necks, and systemic ossification failures are not manifested by 12-10146.

Donald Ortner's (2003:491) initial diagnosis for bilateral HVD in an adolescent/young adult from Early Dynastic Egypt was achondroplasia, based on the abnormally short length of the humeri. However, upon further consideration of the humeral head morphology, which is uniquely associated with HVD, he concluded that one of the mucopolysaccharidoses is more likely. Specifically, he favored types II or IV, given the individual's survival beyond childhood. Luigi Capasso (1989) also cites type IV mucopolysaccharidosis ("Morquio syndrome") as the cause of a young adult's HVD from Bronze Age Italy. Certain characteristics of Morquio syndrome, particularly the intermediate (IVB) or mild (IVC) types, are consistent with 12-10146's suite of pathological conditions (Alman and Goldberg 2006:288–91). These include HVD, coxa valga, and short stature. However, this young woman does not exhibit other diagnostic changes, including small or absent femoral heads and flattened vertebral bodies. The second cervical vertebra is not extant, which prevents an identification of another indicator of Morquio's syndrome (i.e., the reduction or absence of the odontoid process). Although Morquio's syndrome presents the closest diagnostic "fit" for 12-10146's condition, the number of inconsistencies makes this etiology doubtful. Septic arthritis and osteomyelitis also are clinically documented causes of HVD (Ogden, Weil, and Hempton 1976; Peterson 2012). Accordingly, M. Özbek (2005) points to traumatic injury with subsequent infection as a cause of unilateral HVD in an ancient Thracian skeleton. But 12-10146 presents no macroscopic evidence of chronic infection.

Unable to diagnose 12-10146's condition based on gross examination alone, we obtained radiographs of her right humerus and femur.[6] Consultation with musculoskeletal radiologists yielded a consensus that genetic or congenital diseases were not to blame for their deformities and short length (R. Boutin, personal communication). More likely, the HVD was acquired, although infection or trauma has left no trace radiologically. The conditions of both bones are best described as idiopathic (i.e., of uncertain or unknown origin). Idiopathic HVD usually manifests unilaterally, as an isolated indicator of skeletal pathology; this is consistent with its occurrence in the wake of postnatal or early childhood trauma, infection, or tumor (Vanderbeck et al. 2009:126). Coxa valga can result from a variety of acquired disorders, which often involve "muscle power imbalance or a decrease in weight-bearing" due to a lack of upright posture (Castriota-Scanderbeg and Dallapiccola 2005:260).

Several case studies in the bioarchaeological literature have cited traumatic injury as the most likely etiology of HVD. T. Anderson (1997), J. E. Molto (2000), and S. P. Kacki et al. (2013) favor traction injuries incurred at the time of birth or during the early postnatal period. Traction injuries often occur during the final stages of vaginal delivery, when the neonate's passage through the pubic arch is hampered and the birth attendant must apply a pulling force. Merbs and Vestergaard (1985:95) and Ortner and Frohlich (2008:67) attribute HVD, respectively, to trauma suffered early in childhood without specifying a birth injury.

In sum, all of 12-10146's pathological conditions are best explained as idiopathic, with an uncertain relationship to one another. The significant shortening of 12-10146's humerus (which is more than five standard deviations below the mean for ancient Near Eastern females) suggests that the premature fusion of the proximal epiphysis occurred during childhood, if not earlier. The lack of visible evidence for infection or trauma in 12-10146 could be attributed to extensive bone remodeling since childhood. Prolonged bed rest could have contributed to the development of coxa valga. The multiple episodes of nutritional, infectious, or metabolic stress that caused hypoplastic lesions on the second and third molars seem to have occurred later in childhood and early adolescence, and therefore may have been only indirectly related to the skeletal anomalies; however, they certainly could have contributed to the young woman's short stature.

IMPLICATIONS ACROSS THE LIFE COURSE

Humerus varus deformity has both cosmetic and functional implications that manifest progressively across the life course. Upper arm length discrepancies associated with HVD average 8 cm, although they can range from 2 to 11 cm (Ellefsen et al. 1994; Ogden, Weil, and Hampton 1976). The length discrepancy between 12-10146's right and left upper arms, although apparently initiated by damage to the proximal growth plate early in childhood, would not have been fully expressed until adolescence; only when she underwent her pubertal growth spurt would its comparatively short length have become outwardly obvious. Her right arm's orientation was also unusual. In a nonpathological humerus, the olecranon fossa is posterior. So, when the arm is flexed at the elbow, the forearm would be raised anteriorly. However, in the case of 12-10146, the posteromedial rotation of the humeral head caused the young woman's olecranon fossa to be medial; when her arm was flexed at the elbow, her forearm would be raised laterally, or abducted from the body's midline.

Given the major impacts that HVD had on the form of this young woman's arm, we would expect that its function also was affected. Because of the way that the malformed humeral head articulates with the glenoid fossa, the acromion process impinges on the range of motion at the shoulder; this is consistent with limited abduction at the glenohumeral joint in clinical cases of HVD (Lucas and Gill 1947). However, restricted abduction is "usually compensated for by increased scapulothoracic motion," and pain is reportedly uncommon (Ellefsen et al. 1994:485). Therefore, loss of function at 12-10146's shoulder probably would have been minimal. Indeed, clinical evidence suggests that patient complaints are primarily cosmetic, based on the discrepancy in arm length, which can induce body image concerns and require special tailoring of clothes (Peterson 2012:103–4).

Evidence from areas of muscle attachment on the young woman's distal humerus suggests that functional limitations at the elbow were minimal. If the function of the young woman's arm had been impacted significantly by her condition, then the biepicondylar width of her humerus (where many flexor and extensor muscles of the forearm attach) should also be unusually small; yet at 5.25 cm, this is not the case. Although smaller than average, it is within one standard deviation of the mean for females from the ancient Near East. Given the dramatically short length of her humerus, its reasonably average biepicondylar width is even more impressive. This suggests that she may have been able to engage in a fairly normal activity load with her right arm despite its shortened length and unusual range of motion.

As described above, the increased neck shaft angle of 12-10146's femurs resulted in moderate femoral anteversion. Although it is not uncommon for children to exhibit mild developmental femoral anteversion, it usually reduces significantly by age eight and disappears by adolescence. Therefore, 12-10146's retention of this condition into young adulthood would have set her apart. The decreased range of motion in her hips would have caused her thighs to rotate inward, her knees to be close together and point toward one another, and in-toeing of her feet. Although her ability to walk was probably not impaired, she almost certainly had a "clumsy" gait (Jacoby and Youngson 2005:1593–94).

COMMEMORATING THE LIFE OF 12-10146

The physical conditions of 12-10146 modified her mobility and differenti-ated her visibly from the surrounding population. But the exceptionally large number of objects interred in her burial suggests that she was commemorated positively in local society upon her death. While most Early Dilmun buri-als contained one or two objects and occasionally a sheep or goat, 12-10146 received at least twelve ceramic vessels of various shapes and sizes. The real objects of value were likely not these vessels but, rather, their contents, which could have ranged from grains to dates to liquids such as wine and olive oil. The value of at least one vessel's contents was high (no. 9-4700), as its interior was sealed with bitumen, a tarlike substance used to make ceramic less per-meable. Provenience studies of bitumen samples from Bahrain demonstrate that such materials were imported from Hit, a still-occupied settlement in northwestern Iraq, in al-Anbar Province on the Euphrates River (Connan and Van de Velde 2010:12–15).[7] In addition, a small alabaster juglet (no. 9-4682), the only calcite alabaster object in the Cornwall collection, accompanied 12-10146 (Figure 4.6). Such vessels were imported into Bahrain, and its rarity in other interments suggests that it was highly valued. Cornwall did not collect any animal remains from this particular mound. Their absence is not too surpris-ing, as animal and objects were not always paired in Dilmun's mortuary com-memoration practices. Unfortunately, Cornwall did not describe the size and

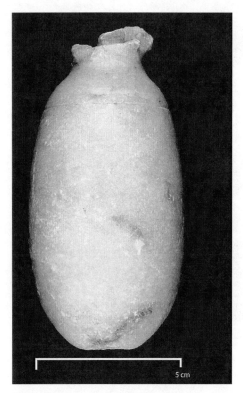
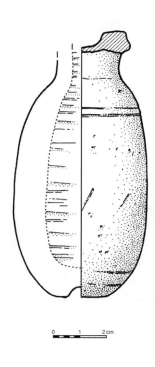

FIGURE 4.6. *A small alabaster juglet (no. 9-4682), the only object of such material in the Cornwall collection, accompanied 12-10146 (Photo: C. Morgan; Drawing: K. Killackey).*

design of the tumulus's architecture nor the body's interred position. If available, this information would have permitted additional insight into 12-10146's commemoration.

One vessel provides evidence for 12-10146's date of interment, an 18 cm high cylindrical jar (9-4680) with a round base, straight body, and a sharp shoulder leading to a vertical neck, the upper part of which is incised with horizontal lines and thickened at the rim (Figure 4.7). The diameter of the vessel's opening is 9.5 cm. The surface appears to have been smoothed, the fabric color is light red (2.5YR7/8), and the clay is well levigated. This is a common vessel type in Bahrain, and previous studies have classified this form as B73A in the Barbar tradition (e.g., Højlund 1987:32–33, fig. 68, type 17; Højlund and Hellmuth Andersen 1994:96, fig. 217, type B73; Højlund 2007:13, fig. 4, type B73A). Although found in limited amounts in settlements, these

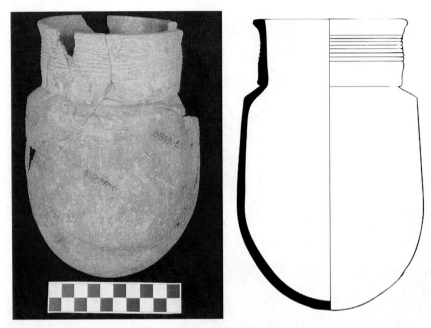

Figure 4.7. *A cylindrical wheel-thrown ceramic jar (9-4680) associated with individual 12-10146. The surface is untreated, and the fabric color is light red (2.5YR7/8) (Photo: C. Morgan; Drawing: K. Leu).*

vessels were commonly used in mortuary practices, as their repeated discovery in tombs indicates (e.g., During Caspars 1980:pls. 14–15; Højlund 2007:figs. 136, 173, 197, 199, 238; Ibrahim 1982:31, fig. 35, pls. 41–43; Mughal 1983:62, fig. 18, pl. 41). Højlund observes this form in datable stratified contexts at Qala'at al-Bahrain IIb-c and Barbar Temple IIb, although it first appears in Qala'at al-Bahrain IIa in limited amounts (Højlund 2007: 13). Based on this link with a dated stratified context, a likely relative date can be assigned to the Tumulus B-5 interment episode at some point between 2000 and 1800 BCE, during the second phase of Early Dilmun's second social formation (Højlund 2007: 125–126).

PLACING DISABILITY IN ITS CULTURAL CONTEXTS

Now more than ever, archaeologists seek to understand alternative forms of personhood in past societies, subjects who were radically different than contemporary Western notions of the autonomous individual (Fowler 2004; Joyce

2008; Meskell and Joyce 2003; Smith 2004). Such a quest has led to new visions of personhoods and the ways that age, gender, class, and so forth shape how persons understood themselves, their places in the social worlds they inhabited, and how others understood them (Clark and Wilkie 2006; Meskell 1999). Surprisingly underemphasized among these vectors of personhood has been the notion of disability, that is, how past societies perceived and classified their members according to their physical and mental capacities (but see Cross 1999 for a rare exception). Because bioarchaeologists study the actual bodies of those persons whose lives they seek to reconstruct, a "bioarchaeology of personhood" (Boutin 2011) offers a unique window into disability in the past.

Social perceptions of people with disabilities are enormously diverse from antiquity to the nineteenth century CE, as revealed by Herbert Covey's (1998) survey of Judeo-Christian and European written traditions. Whether these perceptions were negative (being subhuman or evil) or positive (having unusual spiritual attributes or being entertaining), or connoted helplessness (being poor, intellectual/social "children," or worthy of pity), all of them serve to "Other" people with disabilities from normative identities (Covey 1998:6–25). The dramatic commemoration of 12-10146 similarly set her apart from her peers, albeit in a way that seems to have been positive.

Contextual evidence from the ancient Near East suggests the potential for care and even reverence for persons with disabilities, which would have been expressed in regionally and temporally specific ways. The richest evidence comes from Egypt, where medical papyri, iconographic portrayals, and human remains all speak to experiences of disability (Nunn 1996). Evidence for care may be seen in three individuals from Predynastic Naga-ed-Deir (Podzorski 1990). Poorly healed traumatic fractures of the femur would have jeopardized, if not eliminated, their mobility; yet they survived these injuries, in some cases for decades. David Jeffreys and John Tait characterize Egyptian attitudes toward disability as ambivalent (Jeffreys and Tait 2000). Incurable conditions that were congenital or acquired early—such as club feet and blindness—were tolerated and even associated with noble rank and activities. On the other hand, later-onset diseases like tuberculosis and leprosy were regarded as socially undesirable and decidedly nonelite. People with dwarfism were perceived as liminal in pharaonic Egypt, as full humans with "auspicious and protective" qualities, but also "lifelong children" (Dasen 1993:156, 246). Apparently with little regard for whether the condition was hereditary, congenital, or developmental in origin, people with unusually short stature were well integrated into Egyptian society, based on the regularity of their iconographic representation.

Ancient Near Eastern sources outside Egypt also defy historical and contemporary expectations of reduced tolerance for persons with disabilities. The remains of an elderly Natufian woman have been interpreted as those of a shaman, who may have been imbued with unusual spiritual qualities despite, or even because of, the impaired mobility caused by her deformed pelvis and lumbar vertebrae (Grosman, Munro, and Belfer-Cohen 2008). Another comparandum for 12-10146 may be found in a ca. twenty-eight-year-old female with a leg deformity requiring use of a crutch, who was buried at Jericho in the mid-second millennium BCE with numerous elaborate grave goods (Tubb 2000). Special treatment in death also appears to have been given to a female 18–20 year old with an acquired neuromuscular disease at Tell Abraq (United Arab Emirates) in the late third millennium BCE: unlike the more than 300 other persons buried in the collective tomb, her remains were placed in a container and accompanied by exotic grave goods (Martin and Potts 2012).

Unfortunately, Early Dilmun lacks the abundant written corpora that would place 12-10146's commemoration into a cultural context from which ideologies concerning life, death, and disability could be discerned. Nor do we know much about perceptions of disability, or even dwarfism, in Dilmun's neighbor and trading partner Mesopotamia, despite extensive textual evidence describing disease causation and medical treatment (Scurlock and Andersen 2005). However, in the Sumerian myth of Enki and Ninmah, as Neal Walls (2007) observed, nonnormative bodies were created separately from normative bodies during a drunken contest between the two gods. While disabled individuals were still considered "human" and capable of contributing to society through work, bodily deformities were also interpreted as the result of curses or divine punishments. Still, families and public institutions were obligated to care and provide for such individuals. Birth omens—the best known of which is the Neo-Assyrian series *šumma izbu*—described various physical anomalies of newborns and the consequences of such births for the child, the family, or even the state. Although such connotations were often negative, occasionally positive descriptions of disability also occurred, suggesting that disability was "a meaningful conceptual category regarding physical difference" in the ancient Near East (Schipper 2006:73).

CONCLUSION

Heeding the caveats of Roberts (1999, 2000, 2011) and others (Cross 1999; Dettwyler 1991), we acknowledge that our understanding of how disability was experienced four millennia ago in Dilmun is only one of many possible interpretations. Extracting identities from the archaeological debris of prehistory is always challenging and provocative; perhaps nowhere more so than Bahrain, where even describing its geographic location is fraught with sociopolitical controversy (Insoll 2007). We imagine the bodies of past persons according to contemporary normative aesthetics of the able-bodied. But an approach like the one taken in this chapter helps us to appreciate the past and present diversities of the human body as well as alternative attempts to understand that difference. Although 12-10146's physical anomalies would have modified her mobility and her participation in daily activities, there is no indication that these functions were significantly impaired. Most likely, the repercussions were cosmetic, and were influenced by contemporary social perceptions of disability.

This young woman's experience of her own body during life cannot be reconstructed, but we can state unequivocally that after her death, she was buried with an unusually rich quantity and quality of objects. Yet the reasons for this abundant commemoration remain elusive. This chapter has focused on 12-10146's disability (if one can describe her condition as such) as an example of how archaeologists can engage with bodily and cognitive nonnormativity in the past. However, it would be irresponsible and counterproductive to assume that this aspect of her personhood determined her mortuary treatment. Any number of other factors—specialized knowledge or occupation, inherited status—may have set 12-10146 apart from her peers.

Similarly, we have prioritized Cornwall's deafness over other aspects of his identity solely for the purposes of this anachronistic exercise. Yet his relationship to his own deafness is scarcely more knowable despite its occurrence less than one hundred years ago. The only surviving evidence for its effects on his life is secondary; to our knowledge, Cornwall did not write about his deafness. We do not know whether he engaged with the Deaf clubs, schools, or workplaces that flourished by the 1940s in the United States (Padden 2008). Even labeling his condition a disability might be deemed inappropriate by members of the Deaf community, who refer to themselves as a distinct culture (Lane, Hoffmeister, and Bahan 1996; Senghas and Monaghan 2002). However, we argue that the acquired nature of Cornwall's deafness and the lack of evidence for his identification with Deaf culture (Munoz-Baell and Ruiz 2000), coupled with the documented opinions of his academic peers, makes our interpretation of his deafness as a disability a valid one, although, indeed, not the only one. Cornwall's deafness impeded his doctoral research, apparently complicated his relationship with the Hearst Museum, and may have factored into his self-imposed exile to Italy. Yet he was able to overcome the skepticism of his academic superiors and make a significant contribution to Gulf archaeology.

Despite the fact that Cornwall and the young woman known as 12-10146 lived nearly four thousand years and eight thousand miles apart from one another, he came into contact with her remains for a brief period of time during the early 1940s. In this chapter, we have explored in parallel their experiences during life and their commemoration in death. This endeavor is challenged significantly by the lack of written sources from Early Dilmun, an absence of Cornwall's self-reflection on his deafness, and no record of Cornwall's interpretation of the abnormalities readily evident in 12-10146's skeleton. Nevertheless, we hope to have shown in this case study from the Cornwall collection how careful archival, archaeological, and osteological research can draw out the varying ways that physical differences and abilities can be embodied personally and perceived socially, both in the past and in the present.

ACKNOWLEDGMENTS

The authors would like to thank their colleagues in the Dilmun Bioarchaeology Project. Members who made specific contributions to the research presented here include Athna May Porter (family historian), Jennifer Piro (faunal analyst), Sheel Jagani, and Emily Carleton (research assistants). The authors would also like to thank the Phoebe A. Hearst Museum of Anthropology, particularly its director Mari Lyn Salvador, curator of biological anthropology and professor of integrative biology Tim White, collections manager Leslie Freund, head registrar Joan Knudsen, conservator Madeleine Fang, and HERC-PAHMA liaison Socorro Báez. Jeremiah Peterson provided assistance with Mesopotamian written sources, and Christopher Knüsel with paleopathology identification. Earlier versions of this research were presented in the University of California, Berkeley's Townsend Center for the Humanities "Old Things" Symposium and in the University of Pennsylvania's Kolb Society of Fellows' 2012 symposium. Funding for this research was provided by the University of California, Berkeley, and Sonoma State University (School of Social Sciences and a Research, Scholarly and Creative Activities Program Mini-Grant). Boutin conducted the osteological analysis, and Porter conducted the archival and material cultural analysis for this publication; the chapter was written collaboratively.

NOTES

1. See below for a more nuanced discussion of this age- and gender-based description.
2. Person-first language, which is normative in Disability Studies, emphasizes the person rather than his/her disability (Folkins 1992).
3. These numbers update and supersede Porter and Boutin 2012:tables 2–4.
4. Documents pertaining to Cornwall's life and research are being collected in the DBP's archive. These sources consist of documents and photographs in the Hearst Museum's accession file, student records at Oxford University, and publically available records (e.g., death certificate). Readers with additional information about Cornwall are invited to contact the authors.
5. Stature was calculated with regression equations from Trotter and Gleser (1952), which reflect less secular change than modern forensic databanks. Equations for African Americans were used, based on precedent from other analyses of ancient Near Eastern skeletal remains (Boutin 2008:124).
6. Digital radiography services were generously contributed by Erik Gaensler, M.D. (Alta Bates Summit Medical Center), and film radiography services by Sheila Doney (Tang Center at UC Berkeley). Robert Boutin, M.D. (UC Davis) kindly facilitated diagnostic consultation with musculoskeletal radiologists.
7. Van de Velde examined a sample of bitumen from 9-4700 in 2012 (Van de Velde, personal communication). Gas chromatography–mass spectrometry determined that the material is possibly from the well known bitumen source of Hit, although its chemical composition was altered enough that it could be a mixture of materials from two or more sources. The materials could also come from a yet-to-be-identified source.

REFERENCES

Alman, Benjamin A., and Michael J. Goldberg. 2006. "Syndromes of Orthopaedic Importance." In *Lovell and Winter's Pediatric Orthopaedics*, 6th ed., vol. 1, edited by R. T. Morrissy and S. L. Weinstein, 251–314. Philadelphia: Lippincott Williams & Wilkins.

Anderson, T. 1997. "A Medieval Case of Bilateral Humerus Varus." *Journal of Paleopathology* 9 (3): 143–46.

Ascádi, Gy., and J. Nemeskéri. 1970. *History of Human Life Span and Mortality*. Budapest: Akadémiai Kiadó.

Barnes, Colin, and Geof Mercer. 2010. *Exploring Disability*. 2nd ed. Cambridge: Polity Press.

Bibby, Geoffrey. 1970. *Looking for Dilmun*. London: Collins.

Boutin, Alexis T. 2008. *Embodying Life and Death: Osteobiographical Narratives from Alalakh*. Unpublished PhD diss., Department of Anthropology, University of Pennsylvania.

Boutin, Alexis T. 2011. "Crafting a Bioarchaeology of Personhood: Osteobiographical Narratives from Alalakh." In *Breathing New Life into the Evidence of Death: Contemporary Approaches to Bioarchaeology*, edited by A. Baadsgaard, A. T. Boutin, and J. E. Buikstra, 109–33. Santa Fe: School for Advanced Research Press.

Boutin, Alexis T., Gloria L. Nusse, Sabrina B. Sholts, and Benjamin W. Porter. 2012. "Face to Face with the Past: Reconstructing a Teenage Boy from Early Dilmun." *Near Eastern Archaeology* 75 (2): 68–79.

Brickley, Megan, and Rachel Ives. 2008. *The Bioarchaeology of Metabolic Bone Disease*. San Diego: Academic Press.

Brooks, S., and J. M. Suchey. 1990. "Skeletal Age Determination Based on the Os Pubis: A Comparison of the Ascádi-Nemeskéri and Suchey-Brooks Methods." *Human Evolution* 5 (3): 227–38. http://dx.doi.org/10.1007/BF02437238.

Buikstra, Jane E., and Douglas H. Ubelaker. 1994. *Standards for Data Collection from Human Skeletal Remains*. Fayetteville: Arkansas Archaeological Survey.

Capasso, Luigi. 1989. "Paleopathology of the Bronze Age Population from the Grotta dello Scoglietto (Tuscany, Italy)." In *Advances in Paleopathology: Proceedings of the VII European Meeting of the Paleopathology Association, Lyon, September 1988*, edited by L. Capasso, 21–26. Chieti, Italy: Paleopathology Association.

Castriota-Scanderbeg, A., and B. Dallapiccola. 2005. *Abnormal Skeletal Phenotypes: From Simple Signs to Complex Diagnoses*. Berlin: Springer.

Clark, Bonnie J., and Laurie A. Wilkie. 2006. "The Prism of Self: Gender and Personhood." In *Handbook of Gender Archaeology*, edited by S. M. Nelson, 333–64. Lanham, MD: AltaMira Press.

Connan, Jacques, and Thomas Van de Velde. 2010. "An Overview of Bitumen Trade in the Near East from the Neolithic (c.8000 BC) to the Early Islamic Period." *Arabian Archaeology and Epigraphy* 21 (1): 1–19. http://dx.doi.org/10.1111/j.1600-0471.2009.00321.x.

Cornwall, Peter B. 1943. "The Tumuli of Bahrain." *Asia and the Americas* 42:230–34.

Cornwall, Peter B. 1944. *Dilmun: The History of Bahrein Island before Cyrus*. Unpublished PhD diss., Department of History, Harvard University.

Cornwall, Peter B. 1946a. "Ancient Arabia: Explorations in Hasa, 1940–41." *Geographical Journal* 107 (1/2): 28–50. http://dx.doi.org/10.2307/1789083.

Cornwall, Peter B. 1946b. "On the Location of Dilmun." *Bulletin of the American Schools of Oriental Research* 103: 3–11. http://dx.doi.org/10.2307/1354777.

Covey, Herbert C. 1998. *Social Perceptions of People with Disabilities in History.* Springfield, IL: Charles C. Thomas.

Cross, Morag. 1999. "Accessing the Inaccessible: Disability and Archaeology." *Archaeological Review from Cambridge* 15 (2): 7–30.

Currarino, Guide, and Marion E. Erlandson. 1964. "Premature Fusion of Epiphyses in Cooley's Anemia." *Radiology* 83:656–65.

Dasen, Véronique. 1993. *Dwarfs in Ancient Egypt and Greece.* Oxford: Clarendon Press.

Davis, Lennard J., ed. 1997. *The Disability Studies Reader.* New York: Routledge.

Dettwyler, K. A. 1991. "Can Paleopathology Provide Evidence for 'Compassion'?" *American Journal of Physical Anthropology* 84 (4): 375–84. http://dx.doi.org/10.1002/ajpa.1330840402.

During Caspars, Elisabeth C. L. 1980. *The Bahrain Tumuli: An Illustrated Catalogue of Two Important Collections.* Leiden: Nederlands Historisch-Archaeologisch Instituut te Istanbul.

Edwards, Steven D. 1997. "Dismantling the Disability/Handicap Distinction." *Journal of Medicine and Philosophy* 22 (6): 589–606. http://dx.doi.org/10.1093/jmp/22.6.589.

Ellefsen, B. K., M. A. Frierson, E. M. Raney, and J. A. Ogden. 1994. "Humerus Varus: A Complication of Neonatal, Infantile, and Childhood Injury and Infection." *Journal of Pediatric Orthopedics* 14 (4): 479–86. http://dx.doi.org/10.1097/01241398-199407000-00011.

Finlay, Nyree, ed. 1999. *Archaeological Review from Cambridge. Theme Issue: Disability and Archaeology* 15(2).

Folkins, John. 1992. "Resource on Person-First Language: The Language Used to Describe Individuals with Disabilities." Electronic document. http://www.asha.org/publications/journals/submissions/person_first.htm. Accessed June 12, 2012.

Fowler, Chris. 2004. *The Archaeology of Personhood: An Anthropological Approach.* London: Routledge.

France, Diane L. 1998. "Observational and Metrical Analysis of Sex in the Skeleton." In *Forensic Osteology: Advances in the Identification of Human Remains.* 2nd ed., edited by K. J. Reichs, 163–86. Springfield, IL: Charles C. Thomas.

Frohlich, Bruno. 1986. "The Human Biological History of the Early Bronze Age Population of Bahrain." In *Bahrain through the Ages: The Archaeology*, edited by S. H. A. al-Khalifa and M. Rice, 47–63. London: Kegan Paul International.

Frohlich, Bruno, Donald J. Ortner, and Haya Ali al-Khalifa. 1989. "Human Disease in the Ancient Middle East." *Dilmun: Journal of the Bahrain Historical and Archaeological Society* 14:61–73.

Goffman, Erving. 1963. *Stigma: Notes on the Management of Spoiled Identity*. New York: Prentice-Hall.

Goodman, Alan H., and Jerome C. Rose. 1991. "Dental Enamel Hypoplasias as Indicators of Nutritional Status." In *Advances in Dental Anthropology*, edited by M. A. Kelley and C. S. Larsen, 279–93. New York: Wiley-Liss.

Grosman, Leore, Natalie D. Munro, and Anna Belfer-Cohen. 2008. "A 12,000-Year-Old Shaman Burial from the Southern Levant (Israel)." *Proceedings of the National Academy of Sciences of the United States of America* 105 (46): 17665–69. http://dx.doi.org/10.1073/pnas.0806030105.

Hall, Christine. 2005. "Spondyloepimetaphyseal dysplasias." Electronic document. https://www.orpha.net/data/patho/GB/uk-SEMD05.pdf. Accessed June 5, 2012.

Haverkamp, D., and R. K. Marti. 2007. "Bilateral Varus Osteotomies in Hip Deformities: Are Early Interventions Superior?" *International Orthopaedics* 31 (2): 185–91. http://dx.doi.org/10.1007/s00264-006-0147-2.

Hawkey, Diane E. 1998. "Disability, Compassion and the Skeletal Record: Using Musculoskeletal Stress Markers (MSM) to Construct an Osteobiography from Early New Mexico." *International Journal of Osteoarchaeology* 8 (5): 326–40. http://dx.doi.org/10.1002/(SICI)1099-1212(1998090)8:5<326::AID-OA437>3.0.CO;2-W.

Hershkovitz, I., B. Ring, M. Speirs, E. Galili, M. Kislev, G. Edelson, and A. Hershkovitz. 1991. "Possible Congenital Hemolytic Anemia in Prehistoric Coastal Inhabitants of Israel." *American Journal of Physical Anthropology* 85 (1): 7–13. http://dx.doi.org/10.1002/ajpa.1330850103.

Højgaard, Karen. 1980. "Dentition on Bahrain, 2000 B.C." *Scandinavian Journal of Dental Research* 88:467–75.

Højgaard, Karen. 1986. "Dental Anthropological Investigations on Bahrain." In *Bahrain through the Ages: The Archaeology*, edited by S.H.A. al-Khalifa and M. Rice, 64–71. London: Kegan Paul International.

Højlund, Flemming. 1987. *Failaka/Dilmun: The Second Millennium Settlements*. Moesgaard, Denmark: Jutland Archaeological Society Publications.

Højlund, Flemming. 2007. *The Burial Mounds of Bahrain: Social Complexity in Early Dilmun*. Moesgaard, Denmark: Jutland Archaeological Society Publications.

Højlund, Flemming, and H. Hellmuth Andersen. 1994. *Qala'at al-Bahrain*. Moesgaard, Denmark: Jutland Archaeological Society Publications.

Hubert, Jane. 2000. "Introduction: The Complexity of Boundedness and Exclusion." In *Madness, Disability and Social Exclusion: The Archaeology and Anthropology of "Difference"*, edited by J. Hubert, 1–8. London: Routledge.

Ibrahim, Moawiyah. 1982. *Excavations of the Arab Expedition at Sar el-Jisr, Bahrain. State of Bahrain*. Manama: Ministry of Information.

Insoll, Timothy. 2007. "Changing Identities in the Arabian Gulf: Archaeology, Religion, and Ethnicity in Context." In *The Archaeology of Identities: A Reader*, edited by T. Insoll, 308–25. New York: Routledge.

Jacoby, David B., and Robert M. Youngson, eds. 2005. *Encyclopedia of Family Health*. 3rd ed. Tarrytown, NY: Marshall Cavendish.

Jeffreys, David, and John Tait. 2000. "Disability, Madness, and Social Exclusion in Dynastic Egypt." In *Madness, Disability and Social Exclusion: The Archaeology and Anthropology of "Difference,"* edited by J. Hubert, 87–95. London: Routledge.

Johnson, Karl J., and A. Mark Davies. 2006. "Congenital and Developmental Abnormalities." In *Imaging of the Hip and Bony Pelvis: Techniques and Applications*, edited by A. M. Davies, K. Johnson, and R. W. Whitehouse, 93–105. Berlin: Springer. http://dx.doi.org/10.1007/3-540-30000-7_7.

Johnstone, David. 2001. *An Introduction to Disability Studies*. London: David Fulton Publishers Ltd.

Joyce, Rosemary A. 2008. *Ancient Bodies, Ancient Lives: Sex, Gender, and Archaeology*. London: Thames & Hudson.

Kacki, S., P. Duneufjardin, P. Blanchard, and D. Castex. 2013. "Humerus Varus in a Subadult Skeleton from the Medieval Graveyard of La Madeleine (Orleans, France)." *International Journal of Osteoarchaeology* 23:119–26. http://dx.doi.org/10.1002/oa.1249.

Kveiborg, Jacob. 2007. "Appendix 2: Animal Bones from the Aali, Saar and Dar Kulayb Mound Cemeteries." In *The Burial Mounds of Bahrain: Social Complexity in Early Dilmun*, by Flemming Højlund, 149–53. Moesgaard, Denmark: Jutland Archaeological Society Publications.

Lane, Harlan, Robert Hoffmeister, and Ben Bahan. 1996. *A Journey into the Deaf-World*. San Diego: DawnSignPress.

Laursen, Steffen Terp. 2008. "Early Dilmun and Its Rulers: New Evidence of the Burial Mounds of the Elite and the Development of Social Complexity, c. 2200–1750 BC." *Arabian Archaeology and Epigraphy* 19 (2): 156–67. http://dx.doi.org/10.1111/j.1600-0471.2008.00298.x.

Littleton, Judith. 1998a. *Skeletons and Social Composition: Bahrain 300 BC–AD 250*. Oxford: Archaeopress.

Littleton, Judith. 1998b. "A Middle Eastern Paradox: Rickets in Skeletons from Bahrain." *Journal of Paleopathology* 10:13–30.

Littleton, Judith. 2003. "Unequal in Life? Human Remains from the Danish Excavations of Tylos Tombs." *Arabian Archaeology and Epigraphy* 14 (2): 164–93. http://dx.doi.org/10.1034/j.1600-0471.2003.00014.x.

Littleton, Judith. 2007. "The Political Ecology of Health in Bahrain." In *Ancient*

Health, edited by M. N. Cohen and G. M. M. Crane-Kramer, 176–89. Gainesville: University Press of Florida.

Littleton, Judith. 2011. "Moving from the Canary in the Coalmine: Modeling Childhood in Bahrain." In *Social Bioarchaeology*, edited by S. C. Agarwal and B. A. Glencross, 361–89. Chichester, England: Wiley-Blackwell. http://dx.doi.org/10 .1002/9781444390537.ch13.

Littleton, Judith, and Bruno Frohlich. 1989. "An Analysis of Dental Pathology and Diet on Historic Bahrain." *Paléorient* 15 (2): 59–75. http://dx.doi.org/10.3406/paleo .1989.4509.

Littleton, Judith, and Bruno Frohlich. 1993. "Fish-Eaters and Farmers: Dental Pathology in the Arabian Gulf." *American Journal of Physical Anthropology* 92 (4): 427–47. http://dx.doi.org/10.1002/ajpa.1330920403.

Liversidge, H. M., and T. Molleson. 2004. "Variations in Crown and Root Formation and Eruption of Human Deciduous Teeth." *American Journal of Physical Anthropology* 123 (2): 172–80. http://dx.doi.org/10.1002/ajpa.10318.

Lucas, Leo S., and Joseph H. Gill. 1947. "Humerus Varus following Birth Injury to the Proximal Humeral Epiphysis." *Journal of Bone and Joint Surgery: American Volume* 29 (2): 367–69.

Lukacs, John R. 1995. "The 'Caries Correction Factor': A New Method of Calibrating Dental Caries Rates to Compensate for Antemortem Loss of Teeth." *International Journal of Osteoarchaeology* 5 (2): 151–56. http://dx.doi.org/10.1002/oa.1390050207.

Mackay, E. J. H. 1929. "The Islands of Bahrain." In *Bahrain and Hamamieh*, edited by E. J. H. Mackay, G. K. L. Harding, and W. M. F. Petrie, 1–35. London: British School of Archaeology in Egypt.

Martin, Debra L., and Daniel T. Potts. 2012. "Lesley: A Unique Bronze Age Individual from Southeastern Arabia." In *The Bioarchaeology of Individuals*, edited by A. L. W. Stodder and A. M. Palkovich, 13–126. Gainesville: University Press of Florida.

Meindl, Richard S., and C. Owen Lovejoy. 1985. "Ectocranial Suture Closure: A Revised Method for the Determination of Skeletal Age at Death based on the Lateral-Anterior Sutures." *American Journal of Physical Anthropology* 68 (1): 57–66. http://dx.doi.org/10.1002/ajpa.1330680106.

Merbs, Charles F., and Ellen M. Vestergaard. 1985. "The Paleopathology of Sundown, a Prehistoric Site Near Prescott, Arizona." In *Health and Disease in the Prehistoric Southwest*, edited by C. F. Merbs and R. J. Miller, 85–103. Tempe: Arizona State University.

Meskell, Lynn. 1999. *Archaeologies of Social Life: Age, Sex, Class et cetera in Ancient Egypt*. Oxford: Blackwell.

Meskell, Lynn M., and Rosemary A. Joyce. 2003. *Embodied Lives: Figuring Ancient*

Maya and Egyptian Experience. London: Routledge.

Molleson, Theya. 1999. "Archaeological Evidence for Attitudes to Disability in the Past." *Archaeological Review from Cambridge* 15 (2): 69–77.

Molto, J. E. 2000. "Humerus Varus Deformity in Roman Period Burials from Kellis 2, Dakhleh, Egypt." *American Journal of Physical Anthropology* 113 (1): 103–9. http://dx.doi.org/10.1002/1096-8644(200009)113:1<103::AID-AJPA9>3.0.CO;2-A.

Moorey, P. R. S. 1991. *A Century of Biblical Archaeology.* Cambridge: Lutterworth Press.

Moser, Stephanie. 2007. "On Disciplinary Culture: Archaeology as Fieldwork and Its Gendered Associations." *Journal of Archaeological Method and Theory* 14 (3): 235–63. http://dx.doi.org/10.1007/s10816-007-9033-5.

Mughal, M. Rafique. 1983. *The Dilmun Burial Complex at Sar: The 1980–82 Excavations in Bahrain.* Manama: State of Bahrain, Ministry of Information.

Munoz-Baell, Irma M., and M. Teresa Ruiz. 2000. "Empowering the Deaf: Let the Deaf Be Deaf." *Journal of Epidemiology and Community Health* 54 (1): 40–44. http://dx.doi.org/10.1136/jech.54.1.40.

Nelson, Margaret C., Sarah M. Nelson, and Alison Wylie, eds. 1994. *Equity Issues for Women in Archaeology.* Washington, D.C.: Archaeological Papers of the American Anthropological Association.

Nunn, John F. 1996. *Ancient Egyptian Medicine.* Norman: University of Oklahoma Press.

Ogden, John A., Ulrich H. Weil, and Robert F. Hempton. 1976. "Developmental Humerus Varus." *Clinical Orthopaedics and Related Research* (116): 158–66.

Ortner, Donald J. 2003. *Identification of Pathological Conditions in Human Skeletal Remains.* 2nd ed. San Diego: Academic Press.

Ortner, Donald J., and Bruno Frohlich, eds. 2008. *The Early Bronze Age I Tombs and Burials of Bab edh-Dhra', Jordan.* Lanham, MD: AltaMira Press.

Özbek, M. 2005. "Skeletal Pathology of a High-Ranking Official from Thrace (Turkey, Last Quarter of the 4th Century BC)." *International Journal of Osteoarchaeology* 15 (3): 216–25. http://dx.doi.org/10.1002/oa.777.

Padden, Carol. 2008. "The Decline of Deaf Clubs in the United States: A Treatise on the Problem of Place." In *Open Your Eyes: Deaf Studies Talking,* edited by H-Dirksen L. Bauman, 169–76. Minneapolis: University of Minnesota Press.

Perry, Megan A. 2005. "Redefining Childhood through Bioarchaeology: Toward an Archaeological and Biological Understanding of Children in Antiquity." In *Children in Action: Perspectives on the Archaeology of Childhood,* edited by J. E. Baxter, 89–111. Arlington, VA: Archaeological Papers of the American Anthropological Association. http://dx.doi.org/10.1525/ap3a.2005.15.89.

Peterson, Hamlet A. 2012. *Physeal Injury Other than Fracture*. Heidelberg: Springer. http://dx.doi.org/10.1007/978-3-642-22563-5.

Podzorski, Patricia V. 1990. *Their Bones shall not Perish: An Examination of Predynastic Human Skeletal Remains from Naga-ed-Deir in Egypt*. Malden, England: SIA.

Porter, Benjamin W., and Alexis T. Boutin. 2012. "The Dilmun Bioarchaeology Project: A First Look at the Peter B. Cornwall Collection at the Phoebe A. Hearst Museum of Anthropology." *Arabian Archaeology and Epigraphy* 23 (1): 35–49. http://dx.doi.org/10.1111/j.1600-0471.2011.00347.x.

Potts, Daniel T. 1990. *The Arabian Gulf in Antiquity*. Vols. 1 and 2. Oxford: Clarendon Press.

Rashidi, J. S., D. J. Ortner, B. Frohlich, and B. Jonsdottir. 2001. "Brucellosis in Early Bronze Age Jordan and Bahrain: An Analysis of Possible Cases of Brucella Spondylitis." *American Journal of Physical Anthropology* 114:122–123.

Resnick, Donald, ed. 1995. *Diagnosis of Bone and Joint Disorders*. 3rd ed. Philadelphia: W.B. Saunders Company.

Roberts, Charlotte. 1999. "Disability in the Skeletal Record: Assumptions, Problems, and Some Examples." *Archaeological Review from Cambridge* 15 (2): 79–97.

Roberts, Charlotte. 2000. "Did They Take Sugar? The Use of Skeletal Evidence in the Study of Disability in Past Populations." In *Madness, Disability and Social Exclusion: The Archaeology and Anthropology of "Difference"*, edited by J. Hubert, 46–59. London: Routledge.

Roberts, Charlotte. 2011. "The Bioarchaeology of Leprosy and Tuberculosis: A Comparative Study of Perceptions, Stigma, Diagnosis, and Treatment." In *Social Bioarchaeology*, edited by S. C. Agarwal and B. A. Glencross, 252–81. Chichester, England: Wiley-Blackwell. http://dx.doi.org/10.1002/9781444390537.ch9.

Roth, Martha T. 1987. "Age at Marriage and the Household: A Study of Neo-Babylonian and Neo-Assyrian Forms." *Comparative Studies in Society and History* 29 (4): 715–47. http://dx.doi.org/10.1017/S0010417500014857.

Safont, Santiago, Assumpció Malgosa, and M. Eulàlia Subirà. 2000. "Sex Assessment on the Basis of Long Bone Circumference." *American Journal of Physical Anthropology* 113 (3): 317–28. http://dx.doi.org/10.1002/1096-8644(200011)113:3<317::AID-AJPA4>3.0.CO;2-J.

Scheuer, Louise, and Sue Black. 2004. *The Juvenile Skeleton*. London: Elsevier Academic Press.

Schipper, Jeremy. 2006. *Disability Studies and the Hebrew Bible: Figuring Mephibosheth in the David Story*. New York: T & T Clark.

Scurlock, JoAnn, and Burton R. Andersen. 2005. *Diagnoses in Assyrian and Babylonian Medicine*. Urbana: University of Illinois Press.

Senghas, Richard J., and Leila Monaghan. 2002. "Signs of Their Times: Deaf Communities and the Culture of Language." *Annual Review of Anthropology* 31 (1): 69–97. http://dx.doi.org/10.1146/annurev.anthro.31.020402.101302.

Siebers, Tobin Anthony. 2008. *Disability Theory*. Ann Arbor: University of Michigan Press.

Smith, Adam. 2004. "The End of the Essential Archaeological Subject." *Archaeological Dialogues* 11 (1): 1–20. http://dx.doi.org/10.1017/S1380203804211412.

Stiker, Henri-Jacques. 2000. *A History of Disability*. Translated by William Sayers. Ann Arbor: University of Michigan Press.

Stirland, A. J. 1997. "Care in the Medieval Community." *International Journal of Osteoarchaeology* 7 (6): 587–90. http://dx.doi.org/10.1002/(SICI)1099-1212(199711/12)7:6<587::AID-OA340>3.0.CO;2-J.

Suchey, Judy Myers, and Darryl Katz. 1998. "Applications of Pubic Age Determination in a Forensic Setting." In *Forensic Osteology: Advances in the Identification of Human Remains*. 2nd ed., edited by K. J. Reichs, 204–36. Springfield, IL: Charles C. Thomas.

Tilley, Lorna, and Marc F. Oxenham. 2011. "Survival against the Odds: Modeling the Social Implications of Care Provision to Seriously Disabled Individuals." *International Journal of Paleopathology* 1 (1): 35–42. http://dx.doi.org/10.1016/j.ijpp.2011.02.003.

Trigger, Bruce G. 1980. *Gordon Childe: Revolutions in Archaeology*. New York: Columbia University Press.

Trigger, Bruce G. 1989. *A History of Archaeological Thought*. Cambridge: University of Cambridge Press.

Trinkaus, Erik, and M. R. Zimmerman. 1982. "Trauma among the Shanidar Neandertals." *American Journal of Physical Anthropology* 57 (1): 61–76. http://dx.doi.org/10.1002/ajpa.1330570108.

Trotter, Mildred, and Goldine C. Gleser. 1952. "Estimation of Stature from Long Bones of American Whites and Negroes." *American Journal of Physical Anthropology* 10 (4): 463–514. http://dx.doi.org/10.1002/ajpa.1330100407.

Tubb, Johnathan N. 2000. "Two Examples of Disability in the Levant." In *Madness, Disability and Social Exclusion: The Archaeology and Anthropology of "Difference,"* edited by J. Hubert, 81–6. London: Routledge.

Vanderbeck, Jennifer L., John M. Fenlin, Jr., Charles L. Getz, and Anthony F. DePalma. 2009. "Congenital Anomalies and Variational Anatomy of the Shoulder." In *The Shoulder*. 4th ed., vol. 1, edited by C. A. Rockwood Jr. and F. A. Matsen III, 101–43. Philadelphia: Saunders. http://dx.doi.org/10.1016/B978-1-4160-3427-8.50009-X.

Waldron, Tony. 2007. "Hidden or Overlooked? Where are the Disadvantaged in the Skeletal Record?" In *The Archaeology of Identities: A Reader*, edited by T. Insoll, 195–210. New York: Routledge.

Walls, Neal. 2007. "The Origins of the Disabled Body: Disability in Ancient Mesopotamia." In *This Abled Body: Rethinking Disabilities in Biblical Studies*, edited by H. Avalos, S. Melcher, and J. Schipper, 13–30. Atlanta: Society of Biblical Literature.

Weatherall, D. J., and J. B. Clegg. 2001. *The Thalassaemia Syndromes*. 4th ed. Oxford: Blackwell. http://dx.doi.org/10.1002/9780470696705.

White, Tim D., Michael T. Black, and Pieter A. Folkens. 2012. *Human Osteology*. 3rd ed. Burlington, MA: Elsevier.

Willey, Gordon R., and Jeremy A. Sabloff. 1993. *A History of American Archaeology*. New York: W.H. Freeman.

Woolley, Leonard. 1953. *Spadework: Adventures in Archaeology*. London: Lutterworth Press.

5

Bioarchaeological Reconstruction of Group Identity at Early Bronze Age Bab edh-Dhra', Jordan

Susan Guise Sheridan, Jaime Ullinger, Lesley Gregoricka, and Meredith S. Chesson

ABSTRACT

Bab edh-Dhra' has provided the only large, well-excavated, and well-curated skeletal collection spanning the Early Bronze Age (EBA) I–IV for the lower southern Levant. The site demonstrates that mortuary patterns followed settlement changes, allowing detailed analyses of shifting modes of remembrance and commemoration. Dental morphological traits showed that EBIA inhabitants were buried with family members, and EBII–III cranial nonmetric traits suggest the same. Changing social dynamics in the EBA were evidenced archaeologically by the expansion of orchards requiring increased multigenerational commitment (Ullinger, Sheridan, and Guatelli-Steinberg 2015), construction of a large wall indicating enhanced territoriality/exclusivity (Gasperetti and Sheridan 2013), and large visible charnel houses for the dead. By adding demographic profiles, assemblage size estimates, and morphological data to the archaeological evidence, an expanding concept of family/collective lineage (remembrance) and changing investment in the dead (commemoration) emerged.

INTRODUCTION

The necessity of removing dead bodies from a habitation setting is important, given the realities of decomposition and putrefaction. However, burial practices go far beyond the needs of hygiene, providing a glimpse of the wider worldview of those performing the rituals (Andrews and Bellow 2006). Inferring what death meant and to whom, and how that was expressed, however, risks projecting modern values on ancient practices (Ashmore and Geller 2005).

DOI: 10.5876/9781607323295.c005

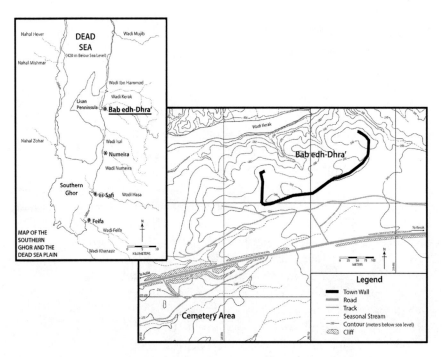

FIGURE 5.1. *Topographic map of Bab edh-Dhraʻ with a map of the Dead Sea Plain inset (Redrawn after Rast and Schaub 2003).*

This chapter will explore changes in mortuary practices as sedentism intensified and population size increased at Early Bronze Age (EBA) Bab edh-Dhraʻ located in modern day Jordan (Figure 5.1). We will assess who was interred in each burial context (age and sex), determine potential kin relations, and look for changes in demographic and genetic diversity with time, in light of the archaeological record showing changes in tomb typology, grave goods, and postmortem handling of the dead. For our purposes, "remembrance" speaks to the forms of burial and to materials included with the human remains. We have defined "commemoration" as an investment in the dead as seen in burial type (creation and maintenance of structures) and as the manipulation of bodies (care of deposition and subsequent handling of bones by successive generations).

Bab edh-Dhraʻ was part of a patchwork of preurban EBIA (ca. 3500–3300 BCE) and EBIB (ca. 3300–3100 BCE) settlements that expanded into fortified towns in EBII–III (ca. 3100–2500 BCE). These settlements were abandoned by the end of EBIV (ca. 2500–2010 BCE) (Falconer and Savage 1995). Changing funerary practices reflect the dynamic social environment of the EBA. No permanent settlements have been found for EBIA at Bab edh-Dhraʻ, but shaft tombs are plentiful. During EBIB and EBII, articulated and disarticulated individuals were interred in aboveground charnel houses (burial structure for numerous individuals) and subterranean shaft tombs (Schaub and Rast 1984). Social changes became increasingly evident in EBII–III, as Bab edh-Dhraʻ underwent a massive expansion and fortification (Schaub 1993). Modifications of funerary practices were likely the result of increased sedentism and population density, illustrating the importance of kinship and social, political, and economic differentiation (Chesson 1999; Schaub 2008). Disarticulated individuals were inhumed in much larger charnel houses, which may have accommodated extended kin groups (Chesson 1999). Upon returning to rural agropastoralism in EBIV, these were replaced by shaft tombs (Rast and Schaub 2003).

Mortuary practices as displayed in the built environment, and inclusion of associated grave goods, are shaped by group forces along lines of age, gender, and kinship (Chesson 1999). These social structures help dictate the appropriate forms of mourning by its members. Biologically, demographic parameters of age, sex and genetic relatedness can be assessed about the decedent, thus giving us insight into mortuary behaviors. In this study, we argue that the bioarchaeological data for Bab edh-Dhraʻ illustrate an expanding definition of family and lineage (remembrance) alongside a corresponding change in investment in the dead (commemoration). We compare two distinct stages of settlement: the shaft tombs associated with seasonal EBIA campsites, and an EBII–III charnel house contemporaneous with the large townsite. Commemoration involves the interactions between the living and the dead, and occurs during the burial event itself, as well as after the funerary rites. Biological information offers clues about who was being commemorated and to whom the living "invested" their time and resources.

BACKGROUND AND RATIONALE

The skeletal collection exhumed from Bab edh-Dhraʻ is massive; however, human remains from each period differ considerably in quality. Bones from EBIA tombs were largely complete, carefully excavated, and properly curated. Although the remains were commingled, it was possible to individualize many of the skeletons, and hence, determine the number of people per tomb. In contrast, the EBII–III bones were burned in prehistory, commingled, damaged by the collapse of the charnel house roof, and poorly stored at Kansas State University for over two decades, so determination of individual burials was not possible. Differences in formation processes thus affected various parameters of our study.

FORMATION PROCESSES

Interpreting past agency is complicated by activities prior to death and to site formation processes that may disturb cemetery stratigraphy, preservation, recovery, and curation (Weiss-Krejci 2011). Antemortem activities and health of the decedent can affect the location, timing, and cause of interment. Disease, conflict, accidents, childbirth, and age-related conditions may bias representation far beyond the morbidity/mortality profiles of the population contributing to the burial assemblage. Death away from one's home due to travel, war, and/or marriage likewise shifts burial profiles.

Diagenetic changes often result in differential preservation, as can degree of bone calcification, composition (trabecular/cortical bone), and size (Ashmore and Geller 2005). Disturbance by burrowing animals, excavation methods, looting, depth, and/or entombment can influence the likelihood of later detection (Weiss-Krejci 2011). The preservation of a skeletal assemblage is shaped in part by chance: pre- and postdepositional conditions, discovery, recovery, and curation all conspire to shape the final study collection. It is therefore the job of the investigator to remain cognizant of the questions the collection is capable of answering. In the present study, the burned, commingled, and fragmentary nature of the EBII–III remains limited aspects of our diachronic comparisons, as detailed below.

STUDY SITE

Bab edh-Dhra' is located southeast of the Dead Sea, just east of the Lisan Peninsula. The EBII–III town was situated on the Wadi Karak and occupied for approximately 1,200 years (Rast and Schaub 2003). The location offered a reliable water supply, access to wildlife, and arable land (Donahue 1985; Grigson 1998; McCreery 2002).

Cooler temperatures and increased rainfall in EBIA coincided with the first evidence of scattered, seasonal campsite-like settlements (Harlan 2003). By EBIB, these became permanent, with hallmark characteristics of village life such as mudbrick dwellings and intensified agriculture (Rast and Schaub

2003). In EBII, residential buildings, fortifications, and a sanctuary were erected near the charred remains of the EBIB village; however, the majority of the town's construction took place during EBIII. The urban settlement was extended, terraced dwellings were built, a new sanctuary was erected, fortifications were expanded, and agriculture intensified (McCreery 2002). It is worth noting that although population agglomeration occurred, EBA sites are better described as villages or towns, rather than urban centers (Joffe 1993; Schaub 1982). Indeed, settlement size differed greatly from other "urban" systems of the time (e.g., Egypt, Mesopotamia), and a corporate village model more accurately explains the EBA occupation of Bab edh-Dhra'. (Philip 2001).

EBA BURIALS AT BAB EDH-DHRA'

Treatment of the dead serves a variety of purposes for survivors: from emotional release to connection to and/or acknowledgment of ancestors; distillation of remembrances to memory; even mechanisms for forgetting (Ashmore and Geller 2005; Charles and Buikstra 2002; Chesson 2007). These methods provide insights about a group's belief systems, in addition to their relation to the environment and surrounding communities. Interpreting these references is difficult, as it is easy to over or under infer agency by ascribing symbolic meaning where none was intended.

With these limitations in mind, we employed a bioarchaeological approach to understanding burial behavior at EBA Bab edh-Dhra'. Mortuary practices and settlement and subsistence patterns clearly changed with time. Indicators include a marked increase in multigenerational commitment required by orchard crops in EBII–III, a potential increase in territoriality as evidenced by the construction of a large wall, interment of significantly more individuals in group tombs, diminishing representation of the very young in EBII–III charnel house A22, and increased visibility of tombs over time.

Levantine burial practices and community structure indicate the importance of kinship to sociopolitical organization during this time (Joffe 1993). This is quite evident at Bab edh-Dhra', where ongoing use of burial areas suggests generational continuity. Nevertheless, as population density increased, burial patterns changed. Vertical shifts in burial procedures altered the conspicuousness of death considerably, as did the horizontal expansion/contraction reflected in the size of the cemeteries (Chesson 2007). For this study we compared the two periods reflecting distinctive changes in burial style: EBIA and EBII–III.

EARLY BRONZE AGE IA

The only substantial evidence for human occupation of the eastern Dead Sea region at this time are the extensive cemeteries at Feifa, Safi, and Bab edh-Dhraʿ (Chesson 2007). The EBIA tombs consisted of meters-long shafts with one or more chambers (Figure 5.2), housing disarticulated individuals along with pottery, jewelry, figurines, and other grave goods (Schaub 2008; Schaub and Rast 1984). All interments were secondary to burial of other goods.

Semipermanent campsites have been found near the large cemetery. Walter Rast and Thomas Schaub (2003) viewed these settlements as indicative of seminomadic pastoralism. Meredith Chesson (2007) envisioned the users of the cemetery moving disinterred remains from another location to their final resting place at Bab edh-Dhraʿ. David McCreery (2011) noted that the dearth of permanent structures near the cemetery might support the idea of a mobile community. There are some intrusive chambers that may suggest periodic return to the area by people unaware of the exact location of earlier tomb locations (Schaub 1981).

McCreery (2011) also noted, however, the continuity of occupation evidenced by a nearby Chalcolithic settlement, the existence of a permanent structure dating to an EBIA stratum, and the presence of fine pottery (which would have been time consuming to produce and difficult to transport). Regular spacing of most tombs *may* also suggest a well-planned cemetery (Rast and Schaub 1980), indicative of a more sedentary community maintaining generational continuity. Gillian Bentley and Victoria Perry (2008) cited the large formal cemetery, the group size required to support a large burial complex, and cultural links with earlier Chalcolithic peoples as possible evidence of such an interpretation. The relatively fine ceramics found as grave goods in the tombs and the sheer number of work hours required to dig the sophisticated tombs, as well as the allure of a nearby permanent water source, may indicate greater sedentism by some members of the group. While it can be argued that secondary burial in a common location is a documented pattern for nomadic groups, Donald Ortner and Bruno Frohlich (2011) counter that the same has been seen in sedentary groups.

Alternatively, less than 3 km from Bab edh-Dhraʿ, the Middle Bronze II (1950–1500 BCE) site of Zahrat adh-Dhraʿ offers evidence that people seasonally farmed one site while living in different villages at other times of the year (Berelov 2006). EBIA Bab edh-Dhraʿ may have been occupied in a similar fashion, with burial occurring during the time that the people (or at least some of them) lived at the location. Regardless of what they called "home," these remains provide the best available window on remembrance and commemoration at the

FIGURE 5.2. *Tomb configurations at Early Bronze Age Bab edh-Dhra', showing schematics of an EBIA multichamber shaft tomb (Illustration by Eric Carlson, used with permission of the Expedition to the Dead Sea Plain Project).*

start of the EBA. Dusan Boric noted that "the dead were the first people to become sedentary" (qtd. in Chesson 2007:11) and that may have to suffice for our understanding of residence at EBIA Bab edh-Dhra'.

EARLY BRONZE AGE II–III

The EBII settlement arose shortly after the destruction of the EBIB village, which, along with ceramic continuity and ongoing use of the cemetery, suggested that the inhabitants were survivors of the earlier community (Rast and Schaub 2003). Improving climatic conditions with access to reliable fresh water may have spurred a transition to settled town life (Donahue 2003). At its zenith around 2600 BCE, Bab edh-Dhra' covered approximately six hectares. Although the EBII–III settlement cannot be deemed an urban center (Broshi and Gophna 1984), factors associated with nascent urbanism are plentiful, including investment in a massive town wall, increased population density, municipal and administrative buildings, roads, large storage spaces, and irrigation structures (Chesson 2007).

In late EBII–early EBIII, the mudbrick wall became a substantial stone-and-brick structure, seven meters wide at the base (McCreery 2011; Rast and Schaub 2003). Construction of a closed space limited expansion, requiring more careful planning of the settlement (Douglas 2011). Burial practices shifted to large rectangular aboveground charnel houses, located near the earlier cemetery, outside the town walls (Schaub 1993). Terraced housing and agricultural fields were expanded, with a greater multigenerational investment needed for orchard crops. It even appears that an offshoot of Bab edh-Dhra', a settlement called Numeira, was founded within view of the town, possibly by related kin groups (Chesson 2007).

Despite increasing population density throughout the region (Joffe 1993), Bab edh-Dhra' provides the only sizable mortuary area for the southern Levant dating to the height of EBII–III town life. This may explain why its charnel houses became such a visible presence, as a reminder of the inhabitants' ancestors. Despite extensive surveys of the region, no other sites have produced a large collection of human skeletons for EBII–III (Ilan 2002), including Jericho (Ullinger and Sheridan 2014).

The built environment and associated grave goods serve as expressions of the community's relationship with the dead, providing evidence of both social cohesion and differentiation reflective of urban life (Broeder and Skinner 2003; Maddin, Muhly, and Stech 2003; McConaughy 2003). The presence of men, women, children, and infants suggests that there may not have been significant vertical stratification, but that social status was inherited "horizontally" through family (Chesson 2001). Chesson (1999) posited that the charnel houses represented extended kin groups. Interestingly, the establishment of a durable, visible settlement matches the emergence of durable, visible mortuary monuments. Further, the construction of broadroom sanctuaries—large rectangular rooms of a religious architectural tradition common in the Levant during the Chalcolithic (Nigro 2010)—is mirrored in the rectangular shape of EBII–III charnel houses (Rast and Schaub 2003). Following Pierre Bourdieu (1977), this may reflect habitus at Bab edh-Dhra'. Physical buildings, both domestic and funerary, may have created and reinforced social memory. Given the unique nature of the cemetery at Bab edh-Dhra', these ideas may have been a significant force in shaping/maintaining group identity.

EBII–III charnel house A22 represents a tomb from the period of greatest population density (Figure 5.3). It is the largest such structure found at the site and may have supported a second story (McCreery 2011). Ecological arguments suggest that these were constructed because shaft tombs took up potential agricultural land, and mounting population pressure necessitated more

FIGURE 5.3. *Artistic representation of EB II–III charnel house A22 and its function as a "library of the dead" (Illustration by Eric Carlson, used with permission of the Expedition to the Dead Sea Plain Project).*

efficient means of disposing of the dead (Rast 1981). These structures permitted the interment of significantly more people per unit of land compared to that needed for a comparable number of shaft tombs/graves.

Towards the end of EBIII, security concerns appear to have mounted, illustrated by the massive wall, towers, and a hastily blocked city gate. The site was burned at the end of EBIII, although there is no direct evidence for a foreign attack (Rast and Schaub 2003). After a gap of approimately 150 years, peopple moved back to the site and built an EBIV village on the ruins of the walled town. Approximately four hundred years later (EBIV), the site was abandoned and never reinhabited. This corresponded with a widespread dispersal of people throughout the region, evidenced by the abatement of numerous Levantine sites in EBIV (Joffe 1993). Ian Kuijt (2000) identified a similar transition at the site of Dhra', not far from Bab edh-Dhra', during the Late Pre-Pottery Neolithic B (ca. 6500–6000 BCE); he argued that the abandonment of early agricultural villages resulted from social systems that did not keep pace with increasing population density and sedentism.

EBA BAB EDH-DHRA' BURIAL PRACTICE SUMMARY

Population size changed considerably from EBIA to the EB II–III occupation of Bab edh-Dhra', with a corresponding intensification in agricultural practices. The resultant social adjustments expected with such shifts are manifest in the burial practices of the two periods. The shaft tombs of EBIA were below ground, separated into chambers in which individuals and assorted grave goods were placed. Attention to detail is evident in the deposition of the bones, as even small friable remains were preserved. This is particularly noteworthy if individuals were first buried elsewhere, then exhumed and transported to the large Bab edh-Dhra' cemetery (Ortner and Frohlich 2008). In addition, considerable time was invested in the construction of these shaft tombs, with blocking stones demarcating chambers. Bones were laid on reed mats, with care taken to keep small cranial fragments in bowls with skulls (Ortner and Frohlich 2008). Later manipulation of bodies when tombs were opened for new interments further illustrates the concern regarding remembrance of the dead.

The EBII–III charnel house A22 would have required an investment to create, particularly if it was a two-story structure. Built outside the walled town, charnel houses would have been visible reminders of the dead, a mnemonic mechanism for remembrance and for the construction of genealogies, as proposed by Howard Williams (2007). Gold items and other grave goods were interred with the deceased. It is clear that these were secondary burials, as the bones were disarticulated and, in some places, grouped by type. The ongoing maintenance of the structure, the care taken in sorting and moving remains as new individuals were added, and the wealth and quality of material culture placed with these bodies indicate the importance of the commemoration of the dead. Reuse of the same graveyards and charnel houses likely added continuity to burial procedures and enhanced social memory (Joyce 2001).

MATERIALS AND METHODS

Demographic shifts, the number of people associated with different burial styles, and the degree of relatedness among individuals were analyzed for this study. We examined changes in group inclusion and commemoration as the large, fortified townsite developed; compared shifts in age and sex between periods (subadults/adults, males/females, young/older adults); calculated a more accurate number of individuals in the largest burial structure; and explored genetic indicators of relatedness across time.

The current investigation specifically focused on EBIA, where definitive evidence of a settlement is lacking, and EBII–III, which experienced the site's highest population density. The EBIB remains (representing the 100 years between periods) were excluded due to their transitional nature, the low number of excavated remains, and the lack of clarity about dating (Ortner and

Frohlich 2008; Schaub 1981). Bones from EBIV, exhumed during the Lapp excavations in the late 1960s, were destroyed when a shed roof collapsed at the Albright Institute of Archaeological Research in Jerusalem, and the skeletons were "discarded" (Schaub and Rast 1989:9). Table 5.1 provides a list of skeletal material from Bab edh-Dhraʻ available upon excavation, by time period, tomb type, and grid location, as well as the material's current provenience. Today, EBIA remains are housed at the Smithsonian Institution's National Museum of Natural History, while the EBII–III collection is located at the University of Notre Dame Department of Anthropology.

Both collections were commingled. It was possible to gather data for individual EBIA skeletons; however, the fragmentary nature of the EBII–III collection and its much larger excavated sample size precluded such study. Therefore, EBIA data were recorded by bone element to permit direct comparison between time periods for age and sex determination. These remains represent the same EBIA collection described by Ortner and Frohlich (2008), with a focus on appropriate subsections of that material for the studies described below.

Age – For adults, the primary bone for determining age was the os coxa (innominate), using pubic symphysis morphology (Todd 1920). Degree of cranial suture closure (Meindl and Lovejoy 1985) was also applied. The "vault system" (midlambdoid through midcoronal areas) and the "lateral-anterior system" (pterion through superior sphenotemporal) were considered together. Stages were compared, not mean age at death. To avoid duplicating individuals, the left side was used, unless damaged.

Subadult age was assessed through measurements of long bone diaphyses and cranial bones (Scheuer and Black 2000). Femoral length, width of the distal femur, ischium width, and pubis length were also measured. The basilar portion of the occipital (sagittal length and width) was used when long bones were too damaged (Fazekas and Kosa 1978).

Sex – Due to the fragmentary, commingled nature of the EBII–III material, sex could often be recorded on only one portion of a given bone type (e.g., pubic symphysis). Therefore, sex was determined on a landmark-by-landmark basis, not as an aggregate sum of "male" or "female" traits across an entire skeleton.

While features of the pubis have proven accurate for sex determination (Buikstra and Ubelaker 1994; Phenice 1969), the relative fragility of the innominates proved challenging. Femoral heads tended to be more resistant to taphonomic processes; therefore, their diameters were measured for the two collections as well (Ubelaker 1999).

A technique developed by John Albanese, Hugo Cardoso, and Shelley Saunders (2005) was used to address the issue of applying standard measurements from reference collections far removed from the study group. This approach is sample specific, yet can be used on highly fragmented, commingled remains. A measurement is taken from a joint using as many individual elements of the same bone type as possible, and the mean becomes the sectioning point: those bones above this point are deemed male, those smaller, female. This approach has worked for sample sizes over 40 and a sex ratio up to 1.5:1.

Sex determination for the crania focused on the rugosity of key morphological areas and was scored on a five-point system (Buikstra and Ubelaker 1994). The nuchal crest, mastoid process, glabella, and mental eminence were assessed, as was the sharpness of the supraorbital margin.

Burial Assemblage Size

An accurate assessment of collection size is essential to understanding demographic and health patterns in a burial context. The MNI is most commonly calculated in paleodemographic studies, representing the fewest possible people present (Cruse 2003). Multiple permutations have been used, from simply separating bones by side and basing the MNI on whichever antimere produces the highest yield; to summing lefts and rights of a given bone and dividing by two; to dividing the number of lefts/rights combined, subtracted from the number of pairs. The MNI inherently underestimates original collection size, barring a 100 percent recovery rate (Adams and Konigsberg 2004).

Bradley Adams and Lyle Konigsberg (2004) argued that the most likely number of individuals (MLNI) is a more accurate tool. This method calculates the survival probability of homologous pairs of a single element, while assuming that skeletal elements from the side that occurs with less frequency *must* be paired with their counterparts. As a result, MLNI addresses the effects of taphonomic processes and their resultant bias by permitting a count of unpaired elements as well as pair matches. Adams and Konigsberg demonstrated that MLNI is capable of estimating collection size despite low recovery rates, while also establishing the decreasing efficiency of MNI with increasing sample size. In a study of known skeletal assemblages, the MNI and MLNI were calculated for artificially commingled remains, and in every situation, MLNI resulted in a much closer estimate than MNI (Adams and Konigsberg 2008).

TABLE 5.1 Descriptions of Bab edh-Dhra' skeletal remains by time period, tomb group, tomb type, and current location as referenced in the published literature

Period	Tomb Group	No.	Type	Year Excavated	Current Location*	Reference	Notes
EB IA	A	2	Shallow tomb	1965–67	Lost	Schaub 1973b:3; Schaub and Rast 1989:25, 36–39	
EB IA	A	3	Shaft tomb	1965–67	Lost	Schaub and Rast 1989:29, 39–41	Latest EB IA Tombs (as noted in Schaub and Rast 1989:29)
EB IA	A	5	Shaft tomb	1965–67	Lost	Schaub and Rast 1989:29, 41, 48, 58	Middle-range EB IA Tombs (as noted in Schaub and Rast 1989:29)
EB IA	A	6	Shaft tomb	1965–67	Lost	Schaub and Rast 1989:28, 58–61; Ortner and Frohlich 2008:26	Latest EB IA Tombs (as noted in Schaub and Rast 1989:29)
EB IA	A	7	Shaft tomb	1965–67	Lost	Schaub and Rast 1989:26, 62–64; Ortner and Frohlich 2008:26	Latest EB IA Tombs (as noted in Schaub and Rast 1989:29)
EB IA	A	9	Shaft tomb	1965–67	Lost	Schaub and Rast 1989:29, 65, 72	Latest EB IA Tombs (as noted in Schaub and Rast 1989:29)
EB IA	A	10	Shaft tomb	1965–67	Lost	Schaub and Rast 1989:29, 72	Earliest EB IA Tombs (as noted in Schaub and Rast 1989:29)
EB IA	A	11	Shaft tomb	1965–67	Lost	Schaub and Rast 1989:29, 72–73	Earliest EB IA Tombs (as noted in Schaub and Rast 1989:29)
EB IA	A	12	Shaft tomb	1965–67	Lost	Schaub and Rast 1989:29, 73–74	Earliest EB IA Tombs (as noted in Schaub and Rast 1989:29)

continued on next page

TABLE 5.1—continued

Period	Tomb Group	No.	Type	Year Excavated	Current Location*	Reference	Notes
EB IA	A	45	Shaft tomb	1965–67	Lost	Schaub and Rast 1989:26, 74–76; Ortner and Frohlich 2008:26	Latest EB IA Tombs (as noted in Schaub and Rast 1989:29)
EB IA	A	46	Shaft tomb	1965–67	Lost	Schaub and Rast 1989:29, 76–77	Latest EB IA Tombs (as noted in Schaub and Rast 1989:29)
EB IA	A	47	Shaft tomb	1965–67	Lost	Schaub and Rast 1989:29, 77	Latest EB IA Tombs (as noted in Schaub and Rast 1989:29)
EB IA	A	65	Shaft tomb	1965–67	Lost	Schaub and Rast 1989:26, 28, 83–85	Latest EB IA Tombs (as noted in Schaub and Rast 1989:29)
EB IA	A	66	Shaft tomb	1965–67	Lost	Schaub and Rast 1989:29, 85, 90	Earliest EB IA Tombs (as noted in Schaub and Rast 1989:29)
EB IA	A	67	Shaft tomb	1965–67	Lost	Schaub and Rast 1989:29, 91, 94, 98	Earliest EB IA Tombs (as noted in Schaub and Rast 1989:29)
EB IA	A	68	Shaft tomb	1965–67	Lost	Schaub and Rast 1989:29, 98–101, 106	Middle-range EB IA Tombs (as noted in Schaub and Rast 1989:29)
EB IA	A	69	Shaft tomb	1965–67	Lost	Schaub and Rast 1989:29, 108–10	Earliest EB IA Tombs (as noted in Schaub and Rast 1989:29)
EB IA	A	70	Shaft tomb	1965–67	Lost	Schaub and Rast 1989:29, 110	Earliest EB IA Tombs (as noted in Schaub and Rast 1989:29)

continued on next page

Table 5.1—*continued*

Period	Tomb Group	No.	Type	Year Excavated	Current Location*	Reference	Notes
EB IA	A	71	Shaft tomb	1965–67	Lost	Lapp 1968a:25; Schaub and Rast 1989:28, 110–13, 116	Latest EB IA Tombs (as noted in Schaub and Rast 1989:29)
EB IA	A	72	Shaft tomb	1965–67	Lost	Schaub and Rast 1989:29, 132–36, 140, 142	Middle-range EB IA Tombs (as noted in Schaub and Rast 1989:29)
EB IA	A	75	Shaft tomb	1965–67	Lost	Schaub and Rast 1989:29, 150–51	Earliest EB IA Tombs (as noted in Schaub and Rast 1989:29)
EB IA	A	76	Shaft tomb	1965–67	Lost	Lapp 1968a:14–41; Schaub 1981; Schaub and Rast 1989: 151–52, 156	Earliest EB IA Tombs (as noted in Schaub and Rast 1989:29)
EB IA	A	77	Shaft tomb	1965–67	Lost	Rast and Schaub 1978:6; Schaub and Rast 1989:29, 156–47, 162	Middle-range EB IA Tombs (as noted in Schaub and Rast 1989:29)
EB IA	A	78	Shaft tomb	1977	SI	Schaub 1981: 45–50; Ortner and Frohlich 2008:28:table 4.1, 52–59	
EB IA	A	79	Shaft tomb	1977	SI	Schaub 1981:45–50; Ortner and Frohlich 2008:28:table 4.1, 59–64	
EB IA	A	80	Shaft tomb	1977	SI	Schaub 1981:45–50; Ortner and Frohlich 2008:28:table 4.1, 64–73	
EB IA	A	81	Shaft tomb	1965–67	Lost	Schaub 1981:50; see Lapp 1968b; Schaub and Rast 1989:162–65	Earliest EB IA Tombs (as noted in Schaub and Rast 1989: 29)

continued on next page

TABLE 5.1—continued

Period	Tomb Group	No.	Type	Year Excavated	Current Location*	Reference	Notes
EB IA	A	82	Shaft tomb	1965–67	Lost	Schaub 1981:50; see Lapp 1968b; Schaub and Rast 1989:166–68	Middle-range EB IA Tombs (as noted in Schaub and Rast 1989:29)
EB IA	A	83	Shaft tomb	1965–67	Lost	Schaub and Rast 1989:28, 169–70	Latest EB IA Tombs (as noted in Schaub and Rast 1989:29)
EB IA	A	84	Niche tomb	1965–67	Lost	Schaub and Rast 1989:170–72	
EB IA	A	85	Shaft tomb	1965–67	Lost	Schaub 1981:50; Schaub and Rast 1989:172–73	Earliest EB IA Tombs (as noted in Schaub and Rast 1989:29)
EB IA	A	86	Shaft tomb	1977	SI	Schaub 1981:50–53; Ortner and Frohlich 2008:28:table 4.1, 73–78	
EB IA	A	87	Shaft tomb	1977	SI	Ortner and Frohlich 2008:78–79	
EB IA	A	89	Shaft tomb	1977	SI	Schaub 1981:50–53; Ortner and Frohlich 2008:28:table 4.1, 83–87	
EB IA	A	91	Shaft tomb	1977	SI	Schaub 1981:50–53; Ortner and Frohlich 2008:28:table 4.1, 87–88	
EB IA	A	92	Shaft tomb	1977	SI	Schaub 1981:50–53; Ortner and Frohlich 2008:28:table 4.1, 88	
EB IA	A	100	Shaft tomb	1977	SI	Ortner and Frohlich 2008:89–107	
EB IA	A	101	Shaft tomb	1977	SI	Schaub 1981: 45–50; Ortner and Frohlich 2008:28:table 4.1, 107–10	

continued on next page

Table 5.1—continued

Period	Tomb Group	No.	Type	Year Excavated	Current Location*	Reference	Notes
EB IA	A	102	Shaft tomb	1979	SI	Rast and Schaub 1980:32; Ortner and Frohlich 2008:28:table 4.1, 147–55	
EB IA	A	105	Shaft tomb	1979	SI	Rast and Schaub 1980:32; Ortner and Frohlich 2008:26, 28:table 4.1, 155–61	
EB IA	A	107	Shaft tomb	1979	SI	Rast and Schaub 1980:32; Ortner and Frohlich 2008:28:table 4.1, 165–73	
EB IA	A	108	Shaft tomb	1979	SI	Rast and Schaub 1980:33; Ortner and Frohlich 2008:28:table 4.1, 173–78	
EB IA	A	109	Shaft tomb	1979	SI	Rast and Schaub 1980:33; Ortner and Frohlich 2008:28:table 4.1, 178–82	
EB IA	A	110	Shaft tomb	1981	SI	Ortner and Frohlich 2008:28:table 4.1, 184–99	
EB IA	A	111	Shaft tomb	1981	SI	Ortner and Frohlich 2008:26, 28:table 4.1, 199–214	
EB IA	A	112	Shaft tomb	1981	No human bone	Ortner and Frohlich 2008:26, 214–16	No human bones recovered (looted)

continued on next page

TABLE 5.1—*continued*

Period	Tomb Group	No.	Type	Year Excavated	Current Location*	Reference	Notes
EB IA	A	113	Shaft tomb	1981	No human bone	Ortner and Frohlich 2008:28:table 4.1, 216	No human bones recovered (looted)
EB IA	A	114	Shaft tomb	1981	SI	Ortner and Frohlich 2008:28:table 4.1, 216–24	
EB IA	A	120	Shaft tomb	1977	SI	Ortner 1981:125; Ortner and Frohlich 2008:28:table 4.1, 110–13	
EB IA	A	121	Shaft tomb	1979	SI	Ortner and Frohlich 2008:28:table 4.1, 110–13	
EB IA	A	100 (E, S, W)	Shaft tomb	1977	SI	Schaub 1981:45–50; Ortner and Frohlich 2008:28:table 4.1	
EB IA	C	1	Shaft tomb	1965–67	Lost	Schaub and Rast 1989:185–87	
EB IA	C	2	Shaft tomb	1965–67	Lost	Schaub and Rast 1989:90–191	
EB IA	C	3	Shaft tomb	1965–67	Lost	Schaub and Rast 1989:192–93	
EB IA	C	5	Shaft tomb	1965–67	Lost	Schaub and Rast 1989:196–97	
EB IA	C	6	Shaft tomb	1965–67	Lost	Schaub and Rast 1989:200–202	
EB IA	C	7	Shaft tomb	1965–67	Lost	Schaub and Rast 1989: 202	
EB IA	C	9	Shaft tomb	1977	SI	Schaub 1981: 56; Ortner 1981:126; Ortner and Frohlich 2008:26, 29:table 4.2, 113–14	

continued on next page

TABLE 5.1—continued

Period	Tomb Group	No.	Type	Year Excavated	Current Location*	Reference	Notes
EB IA	C	10	Shaft tomb	1977	SI	Schaub 1981:55–56; Ortner 1981:126; Ortner and Frohlich 2008:26, 29:table 4.2, 114–16	
EB IA	C	11	Shaft tomb	1981	SI	Ortner and Frohlich 2008:28:table 4.2, 224–27	
EB IA	F	1	Shaft tomb	1975	UND	Rast and Schaub 1978:5; Rast and Schaub 2003:63, 64; Ortner and Frohlich 2008:27	
EB IA	F	2	Shaft tomb	1975	UND	Rast and Schaub 1978:5; Rast and Schaub 2003:63, 64–66; Ortner and Frohlich 2008:27	
EB IA	F	4A	Shaft tomb	1977	UND	Rast and Schaub 2003:66–68; Ortner and Frohlich 2008:27	
EB IA	F	4B	Shaft tomb	1977	UND	Rast and Schaub 2003:68	
EB IA	F	4C	Shaft tomb	1977	No human bone	Rast and Schaub 2003:68	No human bones recovered
EB IA	G	4	Shaft tomb (but possibly transitional to round charnel house)	1977	SI	Schaub 1981:54–55; Ortner and Frohlich 2008:29:table 4.3, 118–21	

continued on next page

TABLE 5.1—*continued*

Period	Tomb Group	No.	Type	Year Excavated	Current Location*	Reference	Notes
EB IA	G	5	Shaft tomb	1977	No human bone	Schaub 1993:132; Ortner and Frohlich 2008:26, 29:table 4-3	May not have contained bone
EB IA	G	6	Shaft tomb	1977	No human bone	Schaub 1981:53–55	
EB IA or IB	A	1	Surface burial w/ assoc. large stones (cairn burial)	1965–67	Lost	Schaub 1973b:3; Schaub and Rast 1989:25, 35–36	Latest EB IA Tombs (as noted in Schaub and Rast 1989:29)
EB IB	A	13	Shallow surface burial	1965–67	Lost	Schaub and Rast 1989:26; 205; Ortner and Frohlich 2008:26	
EB IB	A	53	Round charnel house	1965–67	Lost	Schaub 1981:65; see Lapp 1968c:8, 1968b:5; Schaub 1973:44–46; Rast and Schaub 1978:22–23; Schaub and Rast 1989:25, 209, 222–27, 232; Schaub 1993:132; Rast 1999:172; Ortner and Frohlich 2008:26	
EB IB	A	88	Shaft tomb	1977	SI	Schaub 1981:61–62, 63;fig. 22; Ortner and Frohlich 2008:26, 79–83	

continued on next page

TABLE 5.1—*continued*

Period	Tomb Group	No.	Type	Year Excavated	Current Location*	Reference	Notes
EB IB	A	104	Shallow pit	1979	No human bone	Rast and Schaub 1980:34; Ortner and Frohlich 2008:26, 29:table 4.4	No human bones recovered
EB IB	A	100 (N)	Shaft tomb	1977	SI	Schaub 1981:58–61; Schaub 1993:133; Ortner and Frohlich 2008:26, 29:table 4.4	Reuse of earlier EB IA chamber (Schaub 1993)
EB IB	G	1	Round charnel house	1977	SI	Schaub 1981:53, 62–65; Rast 1999:172; Ortner and Frohlich 2008:26, 29:table 4.4, 123–46	
EB IB	G	2	Shallow shaft	1977	SI	Schaub 1981:57–58; Ortner and Frohlich 2008:26, 29:table 4.4, 116–18	
EB IB	A	43	Shaft tomb	1965–67	Lost	Lapp 1970:110; Schaub 1973a:41–44; Schaub 1973b:4; Schaub 1981:62; Schaub and Rast 1989:25, 205, 209; Ortner and Frohlich 2008:26	
EB II	A	4	Shaft? tomb	1965–67	Lost	Schaub 1973b:4; Schaub and Rast 1989:25:figs. 194–96, 319–22	
EB II	A	56	Round charnel house	1977	UND	Schaub 1981:65–66, 67:fig. 26	

continued on next page

TABLE 5.1—continued

Period	Tomb Group	No.	Type	Year Excavated	Current Location*	Reference	Notes
EB II	A	73	Shallow burial	1965–67	Lost	Schaub and Rast 1989:25,figs. 194–96, 324–25	
EB II–III	A	8	Charnel house	1965–67	Lost	Schaub 1973b:17–18; Schaub and Rast 1989:30, 325–26, 336	Destruction of tomb based on C14 dates—2192 BCE +/- 180 (calibrated 2350 BCE +/- 180 [Schaub 1973b:17–18])
EB II–III	A	20	Charnel house	1965–67	Lost	Schaub and Rast 1989:30, 336–40	
EB II–III	A	21	Charnel house	1965–67	Lost	Rast and Schaub 1980:38:table; Schaub and Rast 1989:3:table 2, 340–43	
EB II–III	A	22	Charnel house	1979	UND	Rast and Schaub 1980:34–39; Schaub 1993:134	
EB II–III	A	41	Charnel house	1965–67	Lost	Schaub and Rast 1989:30, 343–44, 348, 364	
EB II–III	A	42	Charnel house	1965–67	Lost	Schaub and Rast 1989:26, 30, 364–67; Ortner and Frohlich 2008:26	
EB II–III	A	44	Charnel house	1965–67	Lost	Schaub and Rast 1989; cf. Rast and Schaub 2003; Schaub and Rast 1989:3:table 2, 367,371–72	
EB II–III	A	51	Charnel house	1965–67	Lost	Schaub and Rast 1989:30, 381–85; Rast and Schaub 1980:38: table	

continued on next page

TABLE 5.1—*continued*

Period	Tomb Group	No.	Type	Year Excavated	Current Location*	Reference	Notes
EB II–III	A	55	Charnel house	1975	UND	Rast and Schaub 1978:22–24; Finnegan 1978:53	
EB II–III	C	4	Charnel house	1965–67	Lost	Schaub and Rast 1989:25, 385–86, 388	
late EB III	D	1	Shaft tomb	1975	UND	Schaub and Rast 1989:25, 390–92	
EB IV	A	52	Shaft tomb	1965–67	Lost	Schaub and Rast 1989:22, 473–80; Rast and Schaub 1980:40; Schaub 1973b:3–4	
EB IV	A	54	Shaft tomb	1965–67	Lost	Schaub 1973b:2–19; Rast and Schaub 1980:40; Schaub and Rast 1989:22, 480–82	
EB IV	RTT	1	Shaft tomb?	1979	UND	Rast and Schaub 1980:40	
EB IV	RTT	2	Shaft tomb?	1979	UND	Rast and Schaub 1980:40	
EB	B	1	Tholoi	1965–67	Lost	Lapp 1968b:560; Schaub and Rast 1989:22, 32, 483, 489	Schaub and Rast 1989: 32 – no stratigraphic relation; probably dates to the general period
EB	B	2	Tholoi/ tumulus	1965–67	Lost	Lapp 1968b:560; Schaub and Rast 1989:22, 32, 489	Schaub and Rast 1989: 32 – no stratigraphic relation and no parallels or diagnostic material; probably dates to the general period

continued on next page

TABLE 5.1—*continued*

Period	Tomb Group	No.	Type	Year Excavated	Current Location*	Reference	Notes
Unknown	E	1	Shallow surface burial	1975	UND	Finnegan 1978:53	
Unknown	A	103	Shaft tomb—disturbed	1979	SI	Rast and Schaub 1980:33; Ortner and Frohlich 2008:28:table 4.1, 155	
Unknown	A	106	Shaft tomb—disturbed	1979	SI	Rast and Schaub 1980:33; Ortner and Frohlich 2008:28:table 4.1, 161–65	
Unknown	B	3	Tumulus	1975	UND	Finnegan 1978:53; Schaub and Rast 1989:22	

Note: EB = Early Bronze Age; RTT = Road Test Trench; UND = University of Notre Dame; SI = Smithsonian Institution.

* Current Locations as of 2013. Note: not all references cited indicate the 2013 location.

The complete probability function was used to calculate MLNI (see Adams and Konigsberg 2004 for formulae). Visual and metric pair matching was employed for EBII–III, which was not necessary for EBIA, because of individual reconstruction. Elements maintaining the greatest number of landmarks were the calcaneus, talus, and femoral head. For the calcanei, right and left bones were seriated separately by visual estimation of size, then sorted by facet configuration (Bruckner 1987), while maintaining the seriations based on size within each subgroup of facet pattern. Additional morphological features included peroneal and lateral tubercles, tuberosity size, sulci morphology, and size/shape of the sustentaculum tali. For the talus, facet pattern, lateral and medial tubercles, and comparisons of sulci were used. Pathologies used included osteoarthritis, eburnation, osteophytic lipping, and, for the calcanei, heel spurs (with a clear understanding of the bilateral asymmetry associated with these traits). Femora were matched based on visible size of the head, location/size of fovea capitis, and alterations to the femoral neck. Although Ashley Kendell and P. Willey (2014) argued that MNI works better for large fragmentary collections, the substantive nature of the bones selected (Cruse 2003) and preservation of morphological features allowed our use of MLNI.

The visually paired cohorts, where both specimens possessed at least one set of landmarks for measurement, were then sorted metrically (Byrd 2008). Calcaneus measurements included the middle breadth and maximum length. For the talus, the maximum anteroposterior length or talar length and the maximum transverse width or talar width were measured (Koshy, Vettivel, and Selvaraj 2002). The maximum diameter of the femoral head, as well as the anterior-posterior subtrochanteric diameter, were measured to compare femur matches. The metric data were examined to determine whether measurements between the two specimens fell within one standard deviation. If not, the specimens were reexamined using morphological and pathological characteristics.

GENETIC RELATEDNESS

Cranial nonmetric traits are congenital, nonpathological variations that offer information about genetic relationships in a skeletal collection based on the assumption that phenetic similarity reflects genetic similarity (Cheverud and Buikstra 1982; Scott and Turner 1997). Traits were scored according to Gertrud Hauser and Gian DeStefano (1989) and variants in the final analysis included: metopic suture, ossicles at lambda, parietal notch bones, and ossicles at asterion. Traits were chosen based on comparability with regional sites. Pairwise comparisons of the variants using Kendall's tau-b correlation coefficient indicated no intertrait correlation (greatest $\tau_b = 0.30$) (Irish 2006).

Comparative samples from the surrounding area were compiled from published literature: Turkey (Ricaut and Waelkens 2008), Egypt (Berry and Berry 1967; Prowse 1994), Iran/Iraq (Rathbun 1984), and the southern Levant (Hanihara and Ishida 2001). These locations were chosen given evidence of contact and trade with Egypt, Mesopotamia, and the southern Levant, and/or because the sites are geographically close to Bab edh-Dhra'.

STATISTICAL METHODS

Chi-square goodness of fit tests with Yates's correction for continuity were employed in 2×2 tables. Any group of data that contained an expected value less than 5, or with a 0 in a cell, was analyzed with Fisher's Exact Test. Metric data were compared using Student's t-test. All tests were considered significant at $p \leq 0.05$.

Nonmetric traits from both periods were compared to other groups to assess genetic relatedness/distance using the Mean Measure of Divergence statistic (MMD). The MMD determines the relative "distance" of three or more groups by comparing frequencies of discrete traits. This multivariate dissimilarity calculation is an average of the variance present in a suite of characteristics (Sjøvold 1973). The smaller the value, the more similar the comparative groups. A MMD is significant if it is more than twice the standard deviation ($p < 0.025$). A correction for small sample size was added to correct for continuity (De Souza and Houghton 1977).

RESULTS

ADULT AGE

Todd pubic symphysis stages were compressed into broader categories providing a more accurate, if less precise, age distribution for each period (Figures 5.4a–5.4d). The stages roughly correspond to the following ages (in years): Todd stages 1–3 (18–24), 4–6 (25–34), 7–9 (35–49), and 10 (50+). Fisher's Exact tests (with the Freeman-Halton extension) comparing the right pubis by period show no significant difference between stages 1–3, 4–6, and 7–9. Stage 10 was excluded due to the lack of specimens. Using the same statistic to analyze the left side, a significant difference is evident ($p = 0.034$).

There was a similar sample representation problem using cranial suture closure, particularly in EBII–III. An initial rough estimate of MNI ≈ 200 in A22 at excavation was based on crania (Rast and Schaub 2003). However, the plethora of landmarks needed to assess suture closure meant the number of useable skulls was reduced. We found no significant difference by period for age using vault stages S1–S4 (Figures 5.4e–5.4f).

SUBADULT AGE

Table 5.2a lists subadult length and width of the basilar portion of the occipital bone. We found a significant difference between the periods in the number of neonates and infants using sagittal length, with more present in EBIA ($p < 0.001$). There is no significant difference for width by time. There are 16 EBIA fetal crania, some as young as 34 weeks (Scheuer and MacLaughlin-Black 1994). By contrast, there are two possible EBII–III fetuses (Fazekas and Kosa 1978). The majority of EBIA basilar portions are perinatal, while the EBII–III peak between three months and one year. It is unknown whether fetal bones belonged to unborn fetuses, stillborn babies, or premature infants.

Femoral length frequencies are similar for each assemblage (Table 5.2b). Seven right and seven left EBII–III subadult femora were complete enough to measure diaphyseal length, with no significant difference by side. One femur is estimated at 32–34 fetal weeks, four at 40 fetal weeks, and nine as postnatal. There is no side difference for EBIA femoral length. Thirteen are estimated at 34–38 fetal weeks, while 10 are likely from a fetus or neonate between 38 and 40 fetal weeks. Another eight EBIA femora are from babies younger than three months old, while no infants older than three months are identified from EBII–III. There is no significant difference by time period for either side.

Too few ilia could be measured from EBII–III skeletons for inclusion. Only five are complete enough to measure length, three to measure width. The same is true for ischium length, with four available. The portions required for ischium width measurement, however, proved much more durable (Table 5.2c). There is no difference by side for ischium width, with a significant difference between periods for left ischia ($p = 0.028$). Again, there are more young children in EBIA.

SEX

For EBIA, based on the pubis morphology alone, a minimum of 11 males and 6 females could be identified. Due to the fragmentary nature of the

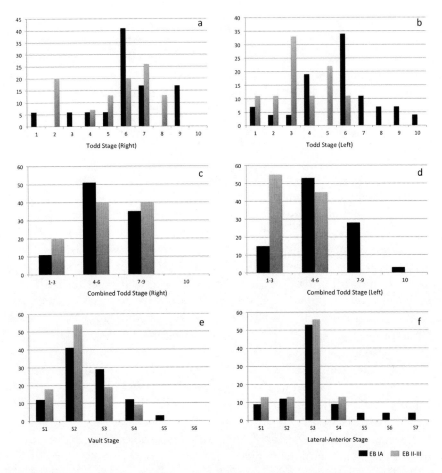

FIGURE 5.4. *Adult aging techniques using the Todd Pubic Symphyseal morphology method: (a) % right faces, (b) % left faces, (c) % right faces with combined stages, and (d) % left faces with combined stages; and cranial suture closure; (e) % crania in each stage on the vault; and (f) % closure on the lateral-anterior portion of the skull.*

EBII–III collection, only 14 have at least one Terrell Phenice (1969) scoring criterion available, with 6 males, 5 females, and 3 indeterminate. There is no difference between periods for sex comparing either side.

Complete innominates with adequate preservation generated a ratio of 18 males:17 females from EBIA. When all elements are considered, using burials with an innominate that preserved at least one scorable attribute, the ratio rises to 25 males:22 females. This is well below the original 120:112 ratio identified

Table 5.2A. Measurements of the basilar portion of the occipital bone for EBIA and EB II–III Bab edh-Dhra‘ subadults

Measure (mm)	Early Bronze IA				Early Bronze II–III			
	Sagittal Length		Width		Sagittal Length		Width	
	n	%	n	%	n	%	n	%
11–11.99	5	12.8	0	0	0	0	0	0
12–12.99	4	10.3	0	0	1	2.5	0	0
13–13.99	11	28.2	1	4.8	2	5.0	0	0
14–14.99	5	12.8	1	4.8	2	5.0	0	0
15–15.99	3	7.7	1	4.8	4	10.0	1	5.0
16–16.99	2	5.1	2	9.5	6	15.0	0	0
17–17.99	1	2.6	1	4.8	5	12.5	2	10.0
18–18.99	1	2.6	2	9.5	5	12.5	0	0
19–19.99	2	5.1	2	9.5	3	7.5	2	10.0
20–20.99	1	2.6	2	9.5	2	5.0	2	10.0
21–21.99	2	5.1	2	9.5	2	5.0	0	0
22–22.99	0	0	1	4.8	1	2.5	1	5.0
23–23.99	1	2.6	0	0	1	2.5	1	5.0
24–24.99	0	0	1	4.8	2	5.0	5	25.0
25–25.99	1	2.6	0	0	0	0	1	5.0
26–26.99	0	0	2	9.5	1	2.5	2	10.0
27–27.99	0	0	1	4.8	2	5.0	0	0
28–28.99	0	0	0	0	0	0	0	0
29–29.99	0	0	1	4.8	1	2.5	2	10.0
30–30.99	0	0	1	4.8	0	0	1	5.0
Total	25		24		4		6	

at excavation when entire individual skeletons were assessed (Ortner and Frohlich 2008).

Sex determination for the crania required the presence of at least two traits: nuchal crest, mastoid process, supraorbital margin, and/or glabella. When the cranium is considered alone, 25 males:49 females were identified in EBIA, 18 males:32 females in EBII–III.

There was likewise no significant difference between bone types (crania vs. innominates) within each period, except when comparing EBIA crania and

TABLE 5.2B. Measurements of femoral length for EBIA and EB II–III Bab edh-Dhra' subadults

Measure (mm)	Early Bronze IA				Early Bronze II–III			
	Right		Left		Right		Left	
	n	%	n	%	n	%	n	%
50–59.99	0	0	0	0	1	14.3	1	14.3
60–69.99	6	19.4	7	22.6	0	0	0	0
70–79.99	4	12.9	6	19.4	1	14.3	3	42.9
80–89.99	2	6.5	2	6.5	0	0	0	0
90–99.99	0	0	0	0	0	0	0	0
100–109.99	3	9.7	1	3.2	0	0	0	0
110–119.99	3	9.7	2	6.5	0	0	1	14.3
120–129.99	0	0	0	0	0	0	0	0
130–139.99	1	3.2	1	3.2	1	14.3	0	0
140–149.99	0	0	1	3.2	0	0	0	0
150–159.99	1	3.2	2	6.5	1	14.3	0	0
160–169.99	1	3.2	0	0	0	0	0	0
170–179.99	4	12.9	1	3.2	0	0	0	0
180–189.99	0	0	0	0	0	0	0	0
190–199.99	0	0	1	3.2	0	0	0	0
200–209.99	0	0	0	0	0	0	1	14.3
Total	25		24		4		6	

right pubis ($p = 0.020$). For all comparisons, we found more females using the crania, and more males using the os pubis.

Vertical femur head diameter (vhd) was used next. In both periods, there is no significant difference by side. Using Albanese, Cardoso, and Saunders (2005), left vhd ≥ 44.0 mm and right vhd ≥ 45.0 mm delimit males, while left vhd ≤ 43.0 mm and right ≤ 44.0 mm define females. There are 14 left femoral heads for each sex in EBIA, and 22 males:26 females in EBII–III. Comparably insignificant are comparisons of right femoral heads in each time period.

BURIAL ASSEMBLAGE SIZE

Ortner and Frohlich (2008) studied shaft tomb chambers that typically contained 1–9 commingled EBIA skeletons, permitting reconstruction of 512 individuals (excluding prenatal remains). Determining MNI using frontal bones for

TABLE 5.2C. Measurements of the width of the ischium for EBIA and EB II–III Bab edh-Dhra' subadults

Measure (mm)	Early Bronze IA				Early Bronze II–III			
	Right		Left		Right		Left	
	n	%	n	%	n	%	N	%
0–4.99	0	0	0	0	0	0	0	0
5–9.99	1	6.3	0	0	0	0	0	0
10–14.99	1	6.3	5	26.3	0	0	0	0
15–19.99	2	12.5	4	21.1	0	0	0	0
20–24.99	2	12.5	1	5.3	1	16.7	2	18.2
25–29.99	2	12.5	2	10.5	1	16.7	2	18.2
30–34.99	4	25.0	2	10.5	1	16.7	1	9.1
35–39.99	0	0	2	10.5	2	33.3	3	27.3
40–44.99	4	25.0	3	15.8	0	0	1	9.1
45–49.99	0	0	0	0	1	16.7	1	9.1
50–54.99	0	0	0	0	0	0	1	9.1
Total	16		19		6		11	

the same EBIA collection, only 81 individuals were estimated, illustrating how MNI can severely underestimate burial assemblage (Adams and Konigsberg 2004). Frontal bones provided the largest single bone MNI for EBIA.

For EBII–III, the fragmentary, commingled nature of the A22 bones did not permit a count of individual skeletons; therefore, assemblage estimation tools were the only mechanism for calculating collection size (Table 5.3). The MNI of the left talus (n = 224) and calcanei (n = 215) are in basic agreement with the original cranial count of ca. 200. The more generous method of summing the sides and subtracting the number of pairs produce a calcaneus MNI of 394. However, the MLNI calculation produces estimates of 1,129 (tali), 2,363 (calcanei), and 1,528 (femora). Within the probability function for each element, the maximum likelihood estimate is 2,363 individuals, the highest point. This is also the MLNI value obtained using Douglas Chapman's (1951) variant of the LI. The highest-density region (HDR) includes 95 percent of the distribution and runs from 1,582 to 3,866.

There are relatively few pair matches given the number of bones present. This is confirmed by low recovery probabilities (r) for the talus (r = 0.184), calcaneus (r = 0.085), and femur (r = 0.086).

TABLE 5.3. MNI/Pair matching /MLNI calculations for the EBII–III collection using the bones best suited to MLNI calculations: the talus, calcaneus, and proximal femur. Graph illustrates the probability function for N at 95 percent highest density region (shaded area).

Bone	*Side*			*MNI Estimates*			*MLNI Values*		
	Left (n)	*Right (n)*	*Pairs (P)*	*Max (L,R)*	*(L+R)/2*	*L+R-P*	*MLNI*	*Recovery*	*Std. Err.*
Calcaneus	215	196	17	215	205	394	2,363	0.085	0.019
Talus	224	200	39	224	212	385	1,129	0.184	0.025
Femur	142	138	12	142	142	268	1,528	0.086	0.023

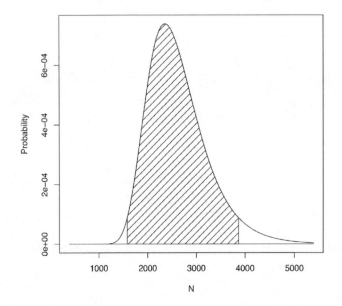

GENETIC RELATEDNESS

Bentley (1987) addressed relatedness among EBIA shaft tombs using dental nonmetric traits, which are largely genetically controlled (Scott and Turner 1997). She proposed that families occupied the tombs, since dental traits clustered by chamber, thus supporting the relationship between the living and their ancestors. There are very few teeth in the EBII–III collection; therefore dental nonmetric traits could not be employed for this study.

Cranial nonmetric traits were collected for both periods. Before using the MMD statistic, we examined each trait independently to identify variation by side, which may result in possible exclusion of the trait from biodistance analysis. No statistically significant differences are found by time period for each sex by side (Table 5.4a) for metopism, ossicles at lambda, coronal suture ossicles, ossicles at asterion, or parietal notch bones. No significant differences are found by period for each side (Table 5.4b). Only one significant difference is identified when comparing time periods: right-side ossicles at asterion ($p^* = 0.030$) (Table 5.4c).

Table 5.5 lists MMD values for Bab edh-Dhra' compared to regional counterparts. The values from EBIA were relatively small, suggesting that the distribution of traits is similar to the values found at other sites. Conversely, EBII–III values are relatively larger, suggesting that the people of EBII–III are less similar to other Near Eastern/Egyptian groups. Nevertheless, values derived from EBII–III trait frequencies indicate that the people of EBII–III were most closely related to EBIA Bab edh-Dhra'.

DISCUSSION

This chapter evaluates shifts in remembrance and commemoration at Bab edh-Dhra' during a time of dynamic social change. Changing practices are compared using demographic information to chart differences in age and sex profiles with time, estimating the number of individuals buried in each assemblage, and gauging genetic continuity.

Demographic Analysis

The commingled nature of the EBII–III material placed limitations upon demographic reconstructions for this site. To permit direct comparison between early and later phases, we were confined to an element-by-element assessment of age and sex indicators. This constraint negatively affected sample sizes, particularly when compared to the reconstructions possible at excavation, and when using complete EBIA individuals.

For adults, a significant difference in age distribution is found between the two periods using left pubic symphysis morphology ($p = 0.034$), most likely the result of missing EBII–III individuals from the oldest age category. We interpret this as an absence of evidence, not evidence of absence. Rather than exclusion from remembrance by EBII–III inhabitants, this is more

TABLE 5.4A. Cranial nonmetric trait frequencies for the EBIA and EBII–III by sex for each side

Time	Sex	Side	Metopic Suture			
			n	+ (%)	– (%)	p*
EB IA	F	L	44	14.7 (5)	88.6 (39)	1
		R				
	M	L	26	11.5 (3)	88.5 (23)	
		R				
EB II–III	F	L	35	8.6 (3)	91.4 (32)	1
		R				
	M	L	47	10.6 (5)	89.4 (42)	
		R				

Time	Sex	Side	Ossicle at Lambda			
			n	+ (%)	– (%)	p
EB IA	F	L	30	10.0 (3)	90.0 (27	1
		R				
	M	L	16	12.5 (2)	87.5 (14)	
		R				
EB II–III	F	L	12	8.3 (1)	91.7 (11)	1
		R				
	M	L	17	11.8 (2)	88.2 (15)	
		R				

Time	Sex	Side	Coronal Suture Ossicles			
			n	+ (%)	– (%)	p*
EB IA	F	L	25	0. (0)	100.0 (25)	0.50
		R	32	6.3 (2)	93.8 (30)	
	M	L	21	9.5 (2)	90.5 (19)	1
		R	18	5.6 (1)	94.4 (17)	
EB II–III	F	L	9	0. (0)	100.0 (9)	1
		R	12	8.3 (1)	91.7 (11)	
	M	L	12	0. (0)	100.0 (12)	1
		R	15	6.7 (1)	93.3 (14)	

continued on next page

TABLE 5.4A—*continued*

				Ossicle at Asterion		
Time	*Sex*	*Side*	*n*	*+ (%)*	*– (%)*	*p**
EB IA	F	L	14	7.1 (1)	92.9 (13)	1
		R	25	8.0 (2)	92.0 (23)	
	M	L	13	23.1 (3)	76.9 (10)	0.08
		R	16	0. (0)	100.0 (16)	
EB II–III	F	L	8	12.5 (1)	87.5 (7)	0.57
		R	8	37.5 (3)	62.5 (5)	
	M	L	12	58.3 (7)	41.7 (5)	0.29
		R	5	20.0 (1)	80.0 (4)	

				Parietal Notch		
Time	*Sex*	*Side*	*n*	*+ (%)*	*– (%)*	*p**
EB IA	F	L	17	35.3 (6)	64.7 (11)	0.73
		R	23	26.1 (6)	73.9 (17)	
	M	L	13	23.1 (3)	76.9 (10)	0.22
		R	13	0. (0)	100.0 (13)	
EB II–III	F	L	6	0. (0)	100.0 (6)	1
		R	9	11.1 (1)	88.9 (8)	
	M	L	9	22.2 (2)	77.8 (7)	0.48
		R	7	0. (0)	100.0 (7)	

Note: $p*$ = Fisher's p.

likely the unfortunate result of postmortem factors conspiring to obscure their memory.

More, and younger, subadults were found in the EBIA death assemblage. Significantly more neonates/infants can be identified using the sagittal length of the occipital basilar portion ($p < 0.001$), distal femur width ($p < 0.001$), and left ilium width ($p = 0.028$). The protected nature of the underground chambers, smaller volume of material excavated from each tomb, and careful oversight by Ortner during excavation likely enhanced the recovery of such delicate remains. Chesson (2007) postulated a ritualized burial ceremony at prescribed time(s) of the year, requiring storage of individuals between interments. If these burials indeed represent people who died quite some distance from the cemetery, it is a testimony to the care taken in handling and commemorating the very young.

TABLE 5.4B. Cranial nonmetric trait frequencies by time periods for each side

Time	Side	Metopic Suture					Ossicle at Lambda				Coronal Suture Ossicles			
		n	+ (%)	- (%)	χ^2	p	n	+ (%)	-	p*	n	+ (%)	- (%)	p*
EB IA	L	81	11.2 (9)	88.9 (72)	0.1	0.71	49	12.2 (6)	87.8 (43)	1	50	6.0 (3)	94.0 (47)	1
	R										51	7.8 (4)	92.2 (47)	
EB II–III	L	150	8.7 (13)	91.3 (137)			34	11.8 (4)	88.2 (30)		24	0 (0)	100 (24)	1
	R										27	7.4 (2)	92.6 (25)	

Note: p^* = Fisher's p.

TABLE 5.4B—*continued*

Time	Side	Ossicle at Asterion				Parietal Notch				
		n	+ (%)	- (%)	p*	n	+ (%)	- (%)	χ^2	p
EB IA	L	27	14.8 (4)	85.2 (23)	0.20	31	32.3 (10)	67.7 (21)	1.22	0.27
	R	42	4.8 (2)	95.2 (40)		39	17.9 (7)	82.1 (32)		
EB II–III	L	20	40.0 (8)	60.0 (12)	0.72	18	11.1 (2)	88.9 (16)	—	1
	R	14	28.6 (4)	71.4 (10)		17	5.9 (1)	94.1 (16)		

Note: p^* = Fisher's p.

Table 5.4C. Cranial nonmetric trait frequencies by side for the EB IA and II–III

Side	Time	Coronal Suture Ossicles				Ossicle at Asterion				Parietal Notch			
		n	+ (%)	–	p^*	n	+	– (%)	p^*	n	+ (%)	– (%)	p^*
L	EBIA	50	6.0(3)	94.0 (47)	0.55	27	14.8 (4)	85.2 (23)	0.09	31	32.3 (10)	67.7 (21)	0.17
	EBII–III	24	0	100 (24)		20	40.0 (8)	60.0% (12)		18	11.1 (2)	88.9 (16)	
R	EBIA	51	7.8 (4)	92.2 (47)	1	42	4.8 (2)	95.2 (40)	0.03	39	17.9 (7)	82.1 (32)	0.41
	EBII–III	27	7.4 (2)	92.6 (25)		14	28.6 (4)	71.4 (10)		17	5.9 (1)	94.1 (16)	

Note: p^* = Fisher's p.

TABLE 5.5. MMD values for EBIA and EBII–III with nineteen comparative sites using metopism, ossicles at lambda, parietal notch bones, ossicles at asterion, and coronal suture ossicles.

	SAG	NAQB	NAQT	NAQG	BAD	KEN	ABY	TRK	N277	QAU
SAG		0.004	0.008	0.007	0.003	0.014	0.009	0.003	0.348	0.006
NAQB	0.018		0.002	0.001	0.003	0.003	0.001	0.001	0.428	0
NAQT	0.085	0.007		0	0.002	0.001	0	0	0.385	0
NAQG	0.079	0.007	0		0	0	0	0	0.349	0
BAD	0.020	0.026	0.037	0.017		0.004	0.001	0.001	0.283	0.001
KEN	**0.172**	**0.040**	0	0.002	**0.114**		0	0.001	0.446	0.001
ABY	**0.117**	0	0	0	0.038	0		0	0.389	0
TRK	0.006	0	0	0	0.003	0.019	0		0.337	0
N277	**2.165**	**2.797**	**2.593**	**2.584**	**2.114**	**3.204**	**2.834**	**2.473**		0.349
QAU	0.055	0	0	0	0.008	0.012	0	0	2.646	
N179	**0.114**	0.039	0	0	0.022	0	0	0	2.680	0
THS	**0.124**	0.074	0	0	0.053	0.059	0.027	0.011	2.291	0.030
TDW	0.007	0.046	0.124	0.096	0.001	**0.228**	0.121	0.064	2.009	0.068
KSH1	**0.361**	**0.171**	0.030	0.051	**0.212**	0	0.034	0.103	3.282	0.089
DKT	0.081	0.060	0	0	0.030	0.023	0.005	0	2.325	0.005
HSN1	0.106	0.048	0	0	0.060	0.031	0.014	0	2.472	0.017
HSN3	0.045	0.047	0	0	0	0.065	0.019	0	2.109	0.006
NIP	**0.115**	0.040	0	0	**0.101**	0	0	0	2.905	0.005
BGD	**0.173**	**0.117**	0	0.020	**0.115**	0.065	0.055	0.034	2.362	0.066
EBIA	0	**0.114**	0.090	0.089	0.015	**0.235**	**0.149**	0.041	1.641	0.094
EBII–III	**0.718**	**1.377**	**1.486**	**1.451**	**1.098**	**1.791**	**1.617**	**1.218**	**1.122**	**1.414**

Notes: MMD values are on the left of the table; standard deviations are to the right of the midline. Bolded values indicate significance (p < 0.025).

ABY = Abydos, Egypt (Prowse 1994); BAD = Badari, Egypt (Prowse 1994); BGD = Baghdad, Iraq (Rathbun 1984); DKT = Dinkha Tepe, Iran (Rathbun 1984); EBIA = Early Bronze Age IA Bab edh-Dhra', Jordan (Ullinger 2010); EBII–III = Early Bronze Age II–III Bab edh-Dhra', Jordan (Ullinger 2010); HSN1 = Hasanlu, Iran (Rathbun 1984); HSN3 = Hasanlu, Iran (Rathbun 1984); KEN = Keneh, Egypt (Prowse 1994); KSH1 = Kish, Iraq (Rathbun 1984); NAQB = Naqada Cem B, Egypt (Prowse 1994); NAQT = Naqada Cem T, Egypt (Prowse 1994); NAQG = Naqada Great Cem, Egypt (Prowse 1994); NIP = Nippur, Iraq (Rathbun 1984); N179 = Nubia site 179 (Prowse 1994); N277 = Nubia site 277, Egypt (Prowse 1994); QAU = Qau, Egypt (Berry and Berry, 1967); SAG = Sagalassos, Turkey (Ricaut and Waelkens, 2008); TDW = Tell Duweir, Israel/Palestine (Hanihara and Ishida 2001); TRK = Tarkhan, Egypt (Berry and Berry, 1967); THS = Tepe Hissar, Iran (Rathbun 1984).

Nr79	*THS*	*TDW*	*KSH1*	*DKT*	*HSN1*	*HSN3*	*NIP*	*BGD*	*EBLA*	*EBII-III*
0.012	0.010	0.002	0.034	0.010	0.009	0.006	0.019	0.021	0.001	0.079
0.005	0.005	0.003	0.013	0.006	0.003	0.004	0.007	0.011	0.008	0.109
0	0	0.004	0.003	0	0	0	0	0	0.006	0.109
0	0	0.002	0.003	0	0	0	0	0.003	0.004	0.093
0.002	0.002	0	0.011	0.002	0.002	0.001	0.010	0.008	0.001	0.071
0	0.003	0.006	0.001	0.002	0.002	0.004	0	0.006	0.011	0.124
0	0.001	0.003	0.003	0.001	0.001	0.001	0.002	0.005	0.007	0.105
0	0	0.002	0.007	0	0	0	0.002	0.004	0.003	0.091
0.401	0.315	0.252	0.513	0.353	0.331	0.304	0.527	0.402	0.219	0.108
0	0.001	0.002	0.006	0.001	0.001	0.001	0.003	0.005	0.005	0.095
	0.002	0.005	0.003	0.001	0.001	0.001	0.002	0.006	0.008	0.128
0.017		0.004	0.004	0	0	0	0.001	0	0.005	0.098
0.122	0.145		0.018	0.006	0.004	0.003	0.018	0.014	0.002	0.061
0.016	0.069	0.382		0.005	0.004	0.008	0.002	0.006	0.025	0.194
0	0	0.127	0.044		0	0	0	0	0.005	0.114
0.011	0	0.151	0.055	0		0	0	0	0.005	0.099
0	0	0.069	0.110	0	0		0.003	0.001	0.002	0.096
0	0	0.221	0	0	0	0		0	0.017	0.186
0.048	0	0.230	0.046	0	0	0	0		0.011	0.153
0.120	0.073	0.028	0.349	0	0.088	0.006	0.147	0.109		0.066
1.526	1.427	0.935	2.166	1.338	1.451	1.190	1.600	1.528	0.734	

The infant remains from EBII–III did not fare as well, possibly resulting from a marked change in burial techniques. Indeed, tomb typology grew to a more pronounced "statement" on the landscape in the form of aboveground, possibly two-story, charnel houses. In the largest of these, we found little evidence of infants. Possible interpretations for this pattern include:

- Charnel house A22 may not have been the final resting place for subadults. Another tomb may have provided special commemoration for infants. Only a few charnel houses were excavated, so it is possible such a structure remains undiscovered. Or, other burial techniques may have been employed for infants in EBII–III.

- Conversely, the near absence of infants may indicate that babies were simply discarded as waste. For example, at Roman Ashkelon, Smith and Kahila (1992) explained the numerous subadult bones found in the sewer system as the unwanted result of prostitution, Thomas Crist (2005) found aborted fetuses in a nineteenth-century New York privy, and Ann Stodder (1996) found the remains of New Mexico children from the Pueblo period in midden piles for tuberculosis sufferers. Each argued that this type of disposal moved the remembrance of "undesirables" out of the community.

- The dearth of remains may represent low infant mortality, although this is unlikely given the realities of diet/disease stress on the young in prehistoric settled communities.

- The very fragile infant bones may not have survived site formation processes. The fetal pubis is small (< 18 mm in length) and may not have preserved equally in both collections. Charnel house A22 was burned, looted, and the remains were not curated or appropriately stored for the two decades following exhumation, resulting in considerable postmortem damage. Thus, commemoration may have been as careful as that of the EBIA, but the extant collection does not let us evaluate this aspect of remembrance.

Sex determination for EBIA individuals was hampered by limiting data collection to individual elements (to permit comparison to EBII–III). However, whether using portions of the innominate in isolation—or the entire innominate, crania, or femoral head diameters—the maximum sex ratio is 25 males:49 females. This calls into question the validity of the 18 male:32 female ratio for the EBII–III collection, where use of complete skeletons is not an option.

The innominate and cranium are ubiquitously cited as the most accurate for adult sex determination. The femoral head and long bones are similarly reliable. We used a technique by Albanese (2002) that considers within-sample variation.

Sex ratios for the two collections were comparable using pubis morphology, cranial traits, and femoral head diameter—except when EBIA crania and right pubis morphology were compared. This discrepancy may be due to the small but robust nature of skulls from both periods resulting in a large number of crania categorized as indeterminate. Despite this anomaly, we conclude that each sex is represented equally in both time periods.

Burial Assemblage Size

Difficulty in determining sex ratios illustrates the weakness of MNI for determining collection size. A direct count of the burial assemblage was possible for EBIA given the number of discernable individuals and better preservation. For EBII–III, a more accurate estimation was required to explore changes in commemoration with time.

Taphonomic processes such as burning may have altered the bones (e.g., warping, heat fractures, color variation), thereby complicating matching; nevertheless, the talus and calcaneus proved particularly robust, as their small, blocky shapes did not offer large, easily deformable surfaces. The size of the building, volume of fragmented remains, and use of the charnel house during the height of the occupation of Bab edh-Dhra' all call the original field estimate based on intact crania (ca. 200) into serious question. Thus, MLNI appears to offer a more reasonable estimate of the EBII–III burial collection, given the size and volume of the A22 charnel house.

Indeed, as no other large EBII–III assemblages have been found (except possibly Jericho) although this is not in evidence in the collection at the Duckworth Museum at the University of Cambridge (Ullinger and Sheridan 2014), it has been suggested that Bab edh-Dhra' may have served as a cemetery for several communities (Chesson 2007). Given the visible statement of A22 on the surrounding terrain, the need to conserve space in a habitation delineated by a substantial wall, the increased value of acreage for agriculture, and the association of Bab edh-Dhra' during EBII–III with at least one nearby city (Numeira), this proposal seems in keeping with the substantially more voluminous assemblage estimate provided by the MLNI. Charnel house A22 was visible from atop the town walls and on the surrounding plain, perhaps even in the wadi below, given its location and the height added by a possible second floor (McCreery 2011).

These daily visible reminders of remembrance have been called "libraries of the dead" (Chesson 1999), containing shelving for storage of bones and grave goods. A larger number of people interred in EBII–III tombs may indeed indicate larger, more inclusive events that reinforced bonds among the living. The promotion of unity as the population grew may have proven an important reinforcement of purpose, in part explaining the success of the EBIII town. Thus, the much larger assemblage size estimate seems consistent with the "prominence of place" for these structures.

GENETIC RELATEDNESS

Our analysis of genetic distance permitted an assessment of the homogeneity of each collection, with comparisons of similarity/distance to each other as well as regional counterparts. Bentley (1987) showed, using dental nonmetric traits, that EBIA individuals likely represented family groups. Teeth preserve poorly when burned (Schmidt 2008); thus comparable analysis was not possible for A22. However, use of cranial traits was feasible. In virtually every comparison of the two groups, there was a high degree of consistency. Based on a relatively small distance statistic between EBIA and EBII–III, it is quite likely that those in the charnel house were descendants of the earlier occupants of Bab edh-Dhra'.

Tell Duweir was the closest site geographically, and the low MMDs compared to Bab edh-Dhra' most likely indicate general gene flow in the southern Levant during the EBA. Both time periods were also relatively similar to Byzantine Sagalassos, suggesting that people from Bab edh-Dhra' may have contributed to later genetic variation in the region.

Bab edh-Dhra' during EBII–III was relatively more distant from most groups than during EBIA. This was somewhat surprising, given the urbanization of EBII–III. It is worth noting that frequencies for some traits may be depressed compared to other collections, because the commingled nature of the Bab edh-Dhra' collections required the use of only one side to ensure individuals were not duplicated. Most of the comparative studies used complete skeletons, often scoring traits as "present" regardless of side or asymmetry in expression (Sutter and Mertz 2004). While distance comparisons of the Bab edh-Dhra' communities were quite reliable given the same methodology (data collection by the same investigator and application of methods to counter intraobserver error), the same assurance of reliability was not possible for comparative sites. Also, while most researchers use a similar scoring system (Hauser and DeStefano 1989), there is no standardization as to how many traits should be used, or which traits are more reliable (and thereby produce consistently low interobserver error).

With these caveats in mind, EBII–III did not show the degree of diversity expected. This may demonstrate that the inhabitants were more homogeneous in prescribed mating patterns, that increased conflict with neighbors limited gene flow, or that individual charnel houses commemorated particular extended family groups (Chesson 1999). The EBIA crania may represent numerous families sampled from across the entire site, and therefore better represent the genetic profile of the whole group. Analysis of additional charnel houses, reexamination of some of the comparative collections on an element-by-element basis, and/or inclusion of stable isotope data may help delineate these possibilities.

In summary, we found more children in the earlier cemetery, with groups of related individuals (Bentley 1991) sorted into burial chambers. While EBII–III people buried in charnel house A22 were clearly related to EBIA predecessors based on the MMD analyses, they show less genetic affinity to regional samples, suggesting that it was perhaps a large tomb for extended kin (as opposed to multiple families). As we analyze more charnel houses, this pattern should become clearer.

CONCLUSIONS

Bab edh-Dhra' offers a unique opportunity to compare people buried at the same site over time. Mortuary practices changed as Bab edh-Dhra' underwent considerable expansion and contraction in size and population density. The EBIA cemetery was an organized, massive complex composed of below-ground tombs with small chambers containing discrete, related individuals (Bentley 1987, 1991) numbering as many as 56,263 burials (Ortner and Frohlich 2008:261). Although the permanence of the EBIA community is debated, ongoing dedication to the cemetery is clear. All age groups and both sexes were represented by those interred in these tomb chambers.

In EBII–III, the community began building visible, aboveground burial monuments. The lack of comparable cemeteries throughout the southern Levant may support the assertion that this was a regional burial center. The A22 charnel house contains males and females in a ratio comparable to EBIA tombs, although the very youngest and oldest age categories are not represented. This is likely due to site formation processes.

While demographic analysis suffered from the poorly preserved EBII–III assemblage, calculations of collection size fortunately did not. The initial MNI of 200 people in A22 grew by almost an order of magnitude using MLNI (approximately 1,100–2,300) to arrive at a more plausible calculation. This is in keeping with the potential long-term use of the charnel house (600 years); the exceptional volume of postcranial material; the projection from archaeological evidence that Bab edh-Dhra' may have been a regional burial center; and the amount, types, and wealth of associated grave goods.

Interestingly, the EBII–III remains appear to be more genetically distant from the comparative groups than their EBIA counterparts. Chesson (1999) and Ullinger (2010) have proposed that charnel house A22 was used by a large extended family over several generations. Thus, while EBIA crania include families from across the community, A22 may have a more limited genetic representation from fewer multigenerational kin.

In this chapter we have added biological data to the exhaustive archaeological record for changing social organization and burial practices at Bab edh-Dhra'. With increasing population size and marked alterations to the landscape came more visible commemoration of the dead. Familial affinity likely determined who was buried in the tombs with time, moving from small discrete chambers to larger, less individualized structures. Regional genetic affinity differed between the two periods, possibly reflecting changing definitions of kinship, as the community grew and lines of lineage became harder to trace or as particular charnel houses began to host specific families, thus rendering a more homogeneous collection from the later period when only a subset of remains are viewed. This will be an interesting area for future exploration.

Chesson (1999:140) predicted, using ethnographic studies, that "expressions of mourning and identity in mortuary contexts are shaped by the structuring forces within a community, such as gender, kinship affiliation, age, and other corporate identity." Our study therefore has looked at changes in these very forces as a means of determining who represented the dead and by whom they were remembered. Babies and neonates were remembered, as were grandparents. Continuity of EBIA and II–III communities was established. With expanding sample size, kinship lines were preserved, though perhaps more loosely, with very large numbers of people being interred together in highly visible "statements" on the landscape.

Although we worked with less-than-ideal collections from the standpoint of postdepositional alteration, it must be remembered that this is the only collection for the entire southern Levant available for the EBA. Given the excellence of excavation, some of the limitations imposed by bone quality could be overcome, permitting a more accurate understanding of the makeup of young and old in the tombs and the sheer number of people buried in the later period. The study has also contributed to the sense of the relationships these subjects had with regional counterparts during the same two periods.

ACKNOWLEDGMENTS

Special thanks to R. T. Schaub, and Lyle Konigsberg for access to collections and statistical guidance; to the National Science Foundation (SES-0097568; SES-0244096; SES-0649088; SES-1005158), the Institute for Scholarship in the Liberal Arts at Notre Dame, the Ohio State University Graduate School, and the Smithsonian's Pre-doctoral Fellowship Program for funding the project. Many thanks to the reviewers of this chapter. This work would not have been possible without the mentorship of the late Prof. Donald Ortner.

REFERENCES

Adams, Bradley, and Lyle Konigsberg. 2004. "Estimation of the Most Likely Number of Individuals from Commingled Human Skeletal Remains." *American Journal of Physical Anthropology* 125 (2): 138–51. http://dx.doi.org/10.1002/ajpa.10381.

Adams, Bradley, and Lyle Konigsberg. 2008. "How Many People? Determining the Number of Individuals Represented by Commingled Human Resources." In *Recovery, Analysis, and Identification of Commingled Human Remains*, edited by Bradley Adams and John Byrd, 241–55. Totowa, NJ: Humana Press. http://dx.doi .org/10.1007/978-1-59745-316-5_12.

Albanese, John, Hugo Cardoso, and Shelley Saunders. 2005. "Universal Methodology for Developing Univariate Sample-specific Sex Determination Methods: An Example Using the Epicondylar Breadth of the Humerus." *Journal of Archaeological Science* 32 (1): 143–52. http://dx.doi.org/10.1016/j.jas.2004.08.003.

Andrews, Peter, and Silvia Bello. 2006. "Pattern in Human Burial Practice." In *Social Archaeology of Funerary Remains*, edited by Rebecca Gowland and Christopher Knüsel, 14–29. Oxford: Oxbow Books.

Ashmore, Wendy, and Pamela Geller. 2005. "Social Dimensions of Mortuary Space." In *Interacting with the Dead*, edited by Gordon Rakita, Jane Buikstra, Lane Beck, and Sloan Williams, 81–92. Gainesville: University Press of Florida.

Bentley, Gillian. 1987. *Kinship and Social Structure at Early Bronze IA Bab edh-Dhra', Jordan.* PhD thesis, University of Chicago.

Bentley, Gillian. 1991. "A Bioarchaeological Reconstruction of the Social and Kinship Systems at Early Bronze Age Bab edh-Dhra', Jordan." In *Between Bands and States*, edited by S. A. Gregg, 5–34. Carbondale: Center for Archaeological Investigations, Southern Illinois University.

Bentley, Gillian, and Victoria Perry. 2008. "Dental Analyses of the Bab edh-Dhra' Human Remains." In *The Early Bronze Age I Tombs and Burials of Bab edh-Dhra',*

Jordan, edited by Donald Ortner and Bruno Frohlich, 281–96. Lanham, MD: AltaMira Press.

Berelov, Ilya. 2006. "Signs of Sedentism and Mobility in an Agro-pastoral Community during the Levantine Middle Bronze Age: Interpreting Site Function and Occupation Strategy at Zahrat adh-Dhra' 1 in Jordan." *Journal of Anthropological Archaeology* 25 (1): 117–43. http://dx.doi.org/10.1016/j.jaa.2005.09.001.

Berry, A. Caroline, and R. J. Berry. 1967. "Epigenetic Variation in the Human Cranium." *Journal of Anatomy* 101:361–79.

Bourdieu, Pierre. 1977. *Outline of a Theory of Practice*. Cambridge: Cambridge University Press. http://dx.doi.org/10.1017/CBO9780511812507.

Broeder, Nancy, and Catherine Skinner. 2003. "Jewelry and Ornaments." In *Bab edh-Dhra': Excavations at the Town Site (1975–1981)*, edited by Walter Rast and Thomas Schaub, 566–98. Winona Lake, IN: Eisenbrauns.

Broshi, Magen, and Ram Gophna. 1984. "The Settlements and Population of Palestine during the Early Bronze Age II–III." *Bulletin of the American Schools of Oriental Research* 253: 41–53. http://dx.doi.org/10.2307/1356938.

Bruckner, Jan. 1987. "Variations in the Human Subtalar Joint." *Journal of Orthopaedic and Sports Physical Therapy* 8 (10): 489–94. http://dx.doi.org/10.2519/jospt.1987.8.10.489.

Buikstra, Jane, and Douglas Ubelaker. 1994. *Standards for Data Collection from Human Skeletal Remains*. Fayetteville: Arkansas Archaeological Survey.

Byrd, John. 2008. "Models and Methods for Osteometric Sorting." In *Recovery, Analysis, and Identification of Commingled Human Remains*, edited by Bradley Adams and John Byrd, 199–220. Totowa, NJ: Humana Press. http://dx.doi.org/10.1007/978-1-59745-316-5_10.

Chapman, Douglas. 1951. "Some Properties of the Hypergeometric Distribution with Applications to Zoological Sample Census." *University of California Public Statistics* 1:131–59.

Charles, Douglas, and Jane Buikstra. 2002. "Siting, Sighting and Citing the Dead." In *The Place and Space of Death*, edited by Helaine Silverman and David Small, 13–25. Arlington, VA: Archaeological Papers of the American Anthropological Association. http://dx.doi.org/10.1525/ap3a.2002.11.1.13.

Chesson, Meredith. 1999. "Libraries of the Dead: Early Bronze Age Charnel Houses and Social Identity at Urban Bab edh-Dhra', Jordan." *Journal of Anthropological Archaeology* 18 (2): 137–64. http://dx.doi.org/10.1006/jaar.1998.0330.

Chesson, Meredith. 2001. "Embodied Memories of Place and People: Death and Society in an Early Urban Community." In *Social Memory, Identity, and Death*, edited by Meredith Chesson, 100–13. Arlington, VA: Archaeological Papers of the

American Anthropological Association. http://dx.doi.org/10.1525/ap3a.2001.10.1 .100.

Chesson, Meredith. 2007. "Remembering and Forgetting in Early Bronze Age Mortuary Practices on the Southeastern Dead Sea Plain, Jordan." In *Performing Death*, edited by Nicola Laneri, 109–39. Chicago: Oriental Institute.

Cheverud, James, and Jane Buikstra. 1982. "Quantitative Genetics of Skeletal Nonmetric Traits in the Rhesus Macaques of Cayo Santiago. III. Relative Heritability of Skeletal Nonmetric and Metric Traits." *American Journal of Physical Anthropology* 59 (2): 151–55. http://dx.doi.org/10.1002/ajpa.1330590205.

Crist, Thomas. 2005. "Babies in the Privy: Prostitution, Infanticide, and Abortion in New York City's Five Points District." *Historical Archaeology* 39:19–46.

Cruse, Karen. 2003. *What's in a Number? The Implementation of the Lincoln/Peterson Index (LI) as a Method of Quantification*. MA thesis, University of Cincinnati.

Donahue, Jack. 1985. "Hydrologic and Topographic Change during and after Early Bronze Occupation at Bab edh-Dhra' and Numeira." *Studies in the History and Archaeology of Jordan IV* 2:131–40.

Donahue, Jack. 2003. "Geology and Geomorphology." In *Bab edh-Dhra': Excavations at the Town Site*, edited by Walter Rast and Thomas Schaub, 18–55. Winona Lake, IN: Eisenbrauns.

Douglas, Khaled. 2011. "Beyond the City Walls: Life Activities outside the City Gates in the Early Bronze Age in Jordan: Evidence from Khirbet ez-Zeraqon." In *Daily Life, Materiality, and Complexity in Early Urban Communities of the Southern Levant*, edited by Meredith Chesson, Walter Aufrecht, and Ian Kuijt, 3–21. Winona Lake, IN: Eisenbrauns.

Falconer, Steven, and Stephen Savage. 1995. "Heartlands and Hinterlands: Alternative Trajectories of Early Urbanization in Mesopotamia and the Southern Levant." *American Antiquity* 60 (1): 37–58. http://dx.doi.org/10.2307/282075.

Fazekas, Istvan, and F. Kosa. 1978. *Forensic Fetal Osteology*. Budapest: Akademiai Kiado.

Finnegan, M. 1978. "Faunal Remains from Bab edh-Dhra'." *Annual of the American Schools of Oriental Research* 43:55–56.

Gasperetti, Matthew, and Susan Guise Sheridan. 2013. "Cry Havoc: Interpersonal Violence at Early Bronze Age Bab edh-Dhra'." *American Anthropologist* 115 (3): 388–410. http://dx.doi.org/10.1111/aman.12024.

Grigson, Caroline. 1998. "Plough and Pasture in the Early Economy of the Southern Levant." In *The Archaeology of Society in the Holy Land*, edited by Thomas Levy, 245–68. London: Leicester University Press.

Hanihara, Tsunehiko, and Hajime Ishida. 2001. "Frequency Variations of Discrete Cranial Traits in Major Human Populations. I. Supernumerary Ossicle Variations."

Journal of Anatomy 198 (6): 689–706. http://dx.doi.org/10.1046/j.1469-7580.2001
.19860689.x.

Harlan, Jack. 2003. "Natural Resources of the Bab edh-Dhra' Region." In *Bab edh-Dhra': Excavations at the Town Site (1975–1981)*, edited by Walter Rast and Thomas Schaub, 56–61. Winona Lake, IN: Eisenbrauns.

Hauser, Gertrud, and Gian DeStefano. 1989. *Epigenetic Variants of the Human Skull*. Stuttgart: Schweizerbart.

Ilan, David. 2002. "Mortuary Practices in Early Bronze Age Canaan." *Near Eastern Archaeology* 65:92–104. http://dx.doi.org/10.2307/3210870.

Irish, Joel. 2006. "Who were the Ancient Egyptians? Dental Affinities among Neolithic through Postdynastic Peoples." *American Journal of Physical Anthropology* 129 (4): 529–43. http://dx.doi.org/10.1002/ajpa.20261.

Joffe, Alexander. 1993. *Settlement and Society in the Early Bronze Age I and II, Southern Levant*. Sheffield: Sheffield Academic Press.

Joyce, Rosemary. 2001. "Burying the Dead at Tlatilco: Social Memory and Social Identities." In *Social Memory, Identity and Death: Anthropological Perspectives on Mortuary Rituals*, edited by Meredith Chesson, 12–26. Arlington, VA: Archaeological Papers of the American Anthropological Association. http://dx.doi .org/10.1525/ap3a.2001.10.1.12.

Kendell, Ashley, and P. Willey. 2014. "Crow Creek Bone Bed Commingling: Relationship between Bone Mineral Density and Minimum Number of Individuals and Its Effect on Paleodemographic Analyses." In *Commingled and Disarticulated Human Remains*, edited by Anna Osterholtz, Kathryn Baustian, and Debra Martin, 85–104. New York: Springer. http://dx.doi.org/10.1007/978-1-4614 -7560-6_6.

Koshy, Shajan, Selvakumar Vettivel, and K. Selvaraj. 2002. "Estimation of Length of Calcaneum and Talus from their Bony Markers." *Forensic Science International* 129 (3): 200–204. http://dx.doi.org/10.1016/S0379-0738(02)00278-5.

Kuijt, Ian. 2000. "People and Space in Early Agricultural Villages: Exploring Daily Lives, Community Size, and Architecture in the Late Pre-Pottery Neolithic." *Journal of Anthropological Archaeology* 19 (1): 75–102. http://dx.doi.org/10.1006 /jaar.1999.0352.

Lapp, Paul W. 1968a. "Bab edh-Dhra' A 76 and Early Bronze I in Palestine." *Bulletin of the American Schools of Oriental Research* 189: 12–41. http://dx.doi.org/10.2307/1356126.

Lapp, Paul W. 1968b. ""Bab edh-Dhra'." In *Chronique Archéologique*." *Revue Biblique* 75:86–93.

Lapp, Paul W. 1970. "Palestine in the Early Bronze Age." In *Near Eastern Archaeology in the Twentieth Century*, edited by James Sanders, 101–31. Garden City, NJ: Doubleday.

Maddin, Robert, James Muhly, and Tamara Stech. 2003. "Metallurgical Studies on Copper Artifacts from Bab edh-Dhra'." In *Bab edh-Dhra': Excavations at the Town Site (1975–1981)*, edited by Walter Rast and Thomas Schaub, 513–21. Winona Lake, IN: Eisenbrauns.

McConaughy, Mark. 2003. "Chipped Stone Tools at Bab edh-Dhra'." In *Bab edh-Dhra': Excavations at the Town Site (1975–1981)*, edited by Walter Rast and Thomas Schaub, 473–512. Winona Lake, IN: Eisenbrauns.

McCreery, David. 2002. "Bronze Age Agriculture in the Dead Sea Basin: The Cases of Bab edh-Dhra', Numeira and Tell Nimrin." In *"Imagining" Biblical Worlds*, edited by David Gunn and Paula McNutt, 251–63. London: Sheffield Academic Press.

McCreery, David. 2011. "Agriculture and Religion at Bab edh-Dhra' and Numeira during the Early Bronze Age." In *Daily Life, Materiality, and Complexity in Early Urban Communities of the Southern Levant*, edited by Meredith Chesson, Walter Aufrecht, and Ian Kuijt, 77–87. Winona Lake, IN: Eisenbrauns.

Meindl, Richard, and Owen Lovejoy. 1985. "Ectocranial Suture Closure: A Revised Method for the Determination of Skeletal Age at Death Based on the Lateral-anterior Sutures." *American Journal of Physical Anthropology* 68 (1): 57–66. http://dx.doi.org/10.1002/ajpa.1330680106.

Nigro, Lorenzo. 2010. "Between the Desert and the Jordan: Early Urbanization in the Upper Wadi az-Zarqa River." In *Proceedings of the 6th International Congress of the Archaeology of the Ancient Near East*, Vol. 2, edited by Licia Romano, 431–58. Wiesbaden: Otto Harrassowitz Verlag.

Ortner, Donald. 1981. "A Preliminary Report on the Human Remains from the Bab edh-Dhra' Cemetery." In *The Southeastern Dead Sea Plain Expedition: An Interim Report of the 1977 Season*, edited by W. E. Rast and R. T. Schaub, 119–32. Vol. 46. Cambridge, MA: American Schools of Oriental Research.

Ortner, Donald, and Bruno Frohlich. 2008. *The Early Bronze Age I Tombs and Burials of Bab edh-Dhra', Jordan*. Lanham, MD: AltaMira Press.

Ortner, Donald, and Bruno Frohlich. 2011. "The EBIA People of Bab edh-Dhra', Jordan." In *Daily Life, Materiality, and Complexity in Early Urban Communities of the Southern Levant*, edited by Meredith Chesson, Walter Aufrecht, and Ian Kuijt, 101–16. Winona Lake, IN: Eisenbrauns.

Phenice, Terrell. 1969. "A Newly Developed Visual Method of Sexing in the Os Pubis." *American Journal of Physical Anthropology* 30 (2): 297–301. http://dx.doi.org/10.1002/ajpa.1330300214.

Philip, Graham. 2001. "The Early Bronze I–III Ages." In *The Archaeology of Jordan*, edited by Burton MacDonald, Russell Adams, and Piotr Bienkowski, 163–232. Sheffield: Sheffield Academic Press.

Prowse, Tracy. 1994. *Biological Affinities of Ancient Egyptians and Nubians: An Analysis of Cranial Nonmetric Traits*. PhD Thesis, University of Alberta.

Rast, Walter. 1981. "Patterns of Settlement at Bab edh-Dhraʻ." In *The Southeastern Dead Sea Plain Expedition: An Interim Report of the 1977 Season*, edited by Walter Rast and Thomas Schaub, 7–34. Cambridge, MA: American Schools of Oriental Research.

Rast, Walter. 1999. "Society and Mortuary Customs at Bab edh-Dhraʻ." In *Archaeology, History and Culture in Palestine and the Near East*, edited by Tomis Kapitan, 164–82. Atlanta: Scholars Press.

Rast, Walter, and Thomas Schaub. 1978. "A Preliminary Report of Excavations at Bab edh-Dhraʻ, 1975." *Annual of the American Schools of Oriental Research* 43:1–32.

Rast, Walter, and Thomas Schaub. 1980. "Preliminary Report of the 1979 Expedition to the Dead Sea Plain, Jordan." *Bulletin of the American Schools of Oriental Research* 240: 21–61. http://dx.doi.org/10.2307/1356536.

Rast, Walter, and Thomas Schaub. 1981. "The Southeastern Dead Sea Plain Expedition: An Interim Report of the 1977 Season." *Annual of the American Schools of Oriental Research*, vol. 46. Cambridge, MA: American Schools of Oriental Research.

Rast, Walter, and Thomas Schaub. 2003. *Bab edh-Dhraʻ: Excavations at the Town Site (1975–1981)*. Winona Lake, IN: Eisenbrauns.

Rathbun, Ted. 1984. "Metric and Discrete Trait Variation among Southwest Asian Populations." *Spectra of Anthropological Progress* 6:25–50.

Ricaut, François-Xavier, and Marc Waelkens. 2008. "Cranial Discrete Traits in a Byzantine Population and Eastern Mediterranean Population Movements." *Human Biology* 80 (5): 535–64. http://dx.doi.org/10.3378/1534-6617-80.5.535.

Schaub, R. Thomas. 1973a. *The Early Bronze IA–IB Pottery of the Bab edh-Dhraʻ Cemetery, Jordan*. PhD thesis, Pittsburgh Theological Seminary.

Schaub, R. Thomas. 1973b. "An Early Bronze IV Tomb from Bab edh-Dhraʻ." *Bulletin of the American Schools of Oriental Research* 210: 2–19. http://dx.doi.org/10.2307 /1356185.

Schaub, R. Thomas. 1981. "Patterns of Burial at Bab edh-Dhraʻ." In *The Southeastern Dead Sea Plain Expedition: An Interim Report of the 1977 Season*, edited by Walter Rast and Thomas Schaub, 45–68. Cambridge, MA: American Schools of Oriental Research.

Schaub, R. Thomas. 1982. "The Origins of the Early Bronze Age Walled Town Culture of Jordan." *Studies in the History and Archaeology of Jordan* 3:247–50.

Schaub, R. Thomas. 1993. "Bab edh-Dhraʻ." In *The New Encyclopedia of Archaeological Excavations in the Holy Land*, edited by Ephraim Stern, 130–36. New York: Simon & Schuster.

Schaub, R. Thomas. 2008. "Cultural Artifacts of the EB I Tombs." In *The Early Bronze Age I Tombs and Burials of Bab edh-Dhra', Jordan*, edited by Donald Ortner and Bruno Frohlich, 25–43. Lanham, MD: AltaMira Press.

Schaub, R. Thomas, and Walter Rast. 1984. "Preliminary Report of the 1981 Expedition to the Dead Sea Plain, Jordan." *Bulletin of the American Schools of Oriental Research* 254: 35–60. http://dx.doi.org/10.2307/1357031.

Schaub, R. Thomas, and Walter Rast. 1989. *Bab edh-Dhra': Excavations in the Cemetery Directed by Paul W. Lapp (1965–67)*. Winona Lake, IN: Eisenbrauns.

Scheuer, Louise, and Susan Black. 2000. *Developmental Juvenile Osteology*. San Diego: Academic Press.

Scheuer, Louise, and Susan MacLaughlin-Black. 1994. "Age Estimation from the Pars Basilaris of the Fetal and Juvenile Occipital Bone." *International Journal of Osteoarchaeology* 4 (4): 377–80. http://dx.doi.org/10.1002/oa.1390040412.

Schmidt, Christopher. 2008. "The Recovery and Study of Burned Human Teeth." In *The Analysis of Burned Human Remains*, 55–74, edited by Christopher Schmidt and Steven Symes. Boston: Academic Press. http://dx.doi.org/10.1016/B978-012372510-3.50005-8.

Scott, Richard, and Christy Turner, II. 1997. *The Anthropology of Modern Human Teeth*. Cambridge: Cambridge University Press.

Sjøvold, Torstein. 1973. "The Occurrence of Nonmetrical Variants in the Skeleton and Their Quantitative Treatment for Population Comparison." *Homo* 24: 204–33.

Smith, Patricia and Gila Kahila. 1992. "Identification of Infanticide in Archaeological Sites: A Case Study from the Late Roman–Early Byzantine Ages at Ashkelon, Israel." *Journal of Archaeological Sciences* 19: 667–75.

de Souza, Peter, and Philip Houghton. 1977. "The Mean Measure of Divergence and the Use of Nonmetric Data in the Estimation of Biological Distances." *Journal of Archaeological Science* 4 (2): 163–69. http://dx.doi.org/10.1016/0305-4403(77)90063-2.

Stodder, Ann. 1996. "Epidemiology of Eastern and Western Pueblo Communities in Proto-Historic and Historic New Mexico." In *Bioarchaeology of Native Americans in the Spanish Borderlands*, edited by Brenda Baker and Lisa Kealhofer, 149–76. Gainesville: University Press of Florida.

Sutter, Richard, and Lisa Mertz. 2004. "Nonmetric Cranial Trait Variation and Prehistoric Biocultural Change in the Azapa Valley, Chile." *American Journal of Physical Anthropology* 123: 130–45.

Todd, T. Wingate. 1920. "Age Changes in the Pubic Bone. I: The Male White Pubis." *American Journal of Physical Anthropology* 3 (3): 285–334. http://dx.doi.org/10.1002/ajpa.1330030301.

Ubelaker, Douglas. 1999. *Human Skeletal Remains: Excavation, Analysis, Interpretation.* Washington, D.C.: Taraxacum

Ullinger, Jaime. 2010. Skeletal Changes and Increasing Sedentism at Early Bronze Age Bab edh-Dhra', Jordan. PhD thesis, Ohio State University, Columbus.

Ullinger, Jaime and Susan Guise Sheridan. 2014. "Social Change and Dental Health in Early Bronze Age Southern Levant (Abstract)." In *American Journal of Physical Anthropology*, 153 (558): 257–8.

Ullinger, Jaime, Susan Guise Sheridan, and Debbie Guatelli-Steinberg. 2015. "Fruits of Their Labour: Urbanisation, Orchard Crops, and Dental Health in Early Bronze Age Jordan." *International Journal of Osteoarchaeology*, 25: 753–64. http://dx.doi.org/10.1002/oa.2342.

Weiss-Krejci, Estella. 2011. "The Formation of Mortuary Deposits: Implications for Understanding Mortuary Behavior of Past Populations." In *Social Bioarchaeology*, edited by Sabrina Agarwal and Bonnie Glencross, 68–106. Chichester, England: Wiley-Blackwell. http://dx.doi.org/10.1002/9781444390537.ch4.

Williams, Howard. 2007. "Depicting the Dead: Commemoration through Cists, Cairns and Symbols in Early Medieval Britain." *Cambridge Archaeological Journal* 17 (2): 145–64. http://dx.doi.org/10.1017/S0959774307000224.

6

Identity, Commemoration,
and Remembrance in
Colonial Encounters

Burials at Tombos during the
Egyptian New Kingdom Nubian
Empire and Its Aftermath

Stuart Tyson Smith and
Michele R. Buzon

ABSTRACT

Burial practice provides a critical arena for the negotiation of identities in colonial encounters through
different acts of commemoration made by individuals. Ancient Egyptian burial practice in particular
emphasized remembrances of ancestors through decorated tomb chapels and grave goods. Initially evoking
Egyptian primordial ties, changes in burial practice at
Tombos, an Egyptian colonial community in Sudanese
Nubia founded in ca. 1400 BCE, eventually led to the
emergence of a new, entangled identity incorporating
both Egyptian and Nubian practices in the empire's
aftermath. By the Napatan period, ca. 747–600 BCE, the
landscape in the cemetery was marked by a strong sense
of multivocality through commemorations that emphasized different cultural memories, Egyptian and Nubian,
stretching back far in time. This chapter investigates the
social and political dynamics of remembrance associated with monuments and burial practice. In order to
accomplish this, we distinguish between practices that
reflect shorter-term commemorations of individual
lived experience versus those that evoke longer-term
cultural memories. In a similar way, a consideration
of inscribed versus incorporated memorialization can
help distinguish between conscious and unconscious
remembrances reflected in the archaeological record.
We suggest that like the distinction between inscribed
and incorporated memory, commemorative practice
and cultural memory at Tombos do not represent contrasting forms. Instead they indicate intersecting social
fields that apply to varying degrees in different cases,
reflecting choices conditioned by individual predispositions as well as larger social and political contexts.

DOI: 10.5876/9781607323295.c006

INTRODUCTION

Commemoration of individuals through burial provides a critical arena for the negotiation of identities in colonial encounters. Burials at Tombos, an Egyptian colonial community in Sudanese Nubia founded in ca. 1400 BCE, reflect remembrances that vary by sex, class, and chronology. While most individuals commemorated their Egyptian identities, the burials also reflect the cultural entanglements common to colonial encounters that eventually led to the emergence of a new, hybrid identity in the empire's aftermath. By the Napatan period, ca. 747–600 BCE at Tombos, the landscape in the cemetery was marked by a strong sense of multivocality through commemorations that emphasized ties to different cultural memories stretching back far in time. We can better understand the social and political dynamics of remembrance at Tombos through a distinction between the ways monuments and burial practice reflect shorter-term commemorations of individual lived experience versus a resonance to longer-term cultural memories (Meskell 2003) with both Egyptian and Nubian associations. In a similar way, a consideration of inscribed versus incorporated memorialization (Connerton 1989) can help us distinguish between conscious and unconscious remembrances reflected in the archaeological record.

EGYPTIAN COLONIZATION AND NUBIAN RESURGENCE

Pharaoh Thutmose I defeated the king of Kush (Nubia) in 1502 BCE, ushering in 500 years of colonial rule in what is today southern Egypt and northern Sudan (Figure 6.1; Edwards 2004). North of the third cataract of the Nile, the Egyptians established a series of colonial settlements (Kemp 1972), ending at Tombos (Smith 2008), just 10 km north of the former capital of Kush at Kerma, which continued to be an important center (Bonnet 2008). Although temples were located upstream at Kerma, Tabo, Kawa and Gebel Barkal, no evidence of Egyptian colonial cemeteries or establishments has been found upstream from Tombos, suggesting that the site played an important role as an internal boundary between imperial strategies reflecting incorporation to the north and a more hegemonic strategy upstream (Edwards 2004; Morkot 2001; Smith 2003). Panehesy, the last real viceroy of Kush, rebelled against Pharaoh Ramesses XI in ca. 1079 BCE, resulting in the secession of Nubia from the Egyptian empire. Attempts to reconquer the former colony were ultimately unsuccessful. About 350 years later (ca. 727 BCE), a Nubian king named Piankhi (sometimes read as Piye) conquered all of Egypt from a new capital at Napata, portraying himself as the legitimate successor to Pharaonic

FIGURE 6.1. *Map of Egypt and Nubia showing sites mentioned in the text.*

rule at a time of political fragmentation in Egypt (Morkot 2000). Because of its strategic position and continuity of use from the New Kingdom (ca. 1500–1070 BCE) to the Napatan period (ca. 1070–300 BCE), the cemetery at Tombos provides an excellent opportunity to investigate the intersection of commemoration, remembrance, and the dynamics of identity as former colonists and Nubians negotiated their way through this dramatic historical transition.

Egyptologists often place interactions between Egypt and Nubia within a classic relationship of dominant core and subordinate periphery. As a result, the use of Egyptian material culture and emulation of Egyptian practices by Nubians during the New Kingdom together are often framed as a natural acculturation toward a more sophisticated and therefore inherently appealing Egyptian culture. Moreover, the possibility that the conquered Nubians might have maintained native practices or even influenced Egyptian society is either ignored or denied (Adams 1977; David 1988; Emery 1965; Grimal 1992; Van De Mieroop 2011). In a similar way, Egyptologists have interpreted the strong emulation of Egyptian practices by Napatan rulers and key elites as a process of assimilative acculturation driven by an Egyptian or Egyptianized remnant of the old New Kingdom colony, or alternatively an influx of Egyptian influence producing a new wave of Egyptianization after a native revival (Arkell 1961; Breasted 1909; David 1988; Emery 1965; Reisner 1919, 1920; Fairservis 1962). Other scholars have adopted a mixed view, arguing for Egyptianization and some lasting influence from the colony, while acknowledging the importance of internal dynamics and native agency (Adams 1977; Dixon 1964; O'Connor 1993; Gardiner 1961). More recent studies take an alternative view, which attributes the development of the Napatan state to internal factors and a deliberate strategy of cultural adaptation that co-opted and transformed elements of Egyptian theology and ideology, including burial practice, within an indigenous framework (Bard 2008; Smith 1998, 2008; Török 1997, 2008, 2009).

Barry Kemp (1978:34–35) articulated a common view of Egyptianization when he argued that New Kingdom "Egyptian culture must have had a considerable glamour in the eyes of Nubians ... It is not hard to understand how, in an age innocent of the esoteric delights of 'folk culture', many of the local products, such as the decorated hand-made pottery and mother-of-pearl trinkets, did not survive the flood of cheap mass-produced Egyptian wares." He concludes that "some recognition, at least, should be given to the positive side of this early attempt to extend what, to the Egyptians themselves, was a civilized way of life" (Kemp 1978:56; also Kemp 1997; contra Smith 1997). Models of Hellenization and Romanization founded on a similar set of assumptions have come under increasing scrutiny. As Michael Dietler (2010) points out, the notion of the "civilizing" impulse of Classical civilization was created in the nineteenth century CE to justify modern colonialism with a romanticized appeal to Hellenism, a notion that Kemp echoes with an Egyptological twist. This modern colonial narrative has increasingly been replaced with more nuanced interaction-based models like the one proposed here (see also Alcock 2005; Gardiner 2007; van Dommelen 2005). Lost in these debates about colonization and Egyptianization are the day-to-day interactions between individuals that characterized the colonial experience, including rejection, accommodation, and adoption of different cultural features by both Nubians and Egyptian colonists, in particular those revolving around mortuary practices (cf. Dietler 2010). Theoretical models centering on commemoration and remembrance provide the tools for a more nuanced investigation of the impact of these larger events on local identities at a former Egyptian colonial center.

COMMEMORATION AND MEMORIALIZATION IN ANCIENT EGYPT AND NUBIA

Ancient Egyptian burial practice manifests a close connection with commemoration and remembrance through tomb chapels and burial practices. Using the Theban community of artists and craftsmen at Deir el-Medina as a backdrop, Lynn Meskell (2003) makes a distinction between New Kingdom commemorative activities connected with an ancestor cult and the longer-term creation of cultural memory that was ultimately disassociated with past historical realities during the Greco-Roman Period (ca. 332 BCE to 400 CE). She characterizes commemoration in the form of tomb decoration and ancestor veneration in households as ultimately short term, stretching back hardly two generations into the past. She argues that longer-term cultural memory was largely absent in Egyptian society, even in a prosperous community like Deir el-Medina, whose inhabitants cut and decorated the royal tombs in the Valley of the Kings. In contrast, she draws on the reuse of the Theban Necropolis and in particular Deir el-Medina to illustrate dislocation in the creation of new long-term cultural memories. This memorialization of a new, idealized past divorced from historical reality played a key role in the fusion of Egyptian and Hellenistic features into a new hybrid identity. As we will argue below, a similar process applies to Egyptian and Nubian interactions at Tombos, albeit with less dislocation than in Meskell's case.

As noted above, Meskell (2003) describes the paucity of evidence for long-term memorialization at Deir el-Medina, with cases like Inherkhau's homage to five generations of male ancestors standing as remarkable exceptions (Meskell 2004:62–63). There is, however, more evidence for this kind of cultural memory than she allows. She does cite the cult of deceased Pharaoh Amenhotep I and his mother Ahmose-Nefertari (ca. 1524 BCE), who were founding figures for the village, as an example of remembrance that stretched back hundreds of years. They also had a mortuary temple in the Theban Necropolis that remained in use for a wider audience through at least the end of the New Kingdom. Similarly, Wadjmose, one of Thutmose I's sons (ca. 1510 BCE), was another important focus for veneration throughout the New Kingdom. His Theban mortuary chapel was maintained into the Ramesside Period (ca. 1290–1070 BCE) and contained many votive offerings and stelae dedicated by a wide range of Theban society (Petrie and Spiegelberg 1897). Inherkhau (ca. 1150 BCE) also shows himself venerating a series of royal ancestors stretching back nearly a thousand years to Middle Kingdom Pharaoh Nebhepetre Mentuhotep (ca. 2060–2010 BCE; Figure 6.2). The iconography of the figures indicates that they are statues, implying the existence of a cult place where nonroyals like Inherkhau could commemorate and honor a long series of kings. Mentuhotep played an important role in this cultural memory, since he founded the new Theban dynasty that reunified Egypt after the First Intermediate Period civil war (ca. 2040 BCE). He also left a remarkable mortuary complex at Deir el-Bahari that later inspired the design of Queen Hatshepsut's funerary temple. Deir el-Bahari played an important role in the "Beautiful Festival of the Valley," when families visited the tombs of their ancestors, and the Opet Festival, the most important in the Theban religious calendar (Kemp 2006:61–65, 270–274).

In a similar way, the "Immortality of Writers" (Lichtheim 2006:175–78), "Song of the Harper from the Tomb of King Intef" (Simpson, et al. 2003:1, 308, 332–33), and similar texts memorialize famous literary figures of the past whose works were still popular during the New Kingdom. Some nonroyal individuals like Imhotep, who is mentioned in both texts, were also remembered and ultimately deified (Wildung 1977). Imhotep was the architect of the Step Pyramid complex of Djoser (ca. 2650 BCE) and his cult lasted until the end of Pharaonic history, becoming very popular during the Late Period (ca. 525–332 BCE). The maintenance of his cult may more properly represent Meskell's notion of dislocation, the creation of new cultural memories by evoking historical figures and historical milieus without necessarily being grounded in historical reality. Nevertheless, the deification of Imhotep and continued popularity of literature in the New Kingdom that was written and set in an older historical context, like the "Tale of Sinuhe" (ca. 1900 BCE),

FIGURE 6.2. *King Ramses I and Queen Ahmose-Nefertari from a scene showing Inherkhau venerating statues of New Kingdom and older kings in his tomb at Deir el-Medina (TT 359).*

which was a standard school text during the Ramesside Period at Thebes (ca. 1293–1070 BCE; Simpson, et al. 2003: 54–66), and recognition of Imhotep and other sages of the past in texts like the "Immortality of Writers" and Harper's Song, suggest that a more widespread cultural memory was possible, at least in certain cases (Baines and Lacovara 2002).

Paul Connerton's (1989) concepts of inscribed and incorporated social memory can help access individual agency in the transmission of remembrances through burial practices, especially in the absence of texts. The practice of inscribed memory is deliberate and discursive, in the case of funerary practice resulting in tangible monuments that convey specific messages about the history and identity of people. Monumental tombs and especially tomb chapels served this role in Egypt (Figure 6.3). In particular, New Kingdom tomb decoration served as a commemoration of the lived experience of the deceased and his family, often conveying biographical information about their role in society. Women were included in these commemorations, but always in a secondary role vis-à-vis the male tomb owner, as mother, sister or wife during the New Kingdom (Hartwig 2004:121–30). In addition to material expressions of remembrance, we would add ritual acts that served a similar

FIGURE 6.3. *Scene of a scribal bureau overseen by General (later king) Horemheb from his tomb at Memphis (ca. 1325 BCE).*

purpose for both men and women. Funeral processions displayed material goods that projected an image of the deceased to the mourners. The body itself effectively inscribed a memory of the deceased and his or her identity when it was displayed (wrapped) during funeral rituals that included the placement of amulets and other grave goods with the body and coffin. The construction of monuments, orientation of tombs and burials, and other practices created a structured landscape that memorialized, consciously and unconsciously, ideas about the relationship of the living and dead to society and the cosmos.

In contrast to the deliberate nature of inscribed memory, incorporated memory is the result of habitual practices that may have been unconsciously adopted, akin to Pierre Bourdieu's notion of habitus. In ancient Egyptian and Nubian cemeteries, this memory would consist of routine practices structured by an interaction between social norms and individual desires that were not necessarily meant to convey a specific message about identity. The selection of certain objects as grave goods, for example, may have rested more on individual choice and habit than any deliberate attempt at sending commemorative messages that served some larger agenda. Rosemary Joyce (2003) argues in the case of the Maya for the merging of personal and historical memory though the material world in ways that blur the distinction between Connerton's categories of explicit and implicit memory. Practices on a small scale with a smaller audience can transform implicit memories of narrow social groups into commemorations equivalent in content to more explicit monumental expressions of remembrance, allowing items used in daily social practice to serve as mnemonic tools that ultimately reinforce social identity. Gregory Wilson (2010) observes that transforming Connerton's dichotomy into a continuum in this way allows potential access to a broader sweep of society, avoiding the risk of focusing too much on a narrow, elite, and literate segment of society. As we will see, the memorialized landscape created at Tombos became a potential arena for contested commemorations of identity through both monuments and grave goods in a colonial and postcolonial context.

COMMEMORATION AND REMEMBRANCE AT TOMBOS

Archaeological evidence suggests that Tombos was founded around 1400 BCE, about a hundred years after the Egyptian conquest. Colonial administrators were buried in a group of monumental pyramid complexes, while a more middle-class area located some distance to the north held less monumental underground vault and shaft tombs (Table 6.1, Figure 6.4). Although the monumental character of the cemetery reflects a commemoration of deep Egyptian cultural associations, bioarchaeological analyses using cranial measurements indicate that the population at Tombos was biologically mixed between Egyptians and Nubians (Buzon 2006).

TABLE 6.1 Overview of burials at Tombos

Tomb Type	Burial Style(s)	Time Period	Unit(s)
Egyptian-style pyramid	Egyptian	New Kingdom	1/4, 21, 23/29, 30, 31
Egyptian-style chamber tomb	Egyptian and Nubian	New Kingdom	6, 7, 8
Egyptian-style pit	Egyptian	New Kingdom	5
Nubian-style tumulus	Egyptian and Nubian	Third Intermediate/ Napatan	2–3, 10, 16–20, 22, 24–28, 32–34
Egyptian-style pyramid	Egyptian	Third Intermediate/ Napatan	9, 15

Due to the Egyptianization of Nubians during the New Kingdom Period, determining the identity of individuals buried at Tombos requires a multifaceted approach. While the Tombos cemetery largely reflects an Egyptian ethnic identity, many Nubians adopted Egyptian cultural features during this time. In order to explore whether the individuals buried at Tombos were Egyptian immigrants or native Nubians buried using Egyptian customs, biological identity was also assessed in the Tombos remains. Egyptians and Nubians have a long history of interaction and gene flow; however, there are clinal differences between groups who live in the northern Nile Valley in comparison to the southern Nile Valley that allow for some group distinction in the region (Brace et al. 1993).

Thirty individuals from the New Kingdom component of Tombos, primarily from the middle-class area, were examined in conjunction with relatively contemporaneous skeletal collections excavated from sites in Egypt and Nubia (*N* = 525, Buzon 2006). Egyptian biological features are represented by data collected from the Qurneh and Memphis samples, in addition to published craniometric data from two Egyptian samples (Abydos and Sheikh Ali, [Thomson and Randall-MacIver 1905]). In particular, the sites of Qurneh and Sheikh Ali are important because they are located in the area of Thebes, a likely origin of Egyptian colonists in Nubia (O'Connor 1993). Nubian biological features are represented by data collected from the site of Kerma, the primary cultural group in Upper Nubia located very close to Tombos, as well as C-Group cemeteries, a cultural group of Lower Nubia. In addition, a collection of remains from what are called "Pharaonic" cemeteries, Egyptian-style burials in Lower Nubia, as well as the similar site of Shellal, were included. The remains from Qurneh, Memphis, Shellal, and Kerma are housed at the Duckworth

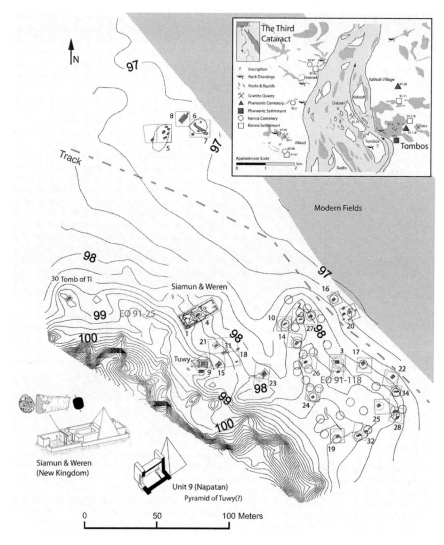

FIGURE 6.4. *Plan of Tombos. Numbers indicate excavation units.*

Collection, University of Cambridge, and the C-Group and Pharaonic collections are housed at the University of Copenhagen (Buzon 2006).

Nine cranial measurements (nasal height, upper facial height, nasal breadth, bizygomatic breadth, basi-bregma height, maximum cranial breadth, maximum cranial length, biauricular breadth, and basi-nasion length; Buikstra and Ubelaker 1994) that correspond with the published data (Thomson and

Randall-MacIver 1905) were recorded from the Tombos and comparative sample remains (Buzon 2006). Principal components analysis and logistic regression equations created from factors with eigenvalues above 1.0 were used to explore how the individual cases clustered and to predict group membership based on these independent variables (Kachigan 1991).

The results of these analyses indicate some differences between the Egyptian and Nubian comparative samples. While there is some overlap between these two groups, Egyptians tend to have higher facial height scores and lower cranial breadth scores than Nubians. The logistic regression results suggest that Egyptians have a more distinctive and comparatively homogenous cranial morphology that allows them to be classified correctly with more frequency than Nubians. In contrast, logistic regression less often correctly identified known Nubians as Nubian based on cranial morphology, a reflection of the more heterogeneous nature of Nubians as a group. With regard to the Tombos sample, the individuals were predicted to be approximately split between the Egyptian and Nubian groups by logistic regression. This split indicates that the individuals buried at Tombos were not simply a community of Egyptian colonists, but likely included Nubians as well (Buzon 2006).

Strontium and oxygen isotopic analysis of human tooth enamel provides additional data to support the idea of a mixed population living at Tombos. Strontium isotopes ($^{87}Sr/^{86}Sr$) are incorporated into the bones and teeth of individuals through the consumption of plants, animals, and groundwater that differ based on local geological context (Faure 1986). A preliminary study to investigate the feasibility of using this method in the Nile Valley to trace human mobility and identify first-generation immigrants at Tombos was conducted (Buzon, Simonetti, and Creaser 2007). Data on $^{87}Sr/^{86}Sr$ were acquired from dental enamel samples (primarily premolars) from 49 individuals buried at Tombos ($^{87}Sr/^{86}Sr$ range = 0.70712 – 0.70911). A local Tombos $^{87}Sr/^{86}Sr$ range was determined using modern and archaeological faunal samples in addition to burial matrix ($^{87}Sr/^{86}Sr$ = 0.70732 – 0.70789). Approximately one-third ($n = 14$) of the Tombos individuals fall outside of this local range, indicating a different, nonlocal source of strontium during childhood development of tooth enamel. These results suggest that the Tombos sample included local Nubians as well as first-generation immigrants. Continuing analyses will assist in determining if the nonlocal values correspond with $^{87}Sr/^{86}Sr$ local ranges found in Egypt (Buzon, Simonetti, and Creaser 2007).

Oxygen isotope ratios ($\delta^{18}O$) in the body are influenced by the oxygen isotope composition of imbibed meteoric water and food sources that vary according to climate, latitude, elevation, and rainfall (Dansgaard 1964). Cultural water practices—such as boiled beverages, storage methods, and irrigation uses—must also be considered when using oxygen isotope ratios to determine origins (White, Longstaffe, and Law 2004). For people living along the Nile and using Nile River water as their primary source for consumption and irrigation, we would expect that the $\delta^{18}O$ values of resident tooth enamel would increase downstream (heading north) due to the preferential loss of ^{16}O from river water during evaporation as the river flows away from its source in central Africa toward the Mediterranean Sea (White, Longstaffe, and Law 2004); thus, Egyptians in the northern Nile Valley would have a different isotopic signature than Nubians living in the southern Nile Valley.

The $\delta^{18}O$ was determined in dental enamel carbonate samples (primarily premolars) from 30 individuals buried at Tombos ($\delta^{18}O$ = 29.2‰ − 35.3‰). This range of values is relatively large, which may be indicative of the presence of nonlocal individuals in the Tombos sample. Comparisons with previously published $\delta^{18}O$ data for sites from various time periods in the Nile Valley reveal that using $\delta^{18}O$ to determine first-generation immigrants is complex in this region, due to numerous factors affecting the isotope composition of water used by Nubian and Egyptian communities, such as the drinking of aquifer groundwater in addition to Nile River water, irrigation practices, and water usage (e.g., brewing of beer; Buzon and Bowen 2010).

These analyses support the earlier suggestion of interaction and likely intermarriage between colonists and locals (Smith 2003), a common phenomenon in colonial contexts generally (Lightfoot and Martinez 1995). The act of colonization can have a significant impact on the people living in the newly incorporated areas. However, research suggests that colonization does not affect all populations equally. The relationship between the colonizer and colonized is not a simple dichotomy but rather is the result of complex interactions based on the precontact situation of the colonized, the goals and methods of the colonizers, and the reaction to these goals and methods by the colonized (Stein 2005).

Bioarchaeological research can make an especially important contribution when exploring contact in the past by investigating patterns of violence in human populations (Robb 1997). Cranial injuries have been shown to be a valuable measure of violent conflict in archaeological conflicts (e.g., Lambert 1997). Parry fractures, injuries to forearms incurred shielding oneself from a blow to the head, have also been used to suggest interpersonal violence (e.g., Wood-Jones 1910). However, researchers caution that forearm fractures could be the result of accidental injury, especially in the absence of craniofacial trauma (e.g.,

Lovell 1997). Aggression between Egypt and Nubia, two culturally different but familiar political communities, has been identified in the archaeological record through fortifications, political documents, victory monuments, and artistic renditions (Adams 1977; Smith 2003). Margaret Judd's (2000, 2004) studies of the Nubian population at Kerma indicated a relatively high level of injuries (11 percent of individuals) reflective of interpersonal violence, which has been associated with a "culture of violence" of the Nubian state (Judd 2000:135).

Cranial trauma as a sign of interpersonal violence has important symbolic value in the Egyptian/Nubian context. Smiting of one's enemy in the head with a club is associated with the Egyptian pharaoh's political power, as seen in depictions of various pharaohs in commemorative stelae and monumental art (Filer 1997). A review of traumatic injuries in Egyptian and Nubian samples reflects the results of these intentions implied in Egyptian texts and art, and attests to the continued use of cranial violence throughout their histories (Filer 1997), especially evident in the high level of injuries seen at Kerma (Judd 2004). This site corresponds to the late Middle Kingdom and Second Intermediate Period, the time of Egypt's aggressive military campaign in Nubia, the era prior to the time of Egyptian colonial activities at Tombos.

The relationship between the mixed community living at Tombos and the imperial Egyptians appears to have been relatively peaceful based on the low frequency of traumatic injuries related to violence. In the Tombos sample, rates of injuries, either due to accidents or intentional violence, are very low with 1.4 percent of the crania and 2.3 percent of all limb bones affected. Only one of seven forearm injuries could be considered a possible parry fracture. This contrasts sharply with the high rates of injuries found in the Nubian population at Kerma located just 10 km south, who were defeated by the Egyptian military prior to the founding of Tombos (ca. 1680–1500 BCE; Buzon and Richman 2007). At Kerma, 11.2 percent of the crania display traumatic injuries and 14 of 23 forearm fractures could be possible parry fractures; these rates are significantly higher than those at Tombos, demonstrating the more peaceful existence of individuals living here (Buzon and Richman 2007).

These data appear to support the hypothesis that traumatic injuries decreased during the New Kingdom Egyptian colonial period in Nubia, which may be due to the increased use of diplomacy and inclusion of Nubians in the administration rather than military action, at least at Tombos. Nubians who followed Egyptian standards appear to have been, to a considerable extent, accepted within society and rewarded (Smith 2003). Native Nubians living at Tombos may have Egyptianized (taking on Egyptian cultural features and behavior) as a way of using these symbols to their advantage and gaining sociopolitical power in the Egyptian system (Buzon 2006; Smith 2003). This adherence to Egyptian standards may have contributed to the more peaceful existence between Egyptians and Nubians at Tombos, as suggested by the low level of traumatic injuries (Buzon and Richman 2007). In contrast, burial styles at Kerma do not indicate the Egyptianization of Nubians at this site during the period prior to Egyptian colonization (Judd 2000, 2004), a reflection of the different relationship between Nubians and Egyptians at Kerma.

In the new social and political milieu that followed colonization, the Egyptian and Egyptianized Nubian elite who served in the colonial bureaucracy built large tombs that overtly signaled their ties to Egypt. Pyramids were the most popular style of tomb among the New Kingdom elite, adopted shortly after being abandoned in royal mortuary complexes at the beginning of the period (Badawy 1968:441–42; Lehner 1997:192). This more modest but still impressive elite version of the previously royal monument connected Egyptian and colonial bureaucrats to a solar theology of rebirth that reflected a deep social memory ultimately stretching back to the royal pyramids of the Old Kingdom (ca. 2650–2181 BCE), which were still admired by contemporary visitors (Lehner 1997:38–39). The provision of funerary cones on at least two pyramids, those of Siamun and Ti, represent not only a commemoration of the tomb owners' privileged position and access to an esoteric level of the solar theology. They also establish specific ties to Thebes, the religious and political capital of Egypt at the time, and the seat of the Viceroy of Kush, chief administrator of the colony. Over four hundred tombs of titled officials at Thebes included friezes of cones as decoration. Only a handful of tombs in the rest of Egypt and only one other tomb outside of Tombos in Nubia were provided with cones, so they represent a distinctively Theban phenomenon (Ryan 1988). As at Tombos, the cones from Thebes name the deceased and usually include titles, in this case "Scribe-Reckoner of the Gold of Kush" for Siamun, an important diplomatic post that is often connected with the assembly of tribute for the annual "Presentation" ceremony held at Thebes (Smith 2003:142). Symbolically, the cones may represent the sun disk, or perhaps more likely given their shape the conical offering loaf used in the ancestor cult (Ryan 1988).

Only scarce fragments of decoration remain, but a small section of a scene from a mudbrick robbed out of a New Kingdom tomb chapel at Tombos and reused in the blocking of a later burial chamber attests to the fact that these structures were elaborately decorated along the lines of their elite counterparts at Thebes. Tomb chapels served as active places of commemoration and remembrance through the regular offering cult and at certain festivals involving the veneration of ancestors. The two small patches of plaster recovered at Tombos in 2011 came from a scene showing two priests (heads shaven) carrying a pole that probably supported a portable shrine, used to convey the statue of a god or goddess in procession during a large festival. The execution of the figures is of the highest quality, equivalent to the elite tombs at Thebes and Memphis, Egypt's two main political and economic centers. Scenes like this reflect an idealized view of the deceased's life and their responsibilities as bureaucrats and, at Tombos, colonial administrators. Monuments like these materialized Egypt's claim over Nubia and established enduring ties to the land through the properly interred dead (Smith 2003:37–43, 193–201). But in this case, they may also reflect a more individual remembrance of the tomb owner's Theban origins demonstrated by the rare use of funerary cones, an overwhelmingly Theban phenomenon (Ryan 1988). In addition, the T-shaped layout of Siamun's tomb resonates with the most common tomb plan at Thebes (Kampp-Seyfried 2003:6–7), contrasting with the typical layout of elite tombs at other Egyptian urban centers, like Saqqara.

Mummification, ushabtis (funerary figurines who did work for the deceased in the afterlife, Figure 6.5), and other specialized goods represent a possible intersection between inscribed and incorporated memory—in some cases habitual, in others signaling identity in the form of deep cultural associations or a combination of the two. Coffins in particular were displayed during funeral processions and rituals performed at the tomb to a family and local audience. Their decoration and inscriptions would provide what Joyce (2003: 105) characterizes as "the transformation of objects employed in practical action into explicit commemorative records." In a similar way, evidence for the deliberate signaling of an alternative past is provided through Nubian burial practices reflecting the commemoration of different cultural attachments during the funeral (Figure 6.6). Four women were placed in Nubian flexed position with head to the east, facing north, lying on the floor of the Unit 6 and 7 chamber tombs (Figure 6.6; Smith 2003; 2007a; 2008). In the Unit 7 tomb, the two women were found lying together in semiflexed position surrounded by traces of wood framing, which points toward the use of a bed, another distinctively Nubian burial practice. At their heads lay a small Kerma-style handmade blacktopped redware cup, the only piece of Nubian pottery found in the tomb and an object that would have been visible during the funeral procession. All four women appear alongside and below contemporaneous coffined burials of women and men in Egyptian supine position. The funerals of these women, who would have been carried out to the cemetery in flexed position, probably on beds, would contrast dramatically with the typical Egyptian procession involving coffins and mummies. The insistence of Nubian women (and/or their families), who likely married into the community (see discussion above), on a Kerma-style burial made a powerful statement about their cultural identity and affiliations, painting a more dynamic picture of cultural interaction than the monuments alone reflect.

At the same time, a consideration of incorporated memorialization through objects placed with the deceased paints a more complex picture of cultural entanglement than the more polarized inscribed commemorations. For example, one of the two women buried in Unit 6 had her arms shifted out of position, apparently to get at a valuable piece of jewelry around her neck. The fact that her skeleton was still completely articulated indicates that her body was disturbed shortly after her funeral. The robbers left glass and faience beads still strung behind the deceased's head, including three amulets dedicated to the god Bes, a popular protective household deity. The unusual dancing Bes was broken in antiquity yet had been saved by stringing through the arms on her necklace. Balancing these Egyptian amulets, the necklace also had a Nerita shell bead more typical of Nubian burials (Smith 2008:19–21, fig. 5; Williams 1983:113). Since they would not have been obvious during the funeral, these items are more likely to reflect habitual patterns relating to the cultural entanglements that resulted from Nubian women intermarrying with Egyptian colonists. The small amount of Nubian pottery appearing in the tombs could be seen in the same light, reflecting an emerging hybrid habitus. In this context of power, however, Nubian pottery perhaps reflects a more deliberate signaling in feasting and display during the funeral. If this were the case, then the use of Nubian pottery would have provided an additional, more subtle ethnic Nubian counterpoint to the monumental inscription of Egyptian cultural traditions on the cemetery landscape (Smith 2003:188–206).

Use of the cemetery continued into the Napatan period in the aftermath of the collapse of the Egyptian colonial empire in both Nubia and Western Asia. Although some posit a withdrawal of the Egyptian colonial communities (Trigger 1976:139), the historical and archaeological records suggest the opposite—that the Nubian colony successfully seceded from the empire. Many of the former colonial sites continued to be occupied during the transition to the Nubian dynasty (ca. 1070–747 BCE). In any case, a large number of tombs at Tombos date to the Third Intermediate Period (1070–747 BCE) and the time of the 25th Dynasty of Nubian Pharaohs (ca. 747–656 BCE). The structure of the cemetery changed, with the middle-class area gradually abandoned and a new cluster of Nubian-style tumuli (circular stone burial monuments) added to the southeast (Figure 6.4). At the same time pyramids continued to be

FIGURE 6.5. *Ushabti of the Scribe and Priest Ti, found in situ inside his coffin in his tomb at Tombos.*

FIGURE 6.6. *New Kingdom Nubian–style flexed burial from the Unit 6 chamber tomb (ca. 1350 BCE).*

built and older tombs within the cemetery reused. Burial practice was mixed between multiple interments in underground chambers and single inhumations in simpler pit and vaulted chamber tombs.

Bioarchaeological analysis points to biological continuity between the New Kingdom and Napatan period populations in the cemetery. Ongoing analyses of the recently excavated Third Intermediate and Napatan period skeletal remains at Tombos using cranial measurements suggests strong similarities to the New Kingdom sample (Buzon 2012). Cranial measurements corresponding to the earlier study of New Kingdom Tombos crania (Buzon 2006) were collected on twenty-six individuals buried in the later Third Intermediate and Napatan component at Tombos. Factor score values generated using principal components analysis from individuals buried during the New Kingdom through Napatan time periods overlap considerably. The range of these values, especially for males in the Third Intermediate and Napatan sample, is slightly smaller, indicating that the individuals became more homogeneous over time at Tombos. These data lend support to the possibility that the Napatan sample may represent the descendants of a community (or communities) reflecting intermarriage between Nubians and Egyptians for centuries.

The construction of new pyramids and modification and reuse of older tombs point toward a deliberate act of inscribed memory evoking long-term cultural associations with an Egyptian past (Figure 6.7). Meskell (2003) correctly cautions that meaning and form are not always connected in the formulation of cultural memories, but in this case there are archaeological indications that the New Kingdom and Napatan period pyramids at Tombos carried similar solar symbolism and were both the focus of an offering cult. For example, Siamun's complex (Unit 1/4) showed evidence of cooking in the form of hearths and cooking pots most likely connected with funeral feasts and/or an offering cult. Similarly, the Napatan pyramid in Unit 9 contained a bin full of ash and a ceramic assemblage including a range of cooking pots and serving vessels, as well as bread molds for producing offering loaves. Both tombs are oriented on an east-west axis with the entrance toward the rising sun, as were most of the burials, evoking an Egyptian solar theology that connected the rebirth of the sun in the morning with the rebirth of the deceased in the afterlife (Hornung 1992:110).

As in the New Kingdom, decorated and inscribed coffins could also have served a deliberate commemorative role drawn from a more routine social practice. The tight position of the legs and other limbs in several burials from Unit 9 and elsewhere in the cemetery indicates the use of binding in mummification. This could also serve as an inscribed memory of Egyptian ties, since the wrapped mummy was displayed during the funeral rituals. The Opening of the Mouth ritual revived the deceased's senses in an elaborate ceremony carried out in the forecourt of the tomb during the funeral (Baines and Lacovara 2002:11–12). The text and depictions of the ceremony indicate that the mummy was set upright, face turned toward the sun. Bathed in light, the deceased was "charged" by the sun's rays (Assmann 2005:317–24). The public performance involved onlookers, family members, and several priests, ideally including the deceased's son and a priest of Anubis wearing a jackal mask. The same can be said for a particularly high-quality inscribed heart scarab of Tuy that was probably thrown out of the Unit 9 pyramid by ancient looters (Figure 6.7, described below). Since they would not have been on display, jewelry and even simple scarabs and other Egyptian amulets like the protective Eye of Horus more likely reflect the performance of an incorporated memory by priests and family members during preparations for burial, which would have reflected the family's and presumably the deceased's long-standing Egyptian cultural ties.

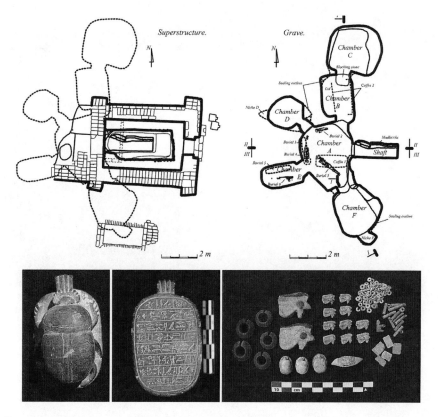

FIGURE 6.7. *Pyramid tomb of the scribe and priest Tuy and finds associated with the complex (ca. 700 BCE), including a heart scarab and Egyptian-style amuletic and ordinary jewelry.*

In contrast to the performance of Egyptian burial practice that inscribed this part of the cemetery, the emergence of a new area devoted entirely to tumuli evoked the remembrance of a different Nubian past (Figure 6.8). Unlike the communal, presumably family crypts in the pyramid cemetery, the tumuli often held only a single burial or occasionally two or three individuals, although the latter could in some cases be the result of reuse. This practice also resonates with earlier Nubian burials during the Kerma period (ca. 2400–1500 BCE) and continued into the New Kingdom in colonial contexts, at least in Lower Nubia and at the fourth cataract (Säve-Söderbergh and Troy 1991; Welsby 2003).

The placement of burials on beds in the tumuli continues this remembrance of a Nubian past in a way that would also be public. Bed burial was a central

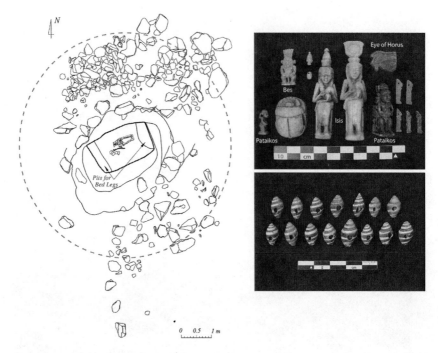

Figure 6.8. *Plan of the Unit 26 tumulus and burial with Nubian-style shell beads and Egyptian-style amulets from a similar burial in the Unit 27 tumulus.*

part of Kerman burial practice (Kendall 1997:92), and as we recently observed the dead continue today to be brought to their graves on beds at Tombos and elsewhere in Sudanese Nubia. The use of coffins and mummification in the tumuli, however, created a more mixed message during funeral rites. Only one burial of a woman was placed upon a bed in the traditional Nubian flexed position. With the exception of one child placed with its head to the east, the rest of the individuals were supine with their heads to the west facing east toward the rising sun, conforming to the Egyptian solar theology. Many of the burials in this area had amulets invoking Egyptian deities, including minor but popular protective gods like Bes and Pataikos as well as goddesses central to the Egyptian pantheon like Isis and Hathor, both of whom represented fertility and motherhood, along with the protective Eye of Horus (Figure 6.8).

Practices like mummification and supine burial as well as the worship of a selection of deities could represent an incorporated remembrance of a new hybrid or entangled identity (Dietler 2010:51–53). In a similar way, at least one burial from a vaulted tomb in the pyramid cemetery consisted of a coffined and mummified individual, its head to the west, but on a bed (Smith 2007b). By the Napatan period these practices might have carried less overt significance, instead reflecting a habitus that blended Egyptian and Nubian elements. Alternatively, it may reflect a diversity in how different individuals, the deceased before death and/or their families after, signaled their identity to a local audience through choices in embodied practices like mummification or the selection of grave goods.

COMMEMORATION IN A CONTESTED LANDSCAPE

The inhabitants of Tombos created enduring monuments that through commemoration of the dead tied the living to different pasts. Although as noted above some tumulus burials were made elsewhere well into the New Kingdom, the use of tumuli and bed burials resonated with the floruit of Nubian civilization during the first kingdom of Kush (ca. 2400–1500 BCE). That society came to an end with the conquest of Kerma by Thutmose I at least five or six hundred years earlier, some twenty generations. Pyramids had ceased as either private or royal funerary monuments at the end of the New Kingdom in Egypt, so the construction of pyramid tombs in the Napatan period evoked the remembrance of an Egyptian colonial past that was by that time around three hundred years old, roughly ten generations (Ambridge 2007; Smith 2007a; Török 1997:118–21).

The continued building of pyramids resonated with contemporary Nubian royal mortuary practice, but also with the colonial past. The reuse of older tombs would have provided access to that Egyptian past for those with more modest means, but also entailed the destruction and/or usurpation of abandoned and/or ruined monuments. This apparent desecration of older tombs would appear to support Meskell's notion of dislocation. The neglect and destruction of New Kingdom tombs seen at Tombos is common at cemeteries in Egypt and Nubia. John Baines and Peter Lacovara (Baines and Lacovara 2002) argue that this neglect of the dead is not incompatible with the mobilization of ruined monuments and sacred ground in memorializing kinship, ethnic, and political ties to the past. They note that the dissonance between an ideal of respect for the dead and the reality of ruined and robbed tombs was mitigated through rituals that granted the dead immortality and, for at least a few individuals like Imhotep, fame that lasted down through the generations.

During the Napatan period, Nubian identity was also inscribed on the landscape at Tombos through the revival of tumuli in a new component of the cemetery that lay directly opposite the pyramids. While the mixture of grave goods may reflect long-term entanglements and a new hybrid culture conditioned by individual choices, the monumental record suggests a more formal structuring of this sacred space. One explanation for the contrasting monumental forms is that there was a social difference between the areas, with the elite buried in the pyramid cemetery and nonelite in the tumuli. Pyramids are more elaborate monuments requiring more effort to build, but the tumuli would still have taken considerable effort to construct. Unlike the communal character of the pyramids, they were made for only one or two individuals. The heart scarab of Tuy that probably came from the principal burial in the Unit 9 pyramid represents the most esoteric level of funerary practice (Smith 1992). This piece compares favorably to those from the contemporary royal tombs at el-Kurru and Nuri (cf. Figure 6.6; Dunham 1950:plate XLVIII, 1955:plate CXXIII), suggesting access to the highest level of craftsmanship. On the other hand, an extraordinarily fine group of amulets from one of the tumulus burials suggests a similar level of wealth and access to craft workshops, since they are of a similar quality to those found in the royal tombs at el-Kurru (cf. Figure 6.7; Dunham 1950:plates XLIX–LVI). Indications of wealth are also provided by the use of valuable materials, like ivory, ebony, copper and gold contained in the jewelry, furniture, and vessels found in this part of the cemetery.

Perhaps a better explanation for the different monuments is an intersection of cultural and political social fields. New pyramids were constructed and older tombs reused in order to explicitly connect the present with the Egyptian colonial past at Tombos. In a similar way, the use of pyramids modeled after those of the New Kingdom colonial elite, heart scarabs, and other Egyptian features in the contemporary royal burials at el-Kurru near Napata created a fictive connection between the colonial past and a new dynasty of kings (Ambridge 2007; Smith 2007a; Török 1997:118–21). These commemorative practices helped legitimate their rule of Egypt not as conquerors but true successors in a line of kingship that stretched back to the beginnings of the Pharaonic state. In this case, the Egyptian features at Tombos appear as a more genuine example of long-term cultural memory, while the royal pyramids at el-Kurru and elsewhere and Nubian tumuli at Tombos might correspond to a greater extent to Meskell's notion of dislocation, although not as strongly as her Greco-Roman period example from Deir el-Medina. We would suggest that like the distinctions between inscribed and incorporated memory, commemorative practice and cultural memory at Tombos do not represent contrasting forms. Instead they indicate intersecting social fields

STUART TYSON SMITH AND MICHELE R. BUZON

that apply to varying degrees in different cases, reflecting choices conditioned by individual predispositions as well as larger contemporary social and political contexts. The combination of archaeological and skeletal analyses applied to the Tombos evidence reveals the ways in which native Nubian individuals used cultural symbols to their advantage in terms of sociopolitical power. Over time, it appears that the incorporation of these Egyptian and Nubian behaviors and material goods became part of the Tombos inhabitants' hybrid identity, as a part of the long-term cultural memory integrated into the new political systems built after the fall of the Egyptian colonial empire.

ACKNOWLEDGMENTS

Principle support for the most recent seasons in 2010 and 2011 came from National Science Foundation grant BCES-0917824. The 2002, 2005, and 2010 excavation seasons were funded in part by grants from the National Geographic Society, and the 2010 and 2011 seasons also benefited from grants by the Schiff-Giorgini Foundation. The project has also benefited from grants by the UCSB Academic Senate and Institute for Social, Behavioral and Economic Research (ISBER). The initial phase of excavation at Tombos (2000 and 2002) was made possible in large part by the generous financial support of James and Louise Bradbury, as well as donations by Nancy Delgado, Francis and Jim Cahill, Jan Bacchi, and Connie Swanson Travel. Bioarchaeological analyses were supported by National Science Foundation grant BCES-0917815, the American Philosophical Society, the American Association of Physical Anthropologists, the Killam Trust, the Institute for Bioarchaeology, the Purdue Alumni Association, and the Purdue College of Liberal Arts.

The people of Tombos have welcomed us into their village and assisted with the excavations each season. We also gratefully acknowledge the support and assistance provided by the Sudanese National Corporation for Antiquities and Museums (NCAM), especially Hassan Hussein Idris, director general of NCAM; Salah Mohammed Ahmed, head of fieldwork; Abdelrahman Ali Mohamed, director of Sudan Museums; and al-Hassan Ahmed Mohamed, senior antiquities inspector. George Pagoulatos and all the staff at the Acropole Hotel proved invaluable to all the logistical aspects of the project, as well as offering us a real haven in Khartoum. Julie Anderson, Bruce Williams, Charles Bonnet, Brigitte Gratien, Jacques Reinold and the late Francis Geus have been generous in their hospitality, encouragement, advice, and assistance. Last but not least, we would like to thank Ali Osman M. Salih (University of Khartoum) and David Edwards (University of Leicester) for their generous suggestions and encouragement to pursue these investigations and kindness in allowing our work to overlap with the University of Khartoum concession.

REFERENCES

Adams, William Y. 1977. *Nubia: Corridor to Africa*. London: Penguin.

Alcock, Susan. 2005. "Roman Colonies in the Eastern Empire: A Tale of Four Cities." In *The Archaeology of Colonial Encounters*, edited by Gil J. Stein, 297–329. Santa Fe: School of American Research Press.

Ambridge, Lindsay. 2007. "Inscribing the Napatan Landscape: Architecture." In *Negotiating the Past: Identity, Memory, and Landscape in Archaeological Research*, edited by N. Yoffee, 128–54. Tucson: University of Arizona Press.

Arkell, Anthony J. 1961. *A History of the Sudan: From the Earliest Times to 1821*. 2nd ed. London: Athlone Press.

Assmann, Jan. 2005. *Death and Salvation in Ancient Egypt*. Translated by David Lorton. Ithaca: Cornell University Press.

Badawy, Alexander. 1968. *A History of Egyptian Architecture: The Empire*. Berkeley: University of California Press.

Baines, John, and Peter Lacovara. 2002. "Burial and the Dead in Ancient Egyptian Society: Respect, Formalism, Neglect." *Journal of Social Archaeology* 2 (1): 5–36. http://dx.doi.org/10.1177/1469605302002001595.

Bard, Kathryn A. 2008. *An Introduction to the Archaeology of Ancient Egypt*. Malden, MA: Blackwell.

Bonnet, Charles. 2008. "L' occupation égyptienne au Nouvel Empire à Doukki Gel: L'apport de l'archéologie." In *Between the Cataracts: Proceedings of the 11th International Conference of Nubian Studies, 27 August–2 September 2006*, edited by Włodzimierz Godlewski and Adam Lajtar, 75–84. Warsaw: Warsaw University.

Brace, C. Loring, David P. Tracer, Lucia Allen Yaroch, John Robb, Kari Brandt, and A. Russell Nelson. 1993. "Clines and Clusters versus "Race": A Test in Ancient Egypt and the Case of a Death on the Nile." *Yearbook of Physical Anthropology* 36 (S17): 1–31. http://dx.doi.org/10.1002/ajpa.1330360603.

Breasted, James H. 1909. *A History of Egypt from the Earliest Times to the Persian Conquest*. 2nd ed. New York: C. Scribner's Sons.

Buikstra, Jane E., and Douglas H. Ubelaker. 1994. *Standards for Data Collection from Human Skeletal Remains*. Fayetteville: Arkansas Archaeological Survey.

Buzon, Michele R. 2006. "Biological and Ethnic Identity in New Kingdom Nubia: A Case Study from Tombos." *Current Anthropology* 47 (4): 683–95. http://dx.doi.org/10.1086/506288.

Buzon, Michele R. 2012. "Diachronic Analysis of Health at Tombos during the Aftermath of the Egyptian New Kingdom Occupation of Nubia." Paper presented at the Paleopathology Association Annual Meeting, Portland, OR.

Buzon, Michele R., and Gabriel J. Bowen. 2010. "Oxygen and Carbon Isotope Analysis of Human Tooth Enamel from the New Kingdom Site of Tombos in Nubia." *Archaeometry* 52 (5): 855–68. http://dx.doi.org/10.1111/j.1475-4754.2009.00503.x.

Buzon, Michele R., and Rebecca Richman. 2007. "Traumatic Injuries and Imperialism: The Effects of Egyptian Colonial Strategies at Tombos in Upper Nubia." *American Journal of Physical Anthropology* 133 (2): 783–91. http://dx.doi.org/10.1002/ajpa.20585.

Buzon, Michele R., Antonio Simonetti, and Robert A. Creaser. 2007. "Migration in the Nile Valley during the New Kingdom Period: A Preliminary Strontium Isotope Study." *Journal of Archaeological Science* 34 (9): 1391–401. http://dx.doi.org/10.1016/j.jas.2006.10.029.

Connerton, Paul. 1989. *How Societies Remember: Themes in the Social Sciences.* Cambridge: Cambridge University Press. http://dx.doi.org/10.1017/CBO9780511628061.

Dansgaard, Willi. 1964. "Stable Isotopes in Precipitation." *Tellus* 16 (4): 436–68. http://dx.doi.org/10.1111/j.2153-3490.1964.tb00181.x.

David, A. Roselie. 1988. *Ancient Egypt.* Oxford: Phaidon.

Dietler, Michael. 2010. *Archaeologies of Colonialism: Consumption, Entanglement, and Violence in Ancient Mediterranean France.* Berkeley: University of California Press. http://dx.doi.org/10.1525/california/9780520265516.003.0002.

Dixon, D. M. 1964. "The Origin of the Kingdom of Kush (Napata-Meroë)." *Journal of Egyptian Archaeology* 50:121–32.

Dunham, Dows. 1950. *El Kurru.* Cambridge: Harvard University Press.

Dunham, Dows. 1955. *Nuri.* Boston: Museum of Fine Arts.

Edwards, David N. 2004. *The Nubian Past: An Archaeology of the Sudan.* London: Routledge.

Emery, Walter B. 1965. *Egypt in Nubia.* London: Hutchinson.

Fairservis, Walter A. 1962. *The Ancient Kingdoms of the Nile and the Doomed Monuments of Nubia.* New York: Crowell.

Faure, Gunter. 1986. *Principles of Isotope Geology.* New York: Wiley-Liss.

Filer, Joyce M. 1997. "Ancient Egypt and Nubia as a Source of Information for Violent Cranial Injuries." In *Material Harm: Archaeological Studies of War and Violence,* edited by J. Carman, 47–74. Glasgow: Cruithne Press.

Gardiner, Alan H. 1961. *Egypt of the Pharaohs: An Introduction.* Oxford: Oxford University Press.

Gardiner, Andrew. 2007. *An Archaeology of Identity: Soldiers and Society in Late Roman Britain*. Walnut Creek: Left Coast Press.

Grimal, Nicholas. 1992. *A History of Ancient Egypt*. Oxford: Blackwell.

Hartwig, Melinda. 2004. *Tomb Painting and Identity in Ancient Thebes, 1419–1372 BCE*. Turnhout, Belgium: Brepols.

Hornung, Erik. 1992. *Idea into Image: Essays on Ancient Egyptian Thought*. New York: Timkin.

Joyce, Rosemary A. 2003. "Concrete Memories: Fragments of the Past in the Classic Maya Present." In *Archaeologies of Memory*, edited by Ruth van Dyke and Susan Alcock, 104–25. Oxford: Blackwell. http://dx.doi.org/10.1002/9780470774304.ch6.

Judd, Margaret A. 2000. *Trauma and Interpersonal Violence in Ancient Nubia during the Kerma Period (ca. 2500–1500 BC)*. PhD thesis. University of Alberta.

Judd, Margaret A. 2004. "Trauma in the City of Kerma: Ancient versus Modern Injury Patterns." *International Journal of Osteoarchaeology* 14 (1): 34–51. http://dx.doi.org/10.1002/oa.711.

Kachigan, Sam K. 1991. *Multivariate Statistical Analysis: A Conceptual Introduction*. New York: Radius Press.

Kampp-Seyfried, Friederike. 2003. "The Theban Necropolis: An Overview of Topography and Tomb Development from the Middle Kingdom to the Ramesside Period." In *The Theban Necropolis: Past, Present and Future*, edited by Nigel Strudwick and John H. Taylor, 2–10. London: British Museum Press.

Kemp, Barry J. 1972. "Fortified Towns in Nubia." In *Man, Settlement and Urbanism*, edited by Ruth Tringam, G. W. Dimbleby, and Peter J. Ucko, 651–54. London: Duckworth.

Kemp, Barry J. 1978. "Imperialism and Empire in New Kingdom Egypt (ca. 1575–1087 B.C.)." In *Imperialism in the Ancient World*, edited by P. D. A. Garnsey and C. R. Whittaker, 7–57. Cambridge: Cambridge University Press.

Kemp, Barry J. 1997. "Why Empires Rise." *Cambridge Archaeological Journal* 7 (1): 125–31.

Kemp, Barry J. 2006. *Ancient Egypt: Anatomy of a Civilization*. 2nd ed. London: Routledge.

Kendall, Timothy. 1997. *Kerma and the Kingdom of Kush, 2500–1500 B.C.: The Archaeological Discovery of an Ancient Nubian Empire*. Washington, D.C.: Smithsonian Institution.

Lambert, Patricia M. 1997. "Patterns of Violence in Prehistoric Hunter-gather Societies of Coastal Southern California." In *Troubled Times: Violence and Warfare in the Past*, edited by Debra L. Martin and David W. Frayer, 77–110. Amsterdam: Gordon and Breach.

Lehner, Mark. 1997. *The Complete Pyramids: Solving the Ancient Mysteries*. New York: Thames and Hudson.

Lichtheim, Miriam. 2006. *Ancient Egyptian Literature: A Book of Readings. The New Kingdom*. Berkeley: University of California Press.

Lightfoot, Kent G., and Antoinette Martinez. 1995. "Frontiers and Boundaries in Archaeological Perspective." *Annual Review of Anthropology* 24 (1): 471–92. http://dx.doi.org/10.1146/annurev.an.24.100195.002351.

Lovell, Nancy C. 1997. "Trauma Analysis in Paleopathology." *Yearbook of Physical Anthropology* 40 (S25): 139–70. http://dx.doi.org/10.1002/(SICI)1096-8644(1997)25+<139::AID-AJPA6>3.0.CO;2-#.

Meskell, Lynn. 2003. "Memory's Materiality: Ancestral Presence, Commemorative Practice and Disjunctive Locales." In *Archaeologies of Memory*, edited by Ruth van Dyke and Susan Alcock, 34–55. Oxford: Blackwell. http://dx.doi.org/10.1002/9780470774304.ch3.

Meskell, Lynn. 2004. *Object Worlds in Ancient Egypt: Material Biographies Past and Present*. Oxford: Berg.

Morkot, Robert. 2000. *The Black Pharaohs: Egypt's Nubian Rulers*. London: Rubicon Press.

Morkot, Robert. 2001. "Egypt and Nubia." In *Empires: Perspectives from Archaeology and History*, edited by Susan Alcock, Terrance D'Altroy, Kathleen Morrison, and Carla Sinopoli, 227–51. Cambridge: Cambridge University Press.

O'Connor, David. 1993. *Ancient Nubia: Egypt's Rival in Africa*. Ann Arbor: Kelsey Museum of Archaeology.

Petrie, W. M. Flinders, and Wilhlem Spiegelberg. 1897. *Six Temples at Thebes. 1896*. London: B. Quaritch.

Reisner, George A. 1919. "Discovery of the Tombs of the Egyptian XXVth Dynasty." *Sudan Notes and Records* 2:237–54.

Reisner, George A. 1920. "The Viceroys of Ethiopia." *Journal of Egyptian Archaeology* 6:28–55 and 73–88.

Robb, John. 1997. "Violence and Gender in Early Italy." In *Troubled Times: Violence and Warfare in the Past*, edited by Debra L. Martin and David W. Frayer, 111–44. Amsterdam: Gordon and Breach.

Ryan, Donald P. 1988. "The Archaeological Analysis of Inscribed Egyptian Funerary Cones." *Varia Aegyptiaca* 4:165–70.

Säve-Söderbergh, Törgny, and Lana Troy. 1991. *New Kingdom Pharaonic Sites: Scandinavian Joint Expedition to Sudanese Nubia*. Uppsala: Almqvist and Wiesel.

Simpson, William K., Robert K. Ritner, Vincent A. Tobin, and Edward F. Wente. 2003. *The Literature of Ancient Egypt: An Anthology of Stories, Instructions, and Poetry*. 3rd ed. New Haven: Yale University Press.

Smith, Stuart T. 1992. "Intact Tombs of the Seventeenth and Eighteenth Dynasties from Thebes and the New Kingdom Burial System." *Mitteilungen des Deutsches Archäologisches Institut Kairo* 48:193–231.

Smith, Stuart T. 1997. "Ancient Egyptian Imperialism: Ideological Vision or Economic Exploitation. Reply to Critics of Askut in Nubia." *Cambridge Archaeological Journal* 7 (2): 301–7. http://dx.doi.org/10.1017/S0959774300002006.

Smith, Stuart T. 1998. "Nubia and Egypt: Interaction, Acculturation, and Secondary State Formation from the Third to First Millennium B.C." In *Studies in Culture Contact: Interaction, Culture Change, and Archaeology*, edited by James G. Cusick, 256–87. Carbondale: Southern Illinois University.

Smith, Stuart T. 2003. *Wretched Kush: Ethnic Identities and Boundaries in Egypt's Nubian Empire*. London: Routledge.

Smith, Stuart T. 2007a. "Death and Tombos: Pyramids, Iron and the Rise of the Napatan Dynasty." *Sudan & Nubia* 11:2–14.

Smith, Stuart T. 2007b. "A New Napatan Cemetery at Tombos." *Cahier de recherches de l'Institut de papyrologie et égyptologie de Lille* 26:347–52.

Smith, Stuart T. 2008. "Tombos and the Transition from the New Kingdom to the Napatan Period in Upper Nubia." In *Between the Cataracts: Proceedings of the 11th International Conference of Nubian Studies*, 27 August–2 September 2006, edited by Włodzimierz Godlewski and Adam Lajtar, 95–115. Warsaw: Warsaw University.

Stein, Gil J. 2005. "Introduction: The Comparative Archaeology of Colonial Encounters." In *The Archaeology of Colonial Encounters*, edited by Gil J. Stein, 3–31. Santa Fe: School of American Research Press.

Thomson, Arthur, and David Randall-MacIver. 1905. *The Ancient Races of the Thebaid: Being an Anthropological Study of the Inhabitants of Upper Egypt from the Earliest Prehistoric Times to the Mohammedan Conquest based upon the Examination of over 1500 Crania*. Oxford: Clarendon Press.

Török, Lázló. 1997. *The Kingdom of Kush: Handbook of the Napatan-Meriotic Civilization*. Leiden: Brill.

Török, Lázló. 2008. "From Chiefdom to "Segmentary State" Meroitic Studies: A Personal View." In *Between the Cataracts: Proceedings of the 11th International Conference of Nubian Studies, 27 August–2 September 2006*, edited by Włodzimierz Godlewski and Adam Lajtar, 149–178. Vol. 1. Warsaw: Warsaw University.

Török, Lázló. 2009. *Between Two Worlds: The Frontier Region between Ancient Nubia and Egypt, 3700 BC–AD 500*. Leiden: Brill. http://dx.doi.org/10.1163/ej.978900 4171978.i-606.

Trigger, Bruce. 1976. *Nubia under the Pharaohs*. London: Thames and Hudson.

van de Mieroop, Marc. 2011. *A History of Ancient Egypt*. Chichester, England: Blackwell.

van Dommelen, Peter. 2005. "Colonial Interactions and Hybrid Practices: Phoenician and Carthaginian Settlement in the Ancient Mediterranean." In *The Archaeology of Colonial Encounters*, edited by Gil J. Stein, 109–42. Santa Fe, NM: School of American Research Press.

Welsby, Derek A. 2003. "The Amri to Kirbekan Survey: The 2002–2003 Season." *Sudan & Nubia* 7:26–32.

White, Christine, Fred J. Longstaffe, Kimberley R. Law. 2004. "Exploring the Effects of Environment, Physiology and Diet on Oxygen Isotope Ratios in Ancient Nubian Bones and Teeth." *Journal of Archaeological Science* 31:233–50.

Wildung, Dietrich. 1977. *Imhotep und Amenhotep: Gottwerdung im alten Ägypten*. Habilitationsschrift. Munich: Deutscher Kunstverlag.

Williams, Bruce B. 1983. *C-Group, Pan Grave, and Kerma Remains at Adindan Cemeteries T, K, U, and J. Excavations between Abu Simbel and the Sudan frontier pt. 5*. Chicago: Oriental Institute, University of Chicago.

Wilson, Gregory. 2010. "Community, Identity, and Social Memory at Moundville." *American Antiquity* 75 (1): 3–18. http://dx.doi.org/10.7183/0002-7316.75.1.3.

Wood-Jones, Frederic. 1910. "Fractured Bones and Dislocations." In *The Archaeology of Nubia Report for 1907–8. Vol. 2: Report on the Human Remains*, edited by G. Elliot-Smith and F. Wood-Jones, 293–42. Cairo: National Printing Department.

7

Abandoned Memories

A Cemetery of Forgotten Souls?

ABSTRACT

While Tell el-Amarna represents a unique period
in ancient Egypt's religious and political history, the
commemoration of the dead progressed in much the
same way as it did during the rest of the New Kingdom.
Spatial organization of the death landscape, as well as
individual mortuary treatment and identity based on
burial goods, is generally congruent with other time
periods in ancient Egypt. Under the assumption that
social class can often be inferred from the burial treatment and items interred with individuals, the South
Tombs Cemetery has proven to contain individuals from a large cross-section of the social hierarchy.
These demographics appear to reflect the settlement
patterns found during the excavation and investigation of Amarna with close associations of all but the
very highest social classes interred beside one another,
just as they lived. The circumstances of what led some
of these people to their demise, however, is proving
to be unexpected. Demographic profiles and paleopathological observations are not what is expected
from a capital city from the most prosperous time in
Egypt's history. The concept of remembering the dead
is yet another complicated issue at Tell el-Amarna.
Extensive contemporary grave robbing suggests that
cemetery use ceased at the same time the city was
abandoned, only fifteen years after its construction.
What are the social and psychological consequences
of abandoning one's ancestors and the objects of their
identity, then for them to be desecrated by the disrup-
tive activities of grave robbers almost instantly? Was
this actual grave robbing, or were memories of the
dead taken away with the living upon return to their

GRETCHEN R. DABBS AND
MELISSA ZABECKI

DOI: 10.5876/9781607323295.c007

original town of origin? Or, much like the entire Amarna heresy, were the dead forgotten and ignored?

INTRODUCTION

The underlying attitude of ancient Egyptians in the commemoration of the dead was one of permanence and persistence of the burial cult as a source of provisions for the dead in the afterlife. Fantastic examples of such are visible in the archaeological record in the form of the pyramids at Giza, mortuary temples at Deir el-Bahri, and tombs in the Valley of the Kings, among many others. Excavations of nonelite cemeteries at sites dating from the pre-Dynastic period (Abydos) through the New Kingdom (Deir el-Medina) demonstrate that while the nonelite population could not hope to mirror the royal and elite burial practices in quantity, they could provision the dead in many of the same ways, appropriate to their own status. Whatever the ideal practice for commemoration and remembrance of Westerners (the ancient Egyptian term for the dead), the reality in Egypt was one of neglect, destruction, and eventual reuse of burial grounds, temples, and sometimes equipment in the medium and long terms (Baines and Lacovara 2002). This chapter addresses the commemoration of the nonelite dead during the Amarna Period. The short period of occupation of the city and its burial ground precluded the slow transition of the mortuary areas at Amarna from active use through neglect, decay, and/or reuse commonly observed in Egypt. As a result, the population had to improvise a much more dramatic final transition for individuals buried in the South Tombs Cemetery.

Pharaoh Amenhotep IV, the "heretic king" of New Kingdom Egypt, ruled for a relatively short period of time (1352–1336 BCE) during the Eighteenth Dynasty. However, during this time he created a great deal of social turmoil. By year 9 of his reign, the pharaoh had already accomplished three feats unparalleled in Egyptian history: the alteration of his name to Akhenaten to reflect his devotion to a once minor Egyptian god (the Aten); the establishment of a new capital city where the land had not been spoiled by worship of, or temples to, gods or goddesses other than the Aten; and the implementation of state-sanctioned monotheism (Hornung 1999; Kemp 2006a; Van Dijk 2000). Represented by the visual sun disc in the sky, the Aten became the focus of Akhenaten's religious vision. The site chosen for the new capital city was perfect for the worship of a sun god, with harsh desert landscapes extending from the Nile River outward to high cliff faces in Middle Egypt. Situated nearly exactly equidistant between the ancient Egyptian religious

(Thebes) and administrative (Memphis) capitals, Akhetaten was the unified capital of Egypt for the duration of Akhenaten's short reign. Craniometric analysis of the skulls from the South Tombs Cemetery (hereafter STC) shows high levels of diversity and supports the interpretation that the population at Amarna originated from throughout Egypt (Dabbs and Zakrzewski 2011). Today, much of the city remains as the archaeological site Tell el-Amarna, or simply Amarna, including the extensive STC.

A long history of amateur and professional archaeological excavation at Amarna has provided insight into the daily lives of the ancient residents. However, the locations of the Amarna residents' cemeteries have only recently been discovered through geophysical survey. Surveyed in 2005 and excavated beginning in 2006, the STC is positioned near the more southern set of cut rock tombs along the cliff face at Amarna. Five seasons of excavation (2006–2010) have yielded skeletal remains of nearly 240 discrete individuals. A large number of isolated skulls and disarticulated skeletal remains have also been excavated from the ancient cemetery surface. The paucity of grave goods, high frequency of disturbed burials, and pattern of skeletal articulation of remains found on the ancient cemetery surface suggest the graves of the STC were disturbed, or more likely robbed, during the original period of use (i.e., in antiquity).

Throughout this chapter, we will use a variety of archaeological and skeletal data to interpret life at Amarna during the short reign of Akhenaten. Topics to be discussed include workloads, nutritional status, and epidemic disease. Both lines of evidence suggest living at Amarna was full of hardships, both physical and psychological. In addition, we suggest one possible explanation for the high frequency of robbed graves excavated at Amarna and discuss the psychological reasons for and implications of such behavior.

THE AMARNA PERIOD

The characteristics of the time period represented by this site and cemetery are without precedent in ancient Egyptian history. The leaders of Egypt were dedicated to polytheism for the 1,800 years preceding the reign of Akhenaten. Temples to the gods and goddesses worshipped from the Old Kingdom, and most likely earlier, were the focus of major construction projects during each pharaoh's reign. Festivals in honor of the deities marked the passing of time in the Egyptian calendar. From the time of the Unification, in about 3,100 BCE, the pharaohs built their tombs in huge necropoli that only changed location when the capital of the unified state changed.

When Akhenaten assumed the throne, not only were the pharaohs constructing temples to the gods and goddesses; they were also expanding Karnak Temple, the largest temple complex in the world, begun almost a thousand years previously in the Middle Kingdom (Grimal 1988:298). The kings' tombs were located in not just any large necropolis, but in the Valley of the Kings, where some of the richest and most beautifully painted tombs in Egypt are found. While these internal projects were occurring, the Egyptian empire had expanded to its furthest extent, to Syria in the north and Nubia in the south, a mere century earlier during the reign of Tuthmosis III (Clayton 1994). Historically speaking, the prosperity of the nation at this point does not seem to warrant the need for a major change in religion or international policy. Yet, this is exactly what happened.

While the first few years of the reign of Akhenaten were much like those of his predecessors, complete with contributions to the Karnak Temple construction (Redford 1984:62), there was an abrupt change during the fourth year of his reign. Akhenaten changed his name from Amenhotep IV to reflect commitment to a different god (Kemp 2006a), closed the long-established temples to the regional gods and goddesses (Kemp 2006a), altered the artistic canon (Van Dijk 2000) to such an extent that for many years it was assumed that he suffered from some extreme birth defect (e.g., Aldred and Sandison 1961; Burridge 1996; Čavka et al. 2010; Marston 2010; Retief and Cilliers 2011; Risse 1971; Smith 1926), and finally, relocated the capital of the country to a desert hinterland now known as Amarna. He succeeded in building a huge city complete with temples, palaces, artisan workshops, outlying villages, quarries, and cemeteries for the royals, elites, and nonelites, all in fewer than fifteen years. This city seemed to grow and flourish, only to be abandoned soon after Akhenaten's death. As is common for almost all pharaohs, no one knows how Akhenaten died, but it is presumed to have been in year 17 of his reign (Kemp 2006a), as all documentation ends there.

Very soon after Akhenaten's reign, the country resumed its traditional religious and military activities (Shaw 2000:281), oftentimes omitting Akhenaten, and sometimes his successor, Tutankhamen, from the records (Hornung 1992), making details of the Amarna Period difficult to reconstruct. Many Egyptologists and historians refer to the period as merely a religious and social experiment. However, religious revolutions and social change rarely begin out of an experiment. Rather, they can begin as a response to some major internal public issue whether economic or spiritual, or related to public health. It is this last issue that appears to be a growing possibility in light of the bioarchaeological analyses.

TELL EL-AMARNA

The ancient city of Akhetaten, the modern archaeological site of Tell el-Amarna, sits on the eastern bank of the Nile River in Middle Egypt. The city was constructed within a large baylike land formation. From the Nile bank a crescent-shaped high desert plateau rises to heights of nearly 100 m. At its maximum, the crescent is nearly 5 km from the bank. Both the high plateau and the cliffs are cut by wadis (water channels) that lead further into the desert.

The Amarna site can be roughly broken into three areas (Figure 7.1). The first area consists of stone architecture cut into the desert cliffs. Along the high cliffs, a series of boundary stelae of rock tablets and statues were carved to mark the limits of Akhetaten (Davies 1903–8; Murnane and van Siclen 1993). Also along the cliffs, two sets of rock tombs (North Tombs and South Tombs) were cut for the courtiers and high officials of Akhenaten's court (Davies 1903–8). In addition, a third group of tombs, the multichambered Royal Tomb, was cut further back, deep inside one of the wadis, intended for the royal family (el-Khouly and Martin 1987; Gabolde and Dunsmore 2004). The city itself was constructed along the riverbank, although a modern strip of cultivated land obscures the city's western edge.

From the northern headland, the city extends southward approximately 6 km and toward the cliffs for about 1 km at the widest point. Within the city itself a number of zones have been identified. The main part of the city is called the Central City in modern times. This area is home to the main palaces, temples to the sun, and administrative buildings. Immediately south was the Main City, an area of densely packed houses and the more open South Suburb. A similar area of housing is located north of the Central City and is known as the North Suburb (Kemp and Garfi 1993; Pendlebury 1951; Petrie 1894). Still further north is the isolated North Palace. Several inscriptions show that throughout the period of Akhenaten's reign the North Palace was the realm of the ladies, being originally built for one of his wives, either Nefertiti or Kiya, and later converted into a palace for the heiress Princess Meritaten, the eldest daughter of Akhenaten and Nefertiti (Newton 1924; Reeves 1988; Spence 1999; Whittemore 1926). At the base of the northern cliffs is the North City, which has been interpreted as the main residence of the royal family (Kemp 1983; Kemp and Garfi 1993; Pendlebury 1931, 1932; Whittemore 1926). Between the city and the distant cliffs lies the intermediate zone, consisting largely of open space. However, along the road leading to the North Tombs lay three desert altars (Frankfort and Pendlebury 1933; Kemp 1995). In addition, the Stone and Workman's Villages are situated on a low plateau running westward from the cliffs and appear to be small centers of manufacture (Kemp 1984, 1985,

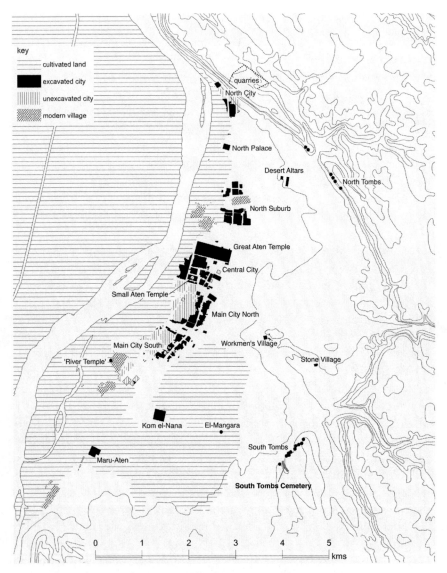

Figure 7.1. *General map of Amarna (Image courtesy of the Amarna Trust).*

1986, 1987a, 1987b; Stevens 2011; Stevens and Dolling 2006, 2007a, 2007b, 2008, 2009).

While small, mostly robbed, cemeteries have been identified in the past, no cemeteries large enough to hold the remains of the large "commoners" population at Amarna could be identified. Extensive GIS survey work in 2005 identified the presence and extent of a large cemetery (over 0.5 km in length) within a wadi bisecting the cliffs amid the South Tombs. This area is now known as the South Tombs Cemetery, which may hold the remains of several thousand individuals of all social classes save the very highest, whose tombs were cut into the cliff walls or in the Royal Wadi (Kemp 2006a, 2007a, 2007b).

EXCAVATIONS AT AMARNA'S SOUTH TOMBS CEMETERY

Since 2006 three distinct areas of the STC have been opened for excavation (Figure 7.2), the Upper Site, the Lower Site, and the Wadi Mouth Site. These area names were not originally meant to suggest significant differences between the individuals buried in them. Rather, this convention was instituted in order to have an easy way to refer to the areas. The few grave goods recovered from the STC are similar in form to objects recovered from the main city excavations, thus linking the STC to the city temporally and culturally (Stevens 2010). The Upper Site lies approximately 0.5 km east of the cliffs of the South Tombs above the eastern side of a wadi cut into the plateau and cliff face. The Upper Site has been excavated over five field seasons (2006–10), which represents the largest scale of cemetery excavation at Amarna, with the largest area of desert and the highest number of burials excavated. The Lower Site lies approximately 150 m east of the wadi mouth, on the western bank of the wadi and extends onto the wadi floor. It was opened in 2009 and was also excavated during the subsequent season. In 2010 excavations were opened at the Wadi Mouth Site on the eastern side of the wadi bank. All of these areas are still under excavation, although the Egyptian Revolution of 2011 interrupted the excavation activities. The following discussion is based on pre-2011 analyses.

Despite likely being one contiguous cemetery, each of the three excavation sites in the STC exhibits markedly different characteristics, which may relate to the social standing of those individuals buried within, temporal differences in the timing of usage, the location of the sites themselves in relation to either the city or the South Tombs, or some other as-of-yet unidentified character. A total of 234 discrete individuals have been excavated from the STC. In addition, numerous isolated skulls, isolated mandibles, and small clusters of largely articulated skeletal remains excavated from the presumed ancient ground surface (designated cluster individuals by the Amarna Project) have been recovered from the cemetery. The presence of isolated skulls is roughly correlated with the number of postcranial remains without skulls, but few have been positively associated with skeletal remains.

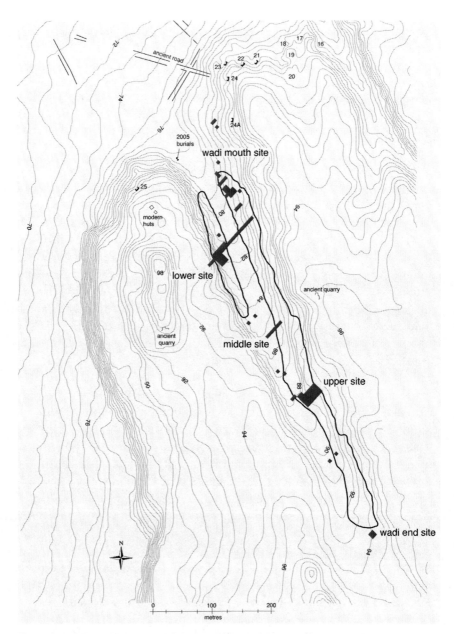

FIGURE 7.2. *Excavation areas of the South Tombs Cemetery (Contours provided by H. Fenwick, image courtesy of the Amarna Trust).*

As the area with the longest period of excavation, the Upper Site unsurprisingly has the largest number of excavated grave pits (n = 156) and is home to the largest portion of the skeletal population (n = 161; 68.8 percent). The Upper Site has the highest density of graves per 5 × 5 m square, with four to six earth-cut grave shaft pits identified within each square. Grave shafts are generally oblong to rectangular pits dug into the desert sand. The influence of topography and matrix depth tends to override that of pit depth and orientation (Kemp et al. 2013). The integrity of the grave shaft depends on the depth of the burial. If the burial is relatively shallow, the grave shaft is almost indistinguishable from the surrounding matrix of loose sand. However, deeper burials have obvious grave cuts that keep their shape upon excavation due to the compacted layer of sand in which they occur. The depth of burials, at present, appears to follow no pattern of age, sex, health, or economic status within the cemetery (Stevens 2010). In general, burial pits are narrow, with the dimensions closely matching the size of the individual(s) interred. Burial treatments are simple, and a full description of the variety found at Amarna can be found later in this chapter.

The orientation of the grave pits demonstrates a wide degree of variation, with no particular dominant one. Multiple burials are common within the Upper Site, and when they occur, the grave pits are cut wider than standard width for the interred individuals to be placed side by side (Shepperson 2010). The Upper Site is much more disturbed than other areas of the cemetery. Eighty-nine percent of the burial pits were disturbed. A later discussion in this chapter will demonstrate that the observed disturbance likely occurred in antiquity. In addition, in comparison to the other areas of the cemetery, the disturbance of the Upper Site is much more complete. Perhaps the robbers, obscured by distance from the main access route to the cemetery, felt safe to spend extended periods of time in their activities at this site (Shepperson 2010). Despite the disturbance of the burial pits, some cultural remains have been recovered from the Upper Site. A persistent feature of the Upper Site is the small number of grave goods recovered. These are concentrated in a few graves, with most containing no grave goods save the burial treatment of the bodies (Ambridge and Shepperson 2006; Dolling 2007, 2008; Shepperson 2009, 2010). In addition, few graves are marked with the stone markers more common in the Lower Site and the Wadi Mouth Site (Shepperson 2010).

Situated much closer to the wadi mouth, the Lower Site was not disturbed as often or as thoroughly as the burials of the Upper Site. Eighty-four percent (47/56) of the Lower Site burials were disturbed, but most of the bodies were found within the burial pit allowing for complete or nearly complete recovery of the skeletal remains (n = 56). The reduced destruction of the burials in the Lower Site allows for observation that the burial pits were only cut wide enough for the body, with little to no extra space allowed. In comparison to the Upper Site, the Lower Site demonstrates increased orderliness and more consistency in burial orientation, individual placement within the burial, and spatial organization of the burials within the cemetery. There are two distinct zones of burial within the Lower Site. When burials were cut into the western slope of the wadi shore, graves were perpendicular to the line of the wadi and individuals were placed within the pit with the head upslope, without exception. Burials on the wadi floor were typically arranged parallel to the line of the wadi, with the head of the buried individual placed at either end of the grave (i.e., there is no consistent orientation of the bodies toward any one direction) (Stevens 2010). The Lower Site has fewer multiple burials than the Upper Site, and in contrast to the Upper Site, the individuals are placed on top of one another inside a single-width grave pit.

Over half of the wooden coffins excavated from the STC have been identified in the Lower Site. The excellent preservation in the STC as a whole suggests this is a true difference in the burials between the cemetery regions, and that the observed difference is not due to differential preservation. This is significant, as the Lower Site only contains 23.9 percent of the individuals. These wooden coffins not only represent greater expenditures of funds to purchase the burial treatment, but also greater expenditures of energy in burial. The average depth of the coffins at the Lower Site was 1.5 m (Stevens 2010). Like the Upper Site, most graves had no goods within, and objects were not common within the cemetery as a whole. The Lower Site is home to six limestone stele with pointed narrow tops, which are characteristic of the total sample (n = 9) from the STC.

The Wadi Mouth Site was opened in 2010, and only one season of excavation is included in this discussion. In total 17 grave pits were excavated and 17 individuals recovered. One pit was completely devoid of skeletal remains, and one contained the double burial of two infants. The Wadi Mouth Site shares characteristics with both the Upper Site and Lower Site. Like the Lower Site, the Wadi Mouth Site has a general consistency in burial orientation. All grave pits are laid out with a southeast-northwest alignment, except one (King-Wetzel 2010). The intergrave spacing is very tight, as was observed at the Upper Site. Graves may have been placed between the observed drainage channels (King-Wetzel 2010). The average grave depth in the Wadi Mouth Site was 50–100 cm, very shallow compared to the other areas of the STC. This may have been due to the shallowness of the sand overlying the limestone bedrock. Many graves were actually cut into the top portion of the bedrock. While the sample size is quite small from this area of the cemetery, it appears as if there is significantly less robbing activity here. Six of the 17 (35.3 percent) excavated pits were entirely intact (p = 0.003, χ^2 = 11.447, df = 2). Unlike either the Upper Site or Lower Site, all intact burials at the Wadi Mouth Site preserved a rough boulder supraburial construction in the form of lines of white limestone boulders (large rock approximately 12" in diameter) placed over the body or the burial pit. One wooden coffin was excavated from the Wadi Mouth Site, but other grave goods were rare, consistent with the remainder of the cemetery (King-Wetzel 2010).

Few grave goods have been excavated from any region in the cemetery. Consistently throughout the cemetery those goods are concentrated in a few graves, while most burials have no cultural materials outside of the body coverings (see next section for a description). When grave goods have been found, they typically fall into one of three general categories. First, offerings of food and drink are common among the burial goods, and can be inferred by the presence of vessels that would have once held these items. The largest cache of this type of artifact was found at the Upper Site, where seven vessels (three bowls, four jars) were identified in 2010. The remains of incense, fruit or seeds, preserved grains, and larger fragments of fruit were identified from these vessels (Shepperson 2010). Personal goods mark the second class of artifact common at the STC. Mostly, these goods are cosmetic implements, such as kohl applicators and jewelry. The most common jewelry is made up of small beads of colored faience. The final artifact category is objects of ritual or symbolic importance, materials meant to secure safe transition to, and security within, the afterlife (Stevens 2010). These kinds of objects are extremely rare at the cemetery.

It is not yet clear how plots were selected and the cemetery was organized. The ground tends to be quite densely occupied by grave pits (Figure 7.3). Neighboring pits usually conform to similar orientations, and there is a clear process of secondary infilling of the ground with pits that tend toward more random orientations. Occasional clusters of graves are apparent that look like they could represent social groupings. The process of infilling blurs this effect, especially at the Upper Site, but on occasions where the ground is not so densely occupied, the infilling itself can probably be read as a desire to be buried within one particular group (Stevens 2010).

Some broader patterns are also emerging across the different excavation areas. One of the clearest is a sense that the Lower Site may have been a slightly "richer" space, evidenced especially by its production of a higher proportion of wooden coffins than other areas. Another is a sense of slight "disorder" in the

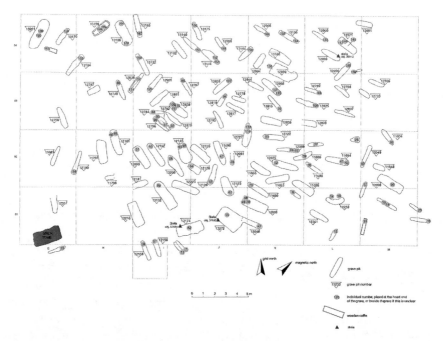

Figure 7.3. *Burial pits of the Upper Site of the South Tombs Cemetery (Image courtesy of the Amarna Trust).*

nature of some of the burials at the Upper Site. This area has produced, for example, proportionately more multiple burials than elsewhere, and of a kind that seem to reflect an economy of approach rather than the development of a more elaborate style of tomb. Excavations here have also revealed a number of interments whose occupants were buried prone (i.e., facedown) rather than supine, as though the correct orientation of the body may have been confused by the time it reached the burial site. There are various ways in which we might explain these circumstances. One intriguing possibility, especially in the case of the multiple burials, is that there was a lessening of control arising from conditions in which multiple individuals were dying at one time, a hypothesis supported by the bioarchaeological data.

COMMEMORATING THE DEAD AT AMARNA

The remarkable preservation of the STC sample at the culturally, temporally, and environmentally unique site of Amarna provides an opportunity to study the rituals and broader patterns of activity and behavior that accompanied the transition between life and death in New Kingdom Egypt. Of particular importance is the occasion to examine the transitions of the nonelite members of society, about whom little has been published (Baines and Lacovara 2002), during a period of religious change. As encountered so far, two aspects best characterize the approach to burial and provisioning of the dead: (1) an overall simplicity, and (2) a consistency of approach, although care must be taken in not assuming these characteristics suggest a lack of complexity of underlying conception and experience.

To date, no indication of deliberate attempts at mummification has been noted in the STC sample. Macroscopic characteristics that could be used to identify potential mummification include removal of the internal organs and the introduction of agents to dry and preserve the tissue. Natural mummification of partial sets of remains has been observed. The most common region preserved in this manner is the lower limbs, although this observation may be skewed by the pattern of disarticulation common at the cemetery.

The majority of burials in the STC at Amarna follow a basic pattern of treatment. The deceased was usually laid out in an extended position, with the head upright and arms either extended by the torso, or with the hands crossed over the pelvis, before being wrapped in textile and placed in a container for burial. The most common burial containers are plain mats made of varying lengths of plant material (Figure 7.4), in which the body was rolled to form a cylinder that was then bound externally with rope. Sometimes a mat of finer plant material was used as an intermediate layer, and often the bodies of children were wrapped only in this finer layer. Rarer still was placement of the body in a wooden coffin. Fifteen examples of wooden coffins have been excavated to date. The coffins range from simple undecorated boxes to anthropoid-style coffins decorated with scenes of offering-bearers and funerary texts (Kemp 2010a:18–21; Kemp and Stevens 2008:35–41). Fragments of pottery coffins have also been identified from the surface collections, although none have been found in situ or in association with skeletal remains (Rose 2005:24).

Occasionally, amulets and jewelry items were placed on the body or among the wrappings. So far, a common trend that is emerging in the recovered evidence is that the interred clutched a single amulet in the left hand. Other goods encountered include cosmetic items such as mirrors and kohl tubes. There is little that has strong ritual associations, one possible exception being a small metal blade with wooden handle recovered in situ under the head of a juvenile, an object that recalls the adze used in the opening of the mouth ceremony to reanimate the deceased and render them capable in the next world

FIGURE 7.4. *Stick matting coffin typical of the South Tombs Cemetery (Image courtesy of the Amarna Trust).*

(Kemp and Stevens 2008:32–34). Its presence may attest to the continuation of this ceremony, or a version thereof, in Akhenaten's reign.

Most of the objects encountered in the STC are familiar from the excavations of the Amarna houses, and are thus firmly situated in the realm of life. The wooden coffins and cut-stone grave markers obviously stand out as two specialized funerary objects. The more common plant stem mats, which were used to wrap the majority of bodies, may well have been standard household provisions used as floor coverings. One burial from the Lower Site was rolled in a mat scattered with potsherds and lumps of mud plaster, as though the body was laid out on a mat that was already in use (Stevens 2010:13), suggesting the preparation of the body was undertaken in a household setting. If this is so, it would seem to leave family members and perhaps close associates the leading participants in this process, following a cultural practice that was likely in place long before and after the Amarna period. If this is correct, it brings death much more viscerally into Amarna's living spaces than has been considered in earlier research. Most research on such spaces focuses on the more distanced practice of domestic ancestor worship (Stevens 2006:293–95).

Transporting bodies the 3 km between the riverside city and the STC required expenditures of time and energy. To facilitate this process, carrying rope(s) have been found surrounding some of the plant stem matting "coffins" in the STC. A distinctive feature of the desert plain between the STC and the city is a network of Amarna Period roadways (Fenwick 2004), which likely represent a series of service roads connected with construction work on the rock-cut officials' tombs. In some cases, perhaps, they were patrol roads helping police monitor movements on the city's perimeter, similar to the security-outpost-dotted rim around the Valley of the Kings. We might also wonder if these roads were used for funerary processions, adding a sense of formality to such events. The recent discovery of a "thoroughfare" devoid of burials in the STC strengthens this interpretation (Stevens 2011).

The body was then lowered into the pit, along with any accompanying goods. Most commonly these objects were plain pottery vessels, similar to those found within the housing areas of the city (Kemp et al. 2013), and in a few cases the remains of foodstuffs have been identified within them (Dolling 2008), although there are again many undisturbed burials that contain no examples of such. The pit was then backfilled with sand and a simple cairn of stones was stacked over the grave to mark its limits (Kemp et al. 2013). Occasionally, a memorial stela was present. While the effect of erosion over the interceding three thousand years has erased many of the finer details of the stela decoration, those that remain visible clearly demonstrate the artistic style of the Amarna Period (e.g., body proportions that differ from the rest of Dynastic art) and often contain small recess areas for images of the deceased (Kemp et al. 2013). More elaborate burial treatments are known, but are uncommon at the STC. For example, excavations at the Upper Site revealed a grave in which a mud-brick chamber had been constructed in the bottom of the grave pit (Ambridge and Shepperson 2006:35), but this more elaborate grave style so far remains unique.

INFERRING SOCIAL CLASS

The presence of burial goods and differences in burial treatment are not always evidence of difference in social status within the archaeological record (Parker Pearson 1993). However, sufficient examples of conspicuous consumption through both the inclusion of rich grave goods and variation in funerary treatments exist in ancient Egypt (pre-Dynastic through Late Periods) to demonstrate that differences in burial treatment and grave goods do represent the social and economic order there (Kemp 2006a). Excellent examples of cemetery organization similar to those observed at Amarna are available from Naga ed-Deir and Beni Hasan (Old and Middle Kingdoms respectively).

The disruption of the STC's mortuary contexts (both burial treatment and loss of grave goods) has made interpretation of social status more difficult at Amarna than perhaps it would be otherwise. However, despite the loss of these significant indicators of social status, multiple lines of evidence still suggest the STC was the final resting place for all social groups at Amarna, save for those individuals with high enough status to warrant a tomb along the cliff face or in the Royal Wadi. There is enough variation in the burial architecture to delineate at least three social statuses. The single mud brick tomb excavated in the Upper Site represents the most exclusive rank (1/234; 0.4 percent). The reported pottery coffins may also fall within this category (Rose 2005). However, they have only been found on the surface and not yet in association with any skeletal remains, so it is a supposition at this time. The next rank of burials would be those individuals buried in wooden coffins (15/234; 6.4 percent). Within this group there is also some degree of variation, as the wooden coffins vary from unadorned wooden boxes to richly decorated anthropoid coffins decorated with the individual's name (Kemp 2010a). The third level of social status at Amarna is represented by those individuals buried in some variation of the typical simple textile and stick mat coffin wrap (174/234; 74.4 percent), which presumably represents the majority of the commoners at Amarna. Forty-four individuals either had no burial treatment, an intriguing idea in and of itself, or it was not preserved (18.8 percent).

The high frequency of undisturbed graves that contain no grave goods (61.3 percent) is sufficient to demonstrate that the inclusion of any such goods was the exception rather than the rule. An initial impression concerning the analysis of burial "richness" based on objects and burial treatment is that socioeconomic rank, or the expressions thereof, may have been somewhat more muted in death than they were in life. From the city, the main source of information on socioeconomic rank is domestic architecture (Crocker 1985; Tietze 1985). Spatial organization of the cemetery reflects the city's settlement pattern in that the individuals seem to be buried together regardless of status (save for the highest elites, of course), similar to the interpretation given by Kemp: "Sometimes groups of larger or smaller houses occur, but the two types are often intimately mixed. Within them, rich and poor lived side by side" (Kemp 1991:294). Similarly, within the cemetery it appears as if the rich and poor were buried side by side. Rather than trying to mask the social differences that would have been clear to the living at Amarna, members of all social ranks apparently felt comfortable with those differences—perhaps with the exception of the highest ranks and royals—as is evidenced by the commingling of small and large houses and rich and poor graves. We conclude that instead of attempts by the low social ranks to mask class differences by mimicking higher status burials, which may have been beyond their economic power, the higher-ranked individuals were making no special efforts to highlight the differences. Perhaps the individually identifying stelae would have been considered sufficient to convey the distinctions.

Bioarchaeological data (see next section for full discussion) demonstrate no significant differences in frequencies of pathological lesions or lifespan between individuals buried in the Upper, Lower, and Wadi Mouth Sites. Frequency or severity of pathological lesions does not stand out in any one section. There appear to be no differences in frequencies of pathological conditions or lifespan between those individuals buried in wooden coffins versus the more prevalent textile and stick mat wraps. The presence of grave goods does not correlate with decreased frequency of pathological lesions, although this is more difficult to interpret because of the extensive robbing at Amarna. However, there is no statistically significant difference between individuals with or without pathological- and nutrition-related lesions whose graves were not disturbed (χ^2 = 3.49; p = 0.3221; df = 3) and those individuals do not display presence or absence of grave goods in any significant pattern (χ^2 = 3.1; p = 0.3765; df = 3).

LIVING AND DYING AT AMARNA

The daily life scenes portrayed in tomb and temple wall reliefs in the rock-cut tombs of the elites at Amarna depict offerings to the Aten consisting of great heaping piles of grain, large shanks of meat, and overflowing vessels of hearty drink. In short, the promise was of a life full of dietary diversity and surplus. With these images and the general prosperity of the Egyptian New Kingdom in mind, a life little affected by disease or nutritional deficiency should be reflected by the skeletal remains of the citizenry. In reality, the skeletal remains of the STC samples present a contrasting picture of a life filled with high levels of general, nutritional, and workload stress (Rose 2006; Zabecki 2008, 2009).

Bioarchaeological data should *always* be interpreted within a particular site's context. Amarna is a unique site in that both the city and cemetery were in use for such a short time that the association between city interpretations and cemetery interpretation is extremely clear. The same people creating the city were also creating the cemetery, or at least people from the same exact place and time. The monumental effort required to build a new city in the harsh desert environment, observed in the city architecture and archaeological evidence, was experienced by and directly affected all of the people buried within the cemetery. There is no issue of extended use of one or the other. The following discussion will focus on three of the most prominent and socially important (anciently speaking) examples of the biological and archaeological evidence from Amarna converging to support a single hypothesis.

PSYCHOLOGICAL AND PHYSICAL STRESS

The archaeological record is full of details of Amarna's occupation that would have caused psychological and physical stress among commoners. With the lens of several thousand years of perspective, it is often much easier to identify the physical stresses and their causes than it would have been during the Amarna Period, when the realities and requirements of daily life would have colored the perceptions of health, life, and death. It is exceptionally clear that Amarna was conceived, built, occupied, and abandoned in a short period of no more than two decades. In order for this pace of progress to be possible, the speed of building production must have been rapid. In part, technological advances, such as the development of the *talatat* block—a uniform block of stone measuring one Egyptian cubit long (approximately 52.5 cm) and half a cubit wide (Barry Kemp personal communication to Dabbs) that was small and light enough for one person to carry (Shaw 2000)—could have partially accounted for the increased building speed. However, the cost was high in terms of human effort.

The bioarchaeological data from the STC sample shows extremely high rates of workload-related physical conditions, including high rates of general trauma (67.4 percent), as well as high levels of pathological lesions of the spine manifest as degenerative joint disease (56.7 percent), compression fractures (37.4 percent), and spondylolysis (28.3 percent) (Dabbs 2012; Kemp et al. 2013; Zabecki 2008, 2009). Basic assessments of age and sex were made using the morphology of the pelvis and cranium (Buikstra and Ubelaker 1994) when possible. When the cranium and pelvis were not available for sex assessments, estimates were made with site-specific metric methods using postcranial remains (Dabbs 2010; unpublished metric data). Using the scoring protocol outlined by the Global History of Health Project (Steckel et al. 2011), no difference was observed between males and females for any of the indicators of health. These indicators include elements of dental health, which elucidate conditions of diet and perhaps oral hygiene. The Amarna residents exhibit low levels of dental abscesses (average per person: females 0.5; males 0.7) and carious lesions on the anterior teeth (average per person: females 0.1; males 0.2), but high levels of carious lesions on the posterior teeth (average per person:

females 1.4; males 1.5), and antemortem tooth loss (average per person: females 3.4; males 2.2). In addition, linear enamel hypoplasia, which represent severe stress during the early childhood years are moderate (frequency: females 0.61; males 0.58), while cribra orbitalia, a consequence of metabolic stress represented by porosity of the superior eye orbits, is high (frequency: females 0.24; males 0.31). Most commonly observed as periosteal reactions of the tibia, nonspecific bacterial infection rates are low in the population (frequency: females 0.19; males 0.12), as is generally observed in Egypt. The rates of both degenerative joint disease and trauma are very high (frequency: females 0.74; males 0.86; frequency: females 0.53; males 0.58, respectively). Degenerative joint disease includes both the development of bony lipping around joint margins, as well as actual joint surface destruction caused by bone-to-bone contact evidenced as polishing of the articular surfaces (eburnation) or subchondral bone destruction. Trauma, which is particularly high at Amarna, was noted very conservatively only when evidence of bone healing, such as callous development or porosity around the fracture margins, was observed. Chi-square comparisons of the frequencies between males and females for all of these conditions indicate no statistically significant differences between the sexes ($0.08 < p < 0.99$) (Dabbs 2012).

The hardships of life at Amarna do not end with the city builders. Nearly everyone in the city was subject to stress of one kind or another. The very nature of the city in its harsh desert environment, the complexity of building a new city and social organization in a land entirely unknown, and living with the general uncertainty that must have accompanied the new venture would have caused severe psychological stress as well as physical and nutritional stresses. The STC sample has high rates of porotic cranial lesions indicative of a complex of nutritional deficiencies (iron, folic acid, vitamin C, vitamin D) such as anemia (cribra orbitalia, porotic hyperostosis, and other porosities of the skull), scurvy, and other indicators of high levels of stress, for example, linear enamel hypoplasias and short stature (Ortner and Ericksen 1997; Steckel 1987, 1995; Walker et al. 2009). In fact, the STC sample at Amarna is the shortest-known sample from any time period in ancient Egypt (Rose 2006; Zabecki 2008, 2009), suggesting the living conditions were stressful for all members of society, adult workers and children alike. In addition, univariate analysis of variance (ANOVA) shows there is no difference in statures for adults who reached maturity before moving to Amarna (35+ years), those who moved to Amarna during adolescence (25–35 years), and those who grew up in Amarna (< 25 years) for either sex (females $p = 0.398$; males $p = 0.939$). Some of the observed indicators of stress can be attributed to noted conditions within the city, such as a generally low level of meat consumption, as is evidenced from analysis of the faunal remains from trash middens within the city (Barry Kemp, personal communication to Zabecki) which may have led to iron deficiency anemia evidenced as cribra orbitalia and porotic hyperostosis in the skeletal remains. The same skeletal lesions also could have been caused by megaloblastic anemia consequent to overexposure to the sun and the destruction of folic acid by UV radiation (Walker et al. 2009).

However, the psychological stress of living within a blended community in a new region must also be considered. Craniometric analysis has demonstrated that the residents of Amarna migrated to the city from all regions of Egypt (Dabbs and Zakrzewski 2011). The sheer fact that the individuals moved to Amarna suggests that they were living in a new environment, away from the people with whom and places with which they were aware of and comfortable. Life at Amarna has all the hallmarks of the physiological stress models proposed by Gordon Ervin Moss (1973) in that the new environment, and population dynamic at Amarna certainly must have caused some uncertainty in the appropriate ways to behave and react to current events, triggering the same stress reaction as the physical stresses previously discussed. It is perhaps this often overlooked underlying stress that contributes to the overall poor health observed from the skeletal remains of the STC sample, as well as the interesting demographic profile of the STC (see next section).

Epidemic Disease

Throughout the excavation and analysis of the STC there has been a consistently high frequency of infant and young child skeletons. This is not uncommon in archaeological sites (cf. Blakely 1971; Jackes 1986; Milner 1991; Mires 1991; Powell 1991; Storey 1985; Wheeler 2010), where the stresses of weaning, poor nutrition, and harsh environments often take their toll on the most vulnerable. Surprising, however, is the high frequency of older children, teenagers, and young adults excavated from the cemetery (Figure 7.5). Forty-three percent of the skeletal remains from the STC represent individuals between the ages of 5 and 25. An additional 14.8 percent of the skeletal sample consists of individuals 25–35 years at death. The high frequencies of postweaning sub-adult and young adults are consistent with demographic profiles constructed from skeletal samples of cemeteries known to house victims of epidemics. For example, the Royal Mint Cemetery in London was used to bury individuals who died from the Black Plague in 1349 CE. The demographic profile of this cemetery shows 34.68 percent of the skeletal population were between 5 and 25.

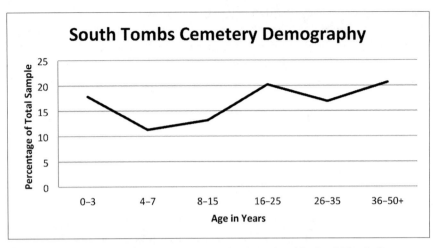

FIGURE 7.5. *Demographic profile of the skeletal remains from the South Tombs Cemetery (2006–10 excavations).*

Another 20.93 percent of the sample died between 25 and 35 years (Margerison and Knüsel 2002). Other examples of the demography typically seen during outbreaks of epidemic diseases have been reported for the plague outbreak in Provence, France, during 1720–22 (Signoli et al. 2002) and the worldwide Spanish influenza epidemic of 1918–19 (Crosby 2003). Both of these examples show much higher than normal mortality for individuals in age categories typically considered childhood through young adulthood (up to 25) (Crosby 2003; Signoli et al. 2002).

Multiple lines of archaeological evidence also support the suggestion that the city was plagued by an epidemic of massive proportions. From a regional archaeological perspective, the "Plague Prayers" of the Hittite king Mursili II are known. In these, he asked to be relieved from the "plague of Egypt," which was brought upon his people subsequent to contact during battle (Singer 2002). Further supporting evidence for an epidemic at Amarna can also be found in the Amarna Letters, a series of communications to and from the rulers of surrounding kingdoms to Akhenaten (EA 11, 35, 96, 932). Although badly damaged, EA 11 mentions that an unnamed individual has died of "the plague," and EA 96 extensively discusses how the king should replace donkeys killed by a "pestilence" attacking people and donkeys. Finally, the spatial patterning of the STC itself lends further support to the interpretation that the Amarna people were suffering from some, as-of-yet-unidentified, epidemic disease. Of particular interest is the Upper Site, where the burials are tightly compacted and often compared to contemporary sites much more haphazard in burial form, body placement within the burial pit, and burial pit arrangement within the space than other areas of the STC (Ambridge and Shepperson 2006; Dolling 2007, 2008; Kemp 2006b, 2007a, 2008, 2009, 2010b; Shepperson 2009, 2010). While interpreting any one of these lines of evidence as an epidemic may be subject to question, the convergence of the osteological evidence (demographic profile), the archaeological evidence (cemetery patterning and organization), and written records (Amarna Letters) does suggest with high probability that the people of Amarna were under significant stress from some sort of epidemic disease.

Eternal Rest? Grave Robbing at Amarna

The degree of disturbance of the STC's burial pits and associated surfaces makes grave robbing nearly an undeniable certainty. It then becomes important to ask who was robbing the graves and when. Mortuary context provides the data necessary to answer these questions. All areas of the STC have been extensively robbed. The lower frequency of robbing in the Wadi Mouth Site may well be an anomaly based on the very small sample size of burial pits excavated to date (n = 17).

Of the total STC sample, 79.5 percent (186/234) of individuals were at least partially disturbed. Of those individuals, over half (58.1 percent; 108/186) were partially articulated and *in situ*. Three individuals (1.6 percent) were completely articulated, but found lying outside of their burial pit. Seventy-three individuals (39.2 percent) were excavated with the upper portion of the body lying outside of the burial pit in a variously articulated heap, and with the legs and feet remaining in situ within the original burial shaft (Figure 7.6), often inside the original burial wrappings. This positioning suggests the burials were disturbed while significant flesh and other soft tissue remained attached to the skeletal remains (cf. Roksandic 2002). The soft tissue held the skeletal remains intact as robbers pulled the bodies from the burial pits. The lower legs are susceptible to separation because of the condyloid joint morphology of the knee. The knee is held together not by bony structures, but instead by soft tissues, which are susceptible to rapid decay. Clearly, the Amarna Period burials were being robbed relatively quickly after death. The three completely articulated individuals lying outside their respective burial pits suggest the interval may have been exceptionally short.

Tomb robbing is often explained as a purely economic activity (Rose and Burke 2004). Alternatively, robbing activity at Amarna was not necessarily

FIGURE 7.6. *Articulated skeletal remains excavated outside of the burial pit (Image courtesy of the Amarna Trust).*

driven entirely by economic motives. Only 38.7 percent of the undisturbed burials contain grave goods beyond the burial treatments described above. Coupled with the suggestion that burial preparation was conducted within the home sphere, presumably by those individuals closest to the deceased, this low occurrence of valuable grave goods suggests the motive for postburial disturbance of the grave is not primarily economic.

Amarna's commoners share many similarities with modern-day refugees. Being beholden to the high status individuals of Amarna, the common resident of Amarna may have not wanted to move to the new capital city. They were brought as members of households of individuals loyal to the Pharaoh. As such, they may be equated to modern refugees who lack the sense of belonging (Götz and Simone 2003; Landau 2006). In a traditional sense, belonging is an idea brought to the fore by historical connections to established social spaces underscored by a long history of settlement, a cohesive sense of community, and stable social institutions (Götz and Simone 2003), all of which were lacking at Amarna. Burial rites are often an important way of expressing one's culture and maintaining ties to the homeland. As such, they are often one of the last cultural elements to be modified by migrant populations (Moore

1970; Parkes 1972). The continuation of burial rituals in the same manner as observed at other sites throughout Egypt suggests the Amarna population burying their dead at the STC was maintaining their burial tradition. This may be because they simply knew nothing else—the new state-sanctioned monotheism being reserved strictly for royalty—or that they were holding on to their traditional practices to ameliorate some of the stress of being strangers in a strange land.

The short time elapsed between burial and the robbing event suggests there is a likelihood that the robbers knew the deceased individuals. One possible explanation for the extremely high rate of disturbance at the Amarna site was not to profit from obtaining and selling the burial goods interred with the dead, as the quantity and quality of goods in the few undisturbed graves suggests this would make for a paltry living, but instead to repossess the goods buried with family or close friends before the city was abandoned. Refugees commonly attempt to repatriate those community members who die in foreign lands, often at great expense (Ayiera 2009). The absence of any skeletal remains in the royal and elite tombs suggests they were either never occupied, or the remains were removed after the abandonment of the city. The commoners at Amarna may have carried out this process of repatriation on a small scale. Instead of taking the whole body back to the homeland, small, portable objects were perhaps removed from the grave and transported away. These "objects" could have been grave goods or even body parts, though with respect to the latter, there are no skeletal elements that appear to be differentially absent in the disturbed burials. While grave robbing may also have been present at the STC, differential treatment between individuals pulled completely from their grave pits and discarded on the ancient surface and those simply disturbed within the pits suggests two different, potentially conflicting, motives for disturbing the burials at Amarna. In this case, analyzing in detail a combination of bioarchaeological and archaeological data allows for understanding the potential motivations for the high rate of disturbance of the STC.

The Psychology of Displacement and its Effect on the Observed Mortuary Patterns

While the STC is the final resting place of thousands of individuals from one of the most unique ancient Egyptian sites ever identified, the mortuary treatment does not generally reflect that uniqueness. Consider the typical pre–Amarna Period New Kingdom mortuary pattern. Royals were buried in the Valley of the Kings in opulent tombs. Elites were buried in somewhat more accessible and visible, albeit somewhat smaller and less richly decorated, tombs. Commoners were buried in cemeteries with varying degrees of social hierarchy reflected in the mortuary treatment and spatial patterning (Kemp 2006a). Such is also the case at Amarna. While no skeletal remains have ever been discovered in the Royal, North, or South Tombs, the rich decoration and placement of these future vaults together suggest the status quo was being maintained in terms of the style of burial, if not the religious representation within the tombs. The STC is even more similar to previous, and later, burials of commoners in Egypt, in that the style of religious artifacts did not even change. With the exception of fragments of the diagnostic blue Amarna pottery and the characteristically Amarna Period artistic representation of human form on the few stelae recovered, there is little within the mortuary treatment at Amarna that would allow someone lacking knowledge of the origins of the burial to identify its place within the New Kingdom. No representations of the Aten have been discovered within the STC. In fact, the few artifacts recovered are inscribed with the symbols of Horus, Taweret, Bes, and an unidentified seated goddess (Shepperson 2010).

Modern studies of refugees in foreign lands have described the importance of maintaining cultural connection to the homeland for the psychological health of displaced people. The question of where one belongs has less to do with physical situation and much more to do with emotional geography and spatial affiliations with place (Bauman 1998; Bloemraad 2004; Castles and Davidson 2000; Götz and Simone 2003; Landau 2006; Zhang 2001). We propose that in maintaining the known burial traditions from earlier places, the inhabitants of Amarna were able to ameliorate some of the social discomfort associated with the difficult transition to life at the new capital city.

We also propose that it is possible to equate Amarna's commoner population to refugees, individuals forced to leave their place of origin due to circumstances beyond their control. The average citizen of Amarna would likely have not made the decision to relocate of his/her own volition, but instead at the command or behest of his/her employer, the high status leaders of the community who were loyal to Akhenaten and supportive of the religious and physical transition he initiated.

Modern ethnographic research has suggested that experiencing the death of a loved one in exile can accentuate the sense of alienation with the country of asylum and create social stress for those surviving (Ayiera 2009; Castles and Davidson 2000; Museum of London 2007). The best way to reduce this stress is to repatriate the remains to the homeland, often at great expense and sometimes at the risk of great danger (Ayiera 2009). However, when that is not possible, maintaining the burial rituals and treatments familiar to the displaced individuals can be substituted to ease the stress associated with death in a foreign land. We propose this may explain a number of characteristics of the STC at Amarna.

The first characteristic explained is the maintenance of the burial rituals through the Amarna Period, despite the major shift in official religion. Unlike the elite tombs—where images of the Aten and the royal couple/family predominate and no other traditional gods of Egypt are identified—the STC is thus far devoid of images of the Aten, and several other gods—especially Taweret and Bes—have been identified on grave goods. While this difference may indicate the transition may not have reached, or was not available to, the common population, an alternate explanation may be that the newly arrived actively chose to ignore the new state religion when burying their dead as a mechanism to ameliorate the stress of burying the dead in an unknown land.

Second, the extensive robbing of the STC at Amarna within a short period after an individual's death may not represent robbing as often thought of as a purely economic activity, but instead an attempt to repatriate at least part of the individual or the individual's burial treatment to the homeland when the city was abandoned at the end of the Amarna Period. In essence, we suggest the grave robbing apparent at Amarna STC may represent the first stage of a *de facto* secondary mortuary context, whereby items—not skeletal elements—were taken for repatriation at/near the end of the Amarna Period in an improvised ritual to deal with the unplanned abandonment of Akhetaten. There is no readily apparent consistency in missing skeletal elements that would point toward part of the body being removed for repatriation. Clearly, the head is probably the skeletal element most easily recognized as human by the lay individual. As such, it would have been one of the prime candidates for repatriation of the deceased. While a large number of postcranial remains without skulls have been recovered from the STC, there is an almost equally large number of skulls found in isolation that cannot be associated positively with postcranial skeletal remains. Thus, it is unlikely the removal of the skull/ head for repatriation was common within the STC. The level of disturbance of many of the robbed graves makes it impossible to guarantee full recovery of widely scattered skeletal remains in a way that would permit positive association of all skeletal remains found on the cemetery surface with individual burial pits. Thus, the possibility exists that skeletal elements were taken for repatriation; however, the nature of the STC precludes any demonstration of this hypothesis. The burial goods alternately may have been taken for symbolic repatriation of the individuals after abandonment of Amarna. When the time came to abandon the city, the inhabitants who could not afford to take the bodies of their loved ones due to lack of sufficient transportation, funds, or other reasons may have removed objects or smaller parts of the individual to be repatriated. So, in actuality, it is not a cemetery of abandoned souls, but a cemetery of remembered souls. The robbing of the cemetery is, in essence, only one, albeit rather dramatic, way to commemorate the dead. The few undisturbed burials at Amarna may represent members of extinct families, those wiped out by the epidemic disease reflected in the written, archaeological, and bioarchaeological evidence. Alternatively, undisturbed individuals may simply represent those individuals without family at Amarna and hence no one present to require a relic.

CONCLUSIONS

While Amarna represents the remains of the social and religious experiments of the "heretic king" Akhenaten, the bioarchaeological and associated mortuary data suggest that this major shift may not have had much of an effect on a majority of residents' original commemoration of the dead. In keeping with traditional New Kingdom disposal practices, the royals and elites built large, richly decorated tombs in high stone cliffs. The common cemetery was much like those from before the Amarna Period, and even the few artifacts recovered were of the style and inscribed with the motifs of earlier gods and goddesses. It seems that while this site and the time period from which it comes do not necessarily represent a "normal" ancient Egyptian city, the inhabitants of Amarna continued remembering and commemorating their dead as their ancestors had before them. However, the hardships of life at Amarna and the state authorized/ordered abandonment of the city after Akhenaten's death may have required a secondary and novel form of commemoration—one whereby living relatives, who had no particular connection to the place of Amarna and suffered physically living there, altered traditional Egyptian burial custom by retrieving objects and potentially body parts to repatriate the deceased in a more hospitable homeland from whence they originally came, a practice observed in modern refugees.

ACKNOWLEDGMENTS

We wish to acknowledge the contributions of Barry Kemp, Anna Stevens, Jerry Rose, Chrissie Sellars, the Ministry of State for Antiquities in Egypt, the King Fahd Center for Middle East and Islamic Studies, and the Amarna Trust, for their support of this project. In addition, the authors thank the editors and reviewers for their helpful comments on earlier drafts of this chapter.

REFERENCES

Aldred, Cyril, and A. T. Sandison. 1961. "The Tomb of Akhenaten at Thebes." *Journal of Egyptian Archaeology* 47:41–65. http://dx.doi.org/10.2307/3855865.

Ambridge, Lindsay, and Mary Shepperson. 2006. "South Tombs Cemetery" In Kemp, B.J., "Tell el-Amarna, 2005–06." *Journal of Egyptian Archaeology* 92:27–37.

Ayiera, Eva A. Maina. 2009. "Burying Our Dead in Your City: Interpreting Individual Constructs of Belonging in the Context of Burial of Loved Ones in Exile." MA thesis, University of Witwatersrand.

Baines, John, and Peter Lacovara. 2002. "Burial and the Dead in Ancient Egyptian Society: Respect, Formalism, Neglect." *Journal of Social Archaeology* 2 (1): 5–36. http://dx.doi.org/10.1177/1469605302002001595.

Bauman, Zygmunt. 1998. *Globalization: The Human Consequences*. New York: Columbia University Press.

Blakely, Robert L. 1971. "Comparison of the Mortality Profiles of Archaic, Middle Woodland, and Middle Mississippian Skeletal Populations." *American Journal of Physical Anthropology* 34 (1): 43–53. http://dx.doi.org/10.1002/ajpa.1330340104.

Bloemraad, Irene. 2004. "Who Claims Dual Citizenship? The Limits of Postnationalism, the Possibilities of Transnationalism, and the Persistence of Traditional Citizenship." *International Migration Review* 38:389–426.

Buikstra, Jane E., and Douglas H. Ubelaker. 1994. *Standards for Data Collection from Human Skeletal Remains*. Fayetteville: Arkansas Archaeological Survey.

Burridge, Alwyn. 1996. "Did Akhenaten Suffer from Marfan's Syndrome?" *Biblical Archaeologist* 59 (2): 127–28. http://dx.doi.org/10.2307/3210517.

Castles, Stephen, and Alastair Davidson. 2000. *Citizenship and Migration: Globalization and the Politics of Belonging*. Houndmills, England: Macmillan Press.

Čavka, Mislav, Tomislav Kelava, Vlatka Čavka, Željko Bušić, Boris Olujić, and Boris Brkljačić. 2010. "Homocystinuria: A Possible Solution of the Akhenaten's Mystery." *Collegium Antropologicum* 34 (Suppl. 1): 255–58.

Clayton, Peter A. 1994. *A Chronicle of the Pharaohs*. London: Thames and Hudson.

Crocker, P. T. 1985. "Status Symbols in the Architecture of el-Amarna." *Journal of Egyptian Archaeology* 71:52–65. http://dx.doi.org/10.2307/3821711.

Crosby, Alfred W. 2003. *America's Forgotten Pandemic: The Influenza of 1918*. Cambridge: Cambridge University Press. http://dx.doi.org/10.1017/CBO9780511586576.

Dabbs, Gretchen R. 2010. "Sex Determination using the Scapula in New Kingdom Skeletons from Tell el-Amarna." *Homo* 61 (6): 413–20. http://dx.doi.org/10.1016/j.jchb.2010.09.001.

Dabbs, Gretchen R. 2012. "Men (and Women) Working? The Interesting Lack of Sexual Dimorphism in Health Status at New Kingdom Amarna, Egypt." [Abstract] *Paleopathology Newsletter* 157:5–19.

Dabbs, Gretchen R., and Sonia R. Zakrzewski. 2011. "Craniometric Variation at Tell el-Amarna: Egyptians or Interlopers at the "Heretic King's" City? (Abstract)." *American Journal of Physical Anthropology* 144:119.

Davies, Norman de Garis. 1903–8. *The Rock Tombs of El Amarna, Part V: Smaller Tombs and Boundary Stelae.* London: Egypt Exploration Fund.

Dolling, Wendy. 2007. "South Tombs Cemetery," In Kemp, B.J. "Tell el-Amarna, 2006–07." *Journal of Egyptian Archaeology* 93:11–35.

Dolling, Wendy. 2008. "South Tombs Cemetery," In Kemp, B.J. "Tell el-Amarna, 2007–08." *Journal of Egyptian Archaeology* 94:13–31.

Fenwick, Helen. 2004. "Ancient Roads and GPS Survey: Modeling the Amarna Plain." *Antiquity* 78:880–5.

Frankfort, Henri, and John Devitt Stringfellow Pendlebury. 1933. *The City of Akhenaten, Part II. The North Suburb and the Desert Altars.* London: Egypt Exploration Society.

Gabolde, Marc, and Amanda Dunsmore. 2004. "The Royal Necropolis at Tell el-Amarna." *Egyptian Archaeology* 25:30–33.

Götz, Graeme, and Abdou Maliq Simone. 2003. "On Belonging and Becoming in African Cities." In *Emerging Johannesburg: Perspectives on the Post-Apartheid City*, edited by R. Tomlinson, 123–47. New York: Routledge.

Grimal, Nicolas. 1988. *A History of Ancient Egypt.* Translated by Ian Shaw. Oxford: Blackwell Publishers.

Hornung, Erik. 1992. "The Rediscovery of Akhenaten and His Place in Religion." *Journal of the American Research Center in Egypt* 29:43–49. http://dx.doi.org/10.2307/40000483.

Hornung, Erik. 1999. *History of Ancient Egypt.* Translated by D. Lorton. Ithaca, NY: Cornell University Press.

Jackes, Mary. 1986. "The Mortality of Ontario Archaeological Populations." *Canadian Journal of Anthropology* 5:33–48.

Kemp, Barry J. 1983. "Preliminary Report on the el-Amarna Expedition, 1981–2." *Journal of Egyptian Archaeology* 69:5–20. http://dx.doi.org/10.2307/3821433.

Kemp, Barry J., ed. 1984. *Amarna Reports. I.* London: Egypt Exploration Society.

Kemp, Barry J., ed. 1985. *Amarna Reports II.* London: Egypt Exploration Society.

Kemp, Barry J., ed. 1986. *Amarna Reports III.* London: Egypt Exploration Society.

Kemp, Barry J., ed. 1987a. *Amarna Reports IV.* London: Egypt Exploration Society.

Kemp, Barry J. 1987b. "The Amarna Workmen's Village in Retrospect." *Journal of Egyptian Archaeology* 73:21–50. http://dx.doi.org/10.2307/3821519.

Kemp, Barry J. 1991. *Ancient Egypt: Anatomy of a Civilization.* 1st ed. London: Routledge.

Kemp, Barry J., ed. 1995. *Amarna Reports VI.* London: Egypt Exploration Society.

Kemp, Barry J. 2006a. *Ancient Egypt: Anatomy of a Civilization.* 2nd ed. London: Routledge.

Kemp, Barry J. 2006b. "Tell el-Amarna, 2006." *Journal of Egyptian Archaeology* 92:21–56.

Kemp, Barry J. 2007a. "The Orientation of Burials at Tell el-Amarna." In *The Archaeology and Art of Ancient Egypt: Essays in Honour of David B. O'Connor,* edited by Zahi A. Hawass and Janet Richards, 21–31. Cairo: Supreme Council of Antiquities Press.

Kemp, Barry J. 2007b. "Tell el-Amarna, 2007." *Journal of Egyptian Archaeology* 93:1–63.

Kemp, Barry J. 2008. "Tell el-Amarna, 2008." *Journal of Egyptian Archaeology* 94:1–67.

Kemp, Barry J. 2009. "Tell el-Amarna, 2009." *Journal of Egyptian Archaeology* 95:1–35.

Kemp, Barry J. 2010a. "Belief on the Edge of Literacy: Two Coffins from the South Tombs Cemetery." *Horizon: The Amarna Project and Armana Trust Newsletter* 7:4–5.

Kemp, Barry J. 2010b. "Tell el-Amarna, 2010." *Journal of Egyptian Archaeology* 96:1–30.

Kemp, Barry J., and Salvatore Garfi. 1993. *A Survey of the Ancient City of el-Amarna.* London: Egypt Exploration Society.

Kemp, Barry J., and Anna Stevens. 2008. "Appendix: Artefacts." In B.J. Kemp, "Tell el-Amarna, 2007–8." *Journal of Egyptian Archaeology* 94:31–41.

Kemp, Barry J., Anna K. Stevens, Gretchen R. Dabbs, Melissa Zabecki, and Jerome C. Rose. 2013. "Life, Death and Beyond in Akhenaten's Egypt: Excavating the South Tombs Cemetery at Amarna." *Antiquity* 87:64–78.

el-Khouly, Aly, and Geoffrey T. Martin. 1987. *Excavations in the Royal Necropolis at El-'Amarna 1984.* Cairo: Institut français d'archéologie orientale.

King-Wetzel, Melinda. 2010. "The Wadi Mouth Site." In Kemp, B.J. "Tell el-Amarna, 2010." *Journal of Egyptian Archaeology* 96:1–7.

Landau, Loren B. 2006. "Transplants and Transients: Idioms of Belonging and Dislocation in Inner-City Johannesburg." *African Studies Review* 49 (2): 125–45. http://dx.doi.org/10.1353/arw.2006.0109.

Margerison, Beverley J., and Christopher J. Knüsel. 2002. "Paleodemographic Comparison of a Catastrophic and an Attritional Death Assemblage." *American Journal of Physical Anthropology* 119 (2): 134–43. http://dx.doi.org/10.1002/ajpa.10082.

Marston, J. E. 2010. "Akhenaten: A Woman, a Eunuch, a Victim of Pathology or a Religious Representation?" *Journal for Semitics* 19:421–64.

Milner, George R. 1991. "Health and Cultural Change in the Late Prehistoric American Bottom, Illinois." In *What Mean these Bones? Studies in Southeastern Bioarchaeology*, edited by Mary Lucas Powell, Patricia S. Bridges, and Marie Wagner Mires Ann, 52–69. Tuscaloosa: University of Alabama Press.

Mires, Ann Marie Wagner. 1991. "Sifting the Ashes: Reconstruction of a Complex Archaic Mortuary Program in Louisiana." In *What Mean these Bones? Studies in Southeastern Bioarchaeology*, edited by Mary Lucas Powell, Patricia S. Bridges, and Ann Marie Wagner Mires, 114–30. Tuscaloosa: University of Alabama Press.

Moore, Joan. 1970. "The Death Culture of Mexico and Mexican-Americans." *Journal of Death and Dying* 1 (4): 271–91. http://dx.doi.org/10.2190/693J-XBM8-HFT1-HBQX.

Moss, Gordon Ervin. 1973. *Illness, Immunity and Social Interaction: The Dynamics of Biosocial Resonation*. New York: John Wiley and Sons.

Murnane, William J., and Charles C. van Siclen, III. 1993. *The Boundary Stelae of Akhenaten*. London: Kegan Paul International.

Museum of London. 2007. "Belonging: Voices of London's Refugees." Electronic document. http://www.museumoflondon.org.uk/Get-involved/Collaborative-projects/Belonging/. Accessed January 7, 2012.

Newton, Francis G. 1924. "Excavations at El-'Amarnah, 1923–24." *Journal of Egyptian Archaeology* 10 (3/4): 289–98. http://dx.doi.org/10.2307/3853931.

Ortner, Donald J., and Mary Frances Ericksen. 1997. "Bone Changes in the Human Skull probably Resulting from Scurvy in Infancy and Childhood." *International Journal of Osteoarchaeology* 7 (3): 212–20. http://dx.doi.org/10.1002/(SICI)1099-1212(199705)7:3<212::AID-OA346>3.0.CO;2-5.

Parker Pearson, Mike. 1993. "The Powerful Dead: Archaeological Relationships between the Living and the Dead." *Cambridge Archaeological Journal* 3 (2): 203–29. http://dx.doi.org/10.1017/S0959774300000846.

Parkes, Collin Murray. 1972. *Bereavement: Studies of Grief in Adult Life*. New York: Pelican.

Pendlebury, John Devitt Stringfellow. 1931. "Preliminary Report on Excavations at Tell el-Amarnah 1930–1." *Journal of Egyptian Archaeology* 17 (3/4): 233–43. http://dx.doi.org/10.2307/3854766.

Pendlebury, John Devitt Stringfellow. 1932. "Preliminary Report on Excavations at Tell el-Amarnah 1931–2." *Journal of Egyptian Archaeology* 18 (3/4): 143–49. http://dx.doi.org/10.2307/3854975.

Pendlebury, John Devitt Stringfellow. 1951. *The City of Akhenaten III*. London: Egypt Exploration Society.

Petrie, William Matthew Flinders. 1894. *Tell El Amarna*. London: Methuen.

Powell, Mary Lucas. 1991. "Ranked Status and Health in the Mississippian Chiefdom at Moundville." In *What Mean these Bones? Studies in Southeastern Bioarchaeology*, edited by Mary Lucas Powell, Patricia S. Bridges, and Marie Wagner Mires Ann, 22–51. Tuscaloosa: University of Alabama Press.

Redford, Donald B. 1984. *Akhenaten: The Heretic King*. Cairo: The American University Press.

Reeves, Carl Nicholas. 1988. "New Light on Kiya from Texts in the British Museum." *Journal of Egyptian Archaeology* 74:91–101. http://dx.doi.org/10.2307/3821749.

Retief, François Pieter, and Louise Cilliers. 2011. "Akhenaten—A Unique Pharaoh." *South African Medical Journal* 101 (9): 628–30.

Risse, Guenter B. 1971. "Pharaoh Akhenaton of Ancient Egypt: Controversies among Egyptologists and Physicians regarding His Postulated Illness." *Journal of the History of Medicine and Allied Sciences* 26 (1): 3–17. http://dx.doi.org/10.1093/jhmas /XXVI.1.3.

Roksandic, Mirjana. 2002. "Position of Skeletal Remains as a Key to Understanding Mortuary Behavior." In *Advances in Forensic Taphonomy: Method, Theory, and Archaeological Perspectives*, edited by William D. Haglund and Marcella H. Sorg, 99–114. New York: CRC Press.

Rose, Jerome C. 2006. "Paleopathology of the Commoners at Tell Amarna, Egypt, Akhenaten's Capital City." *Memórias do Instituto Oswaldo Cruz* 101 (Suppl. II): 73–76. http://dx.doi.org/10.1590/S0074-02762006001000013.

Rose, Jerome C., and Dolores L. Burke. 2004. "Making Money from Buried Treasure." *Culture without Context: The Newsletter of the Near Eastern Project of the Illicit Antiquities Research Centre* 14: 4–8.

Rose, Pamela. 2005. "Preliminary Report on the Pottery from the South Tombs Bone Survey, 2005." In Kemp, B.J., "Tell el-Amarna." *Journal of Egyptian Archaeology* 91:23–24.

Shaw, Ian. 2000. *The Oxford History of Ancient Egypt*. Oxford: Oxford University Press.

Shepperson, Mary. 2009. "The Upper Site." In Kemp, B.J., "Tell el-Amarna, 2009." *Journal of Egyptian Archaeology* 95:21–27.

Shepperson, Mary. 2010. "The Upper Site." In Kemp, B.J., "Tell el-Amarna, 2010." *Journal of Egyptian Archaeology* 96:7–10.

Signoli, Michel, Isabelle Séguy, Jean-Noël Biraben, Olivier Dutour, and Paul Belle. 2002. "Paleodemography and Historical Demography in the Context of an Epidemic: Plague in Provence in the Eighteenth Century." *Population* 57:829–54.

Singer, Itamar. 2002. *Hittite Prayers*. Atlanta: Society of Biblical Literature.

Smith, Grafton Elliot. 1926. "The Diversions of an Anatomist in Egypt." *Cambridge University Medical Society Magazine* 4:34–39.

Spence, Kate E. 1999. "The North Palace at Amarna." *Egyptian Archaeology* 15:14–16.

Steckel, Richard H. 1987. "Growth Depression and Recovery: The Remarkable Case of American Slaves." *Annals of Human Biology* 14 (2): 111–32. http://dx.doi.org/10 .1080/03014468700006852.

Steckel, Richard H. 1995. "Stature and the Standard of Living." *Journal of Economic Literature* 33:1903–40.

Steckel, Richard H., Clark Spencer Larsen, Paul W. Sciulli, and Phillip L. Walker. 2011. "The Global History of Health Project Data Collection Codebook." http:// global.sbs.ohio-state.edu/new_docs/Codebook-01-24-11-em.pdf. Accessed 4 September 2013.

Stevens, Anna K. 2006. *Private Religion at Amarna: The Material Evidence*. Oxford: Archaeopress.

Stevens, Anna K. 2010. "The Lower Site." In Kemp, B.J., "Tell el-Amarna, 2010." *Journal of Egyptian Archaeology* 96:10–16.

Stevens, Anna K. 2011. "The Amarna Stone Village Survey and Life on the Urban Periphery in New Kingdom Egypt." *Journal of Field Archaeology* 36 (2): 100–131. http://dx.doi.org/10.1179/009346911X12991472411367.

Stevens, Anna K., and Wendy Dolling. 2006. "The Stone Village: 2005–2006." In Kemp, B.J., "Tell el-Amarna 2006." *Journal of Egyptian Archaeology* 92:23–27.

Stevens, Anna K., and Wendy Dolling. 2007a. "Shedding Light on the Stone Village at Amarna." *Egyptian Archaeology* 31:6–8.

Stevens, Anna K., and Wendy Dolling. 2007b. "The Stone Village." In Kemp, B.J., "Tell el-Amarna 2007." *Journal of Egyptian Archaeology* 93:1–11.

Stevens, Anna K., and Wendy Dolling. 2008. "The Stone Village." In Kemp, B.J., "Tell el-Amarna 2008." *Journal of Egyptian Archaeology* 94:1–13.

Stevens, Anna K., and Wendy Dolling. 2009. "The Stone Village." In Kemp, B.J., "Tell el-Amarna, 2008–9." *Journal of Egyptian Archaeology* 95:1–11.

Storey, Rebecca. 1985. "An Estimate of Mortality in a Pre-Columbian Urban Population." *American Anthropologist* 87 (3): 519–35. http://dx.doi.org/10.1525/aa.1985 .87.3.02a00010.

Tietze, Christian. 1985. "Analyse der Wonhause und soziale Struktur der Stadtbewohner." *Zeitschrift für Ägyptische Sprache und Alturmskunde* 112:48–84.

Van Dijk, Jacobus. 2000. "The Amarna Period and the Later New Kingdom." In *The Oxford History of Ancient Egypt*, edited by Ian Shaw, 265–307. Oxford: Oxford University Press.

Walker, Phillip L., Rhonda R. Bathurst, Rebecca Richman, Thor Gjerdrum, and Valerie A. Andrushko. 2009. "The Causes of Porotic Hyperostosis and Cribra Orbitalia: A Reappraisal of the Iron-Deficiency-Anemia Hypothesis." *American Journal of Physical Anthropology* 139 (2): 109–25. http://dx.doi.org/10.1002/ajpa.21031.

Wheeler, S. M. 2010. "Nutritional and Disease Stress of Juveniles from Dakhleh Oasis, Egypt." *International Journal of Osteoarchaeology.* http://dx.doi.org/10.1002 .oa.1201.

Whittemore, Thomas. 1926. "The Excavations at el-Amarnah, Season 1924–5." *Journal of Egyptian Archaeology* 12 (1/2): 3–12. http://dx.doi.org/10.2307/3854173.

Zabecki, Melissa. 2008. "Human Bones from the South Tombs Cemetery." In Kemp, B.J., "Tell El-Amarna, 2009–10." *Journal of Egyptian Archaeology* 96:61–67.

Zabecki, Melissa. 2009. "Human Bones from the South Tombs Cemetery." In Kemp, B.J., "Tell El-Amarna, 2008–9." *Journal of Egyptian Archaeology* 95:34–36.

Zhang, Li. 2001. *Strangers in the City: Reconfigurations of Space, Power and Social Networks within China's Floating Population.* Stanford, CA: Stanford University Press.

RACHEL BICHENER is completing a PhD at the University of Manchester on the subject of "The Practical and Symbolic role of the Domestic Dog in the Later Neolithic of Upper Mesopotamia." This research investigates the occurrence of dog remains on sites in southern Anatolia and northern Syria, with a view to developing an idea of what dogs could have been used for, how people related to them, and whether human-dog relations were analogous on different sites. She has previously studied at the University of Liverpool.

ALEXIS T. BOUTIN is an associate professor of anthropology at Sonoma State University. Her bioarchaeological fieldwork and museum collections research focuses on ancient Near Eastern, Gulf, and eastern Mediterranean societies. Boutin's publications use human skeletal remains, archaeological contexts, and ancient texts to explore embodied personhood in all of its iterations.

MICHELE R. BUZON is an associate professor of anthropology at Purdue University. She is a bioarchaeologist whose research focuses on the excavation and analysis of burials in the ancient Nile Valley (Egypt and Nubia). Through the examination of human skeletal remains and mortuary practices at Tombos and numerous collections from additional Nile Valley sites, she examines the effects of Nubian-Egyptian contact on identity and health during the New Kingdom and Napatan periods using paleopathological, isotopic, and biodistance methods.

STUART CAMPBELL is professor of Near Eastern archaeology at the University of Manchester. He has directed and codirected the Domuztepe Project since 1995, and has worked previously on prehistoric sites in Iraq and at the Bronze Age site of Jerablus Tahtani in Syria. His research has involved a wide range of approaches to understanding prehistoric societies, including symbolism and use of ceramics, funerary practices, and the ways in which the past was remembered in prehistoric societies. He also has methodological interests in chronologies, site formation processes, and archaeological practice.

MEREDITH S. CHESSON is an associate professor of anthropology at the University of Notre Dame. She has directed and codirected excavations at prehistoric sites in Jordan and Italy. She is the publication co-editor for the Expedition to the Dead Sea Plain, working with Tom Schaub to publish the results of excavations at Early Bronze Age settlements and cemeteries on the southeastern Dead Sea Plain. She is codirector of the Follow the Pots Project (http://followthepotsproject.org/) with Morag Kersel, tracking looted materials from these same EBA cemeteries and investigating where these materials go and how people think about these artifacts. Her research focuses on the materiality of everyday life, with particular interests in homes, mortuary practices, and identity.

GRETCHEN R. DABBS is an associate professor of anthropology at Southern Illinois University. She is also the director of the Complex for Forensic Anthropology Research at SIU. Her bioarchaeological research focuses mainly on health in ancient history, with particular interest in the effect of harsh environments on health status. She has worked on skeletal remains from the U.S. Great Plains and Southeast, the North American Arctic, and New Kingdom Egypt.

BLAIR DAVERMAN has a master of science in anthropology from Purdue University, where she focused her research on the biological ramifications of imperial conquest in ancient Mesopotamia.

LESLEY GREGORICKA is an assistant professor in the Department of Sociology, Anthropology, & Social Work at the University of South Alabama. She received her BA from the University of Notre Dame and her MA and PhD from The Ohio State University. She specializes in human mobility and the evolution of social complexity in the Near East, mortuary archaeology, and paleodiet using biogeochemical and bioarchaeological approaches. Her recent research examines temporal changes in residential mobility and the negotiation of social identity in southeastern Arabia. She is currently codirector of the Social, Spatial, and Bioarchaeological Histories of Ancient Oman (SOBO) project.

SARAH WHITCHER KANSA is executive director of the Alexandria Archive Institute, where she works to promote data publication in archaeology. She is the editor of Open Context (http://opencontext.org), an open-access, web-based data publication venue. Sarah is also a zooarchaeologist, having worked for fifteen years at Domuztepe, Turkey, and at other sites in Israel, Jordan, the United States, and Italy. She manages BoneCommons.org, a content-sharing site for archaeozoologists worldwide and serves on leadership committees for the International Council for Archaeozoology, the American Schools of Oriental Research, and the Society for American Archaeology.

HANNAH LAU is a graduate student in the Archaeology Program at the University of California, Los Angeles. Her research focuses on zooarchaeology and its implications for reconstructing political economy and historical ecology in the Near East and Southern Caucasus. In addition to her work at Domuztepe, she works in Azerbaijan as part of the Naxçıvan Archaeological Project.

WILLIAM J. PESTLE is an assistant professor in the Department of Anthropology at the University of Miami. In addition to spearheading the Kish Osteology Project, he is actively pursuing research on ancient diet and its ties to power and social stratification in prehistoric Puerto Rico and northern Chile.

BENJAMIN W. PORTER is an assistant professor of Near Eastern archaeology in the University of California, Berkeley's Near Eastern Studies Department, and a curator of Near Eastern Archaeology in the Phoebe A. Hearst Museum of Anthropology. He is a codirector of the Dhiban Excavation and Development Project in Jordan, and the Dilmun Bioarchaeology Project. His research interests focus on the Bronze and Iron Age societies of the ancient Near East.

SUSAN GUISE SHERIDAN is an associate professor of anthropology at the University of Notre Dame. She received her BA and MA from the University of Maryland and her PhD from the University of Colorado. Her research interests include bioarchaeological reconstructions of daily life, health and diet, mobility, and paleopathological indicators of violence. She has worked on collections from the ancient Near East, the Sudan, and the American Southwest.

CHRISTINA TORRES-ROUFF is an associate professor of anthropology at the University of California, Merced, and an associated researcher at the Instituto de Investigaciones Arqueológicas y Museo Le Paige in San Pedro de Atacama, Chile. Her bioarchaeological research is focused on social identities, interregional interaction, mortuary contexts, and body modification.

STUART TYSON SMITH is professor and chair of anthropology at the University of California, Santa Barbara. His methodological focus is on the study of ancient pottery, including the scientific analysis of absorbed residues and clay sources. Smith has worked on archaeological expeditions to Egypt, including Luxor's Theban Necropolis. Since 1996, his archaeological work has focused on the Sudan, in particular the site of Tombos. He also consulted on the films *Stargate*, *The Mummy*, and *The Mummy Returns*.

JAIME ULLINGER is an assistant professor of anthropology at Quinnipiac University. She received her BA from the University of Notre Dame, MA from Arizona State University, and PhD from The Ohio State University. Her research interests include bioarchaeology in the Near East in general, with an emphasis on skeletal and dental health in the southern Levant, particularly during the advent of urbanism in the Early Bronze Age.

MELISSA ZABECKI is a park interpreter at Parkin Archeological State Park in Parkin, Arkansas. She spent multiple years in the field of Egyptian bioarchaeology working at sites such as Hierakonpolis, Abydos, Kafr Hassan Dawood, and Amarna. Her main interest is exploring how muscle attachments contribute to the reconstruction of ancient lives.

disability, 5, 12, 13; archaeological research on, 98–99; of skeleton No. 12-10146, 115–16; social perceptions of, 119–20; sociocultural meaning of, 97–98
Diyala, 82
Djoser, Step Pyramid, 190
dogs, 12; in Domuztepe deposits, 34–37, 42
Domuztepe, 12, 27, *29*, 53, 54(n2); architecture and soil buried in, 49–51; dogs buried at, 34–37; faunal remains at, 37–40, 42–47; funerary practices at, 31–34; objects buried at, 47–49
dwarfism. *See* achondroplasia

Early Bronze Age, 11, 13; at Bab edh-Dhra', 133, *134–37*; burial practices, 137–42; demographic analysis, 164–65; genetic relatedness data, 166–71(tables), 174–75; population age in, 158–59; sex of population in, 159–62, 172–73; skeletal collections, 145–56(table)
Early Bronze IA (EBIA), 13; at Bab edh-Dhra', 138–39, 143, 145–52(table), 159–64, 173; burial practices, 175–76; genetic relatedness data, 166–71(tables), 174–75
Early Bronze II–III (EBII–III): at Bab edh-Dhra', 139–41, 143, 153–56(table), 159, 160–64, 173–74; burial practices, 175–76; charnel houses, 13, 140–*41*; demographic analysis, 164–65, 167, 172–75; genetic relatedness data, 166–71(tables)
Early Dilmun period, 97, 100, 105, 106; grave goods, 116–18; skeletal remains, 107–8, 109–16
Early Dynastic Period, 68, 81, 113; burials, 81, 82; grave goods, 82, 84; Kish, 65–66, 67
Early Dynastic III (EDIII) period, in Kish, 12, 61, 67, 75
Egypt, 2, 11, 113, *187*; commemoration and memorialization practices, 189–91; epidemic disease in, 237–38; New Kingdom in, 6, 217–18; New Kingdom mortuary patterns in, 240–41; and Nubia, 13, 185, 186, 188, 198, 199–200; people with disabilities in, 119–20; social memory in, 191–93; Tell el-Amarna cemetery, 13–14; temples in, 219–20
Egyptianization, 188–89; at Tombos, 194, 198–99

Egyptians, bioarchaeological analysis of, 194–97
elites, 7, 233, 240; in Egyptian Nubia, 199–200, 208
Emberling, Geoff, on archaeology of ethnicity, 63–64
emulation, by Nubians, 188
enamel hypoplasia, 112, 235
Enki, 120
epidemics, at Tell el-Amarna, 236–38
ethnicity, 5, 62; archaeology of, 63–64; at Kish, 70, 85–88; Mesopotamian societies, 61, 64–65

families, 7, 13, 133
Fara, 80
faunal assemblages, from Domuztepe, 37–40, 42–47
feasting, 6, 12, 201
feasting refuse: bone processing and, 45–46; at Domuztepe, 31, 37, 38, 42, 44–45, 47; and human burials, 29–30
Feifa, 138
females: Dilmun, 100, 109–16; from Kish, 77, 78; Mound A (Kish), 85–86; Nubian, 200–201; from Tell el-Amarna, 234–35
femoral anteversion, on skeleton No. 12-10146, 110, *111*, 112
fetuses, in Cornwall collection, 100; at Bab edh-Dhra', 159, 172
Field Museum, Kish collections, 66–67
figurines, 3; burials of, 48–49
Fıstıklı Höyük, 30
food debris, at Domuztepe, 37–47
formation processes, and skeletal remains, 136, 173
fortification, of Bab edh-Dhra', 135, 139, 140
Frohlich, Bruno, 107
funerary practices, 3, 231; as embodied performances, 10–11; Neolithic Mesopotamia, 30–34; New Kingdom Egypt, 191–93, 199; Nubian, 200–201

Gebe Barkal, 186
goats: in Dilmun, 107, 108, 116; in Domuztepe deposits, 37, 38, 39, 43, 45, 46
grave goods/furnishings, 3, 4; A "Cemetery" (Kish), 80–82, *85*; Akkadian period, 82–84; from Bab edh-Dhra', 140; burials of, 52, 53;

in Dilmun burials, 116–18; in Domuztepe deposits, 47–49; Early Bronze Age, 138; Neolithic Mesopotamia, 30; New Kingdom Egypt, 193; with skeleton No. 12-10146, 116–18; South Tombs Cemetery, 223, 227, 229–30, 231, 232, 239, 242; at Tombos, 200, 201, 204–5, *206*, 208

grave markers, South Tombs Cemetery, 230

grave pits, South Tombs Cemetery, 225, 226–27, 231

grave robbing: and repatriation, 242–43; South Tombs Cemetery, 217–18, 219, 238–40

Halaf period: burial practices, 30–31, 53–54; figurine burials, 48–49

Hamad Town, 107–8

Harappan societies, 106

Harper's Song, 191

Harvard University, and Peter Cornwall, 101, 102

Hasa Eastern Province, al- (Saudi Arabia), 105

Hatshepsut, 190

Hearst Museum of Anthropology, Phoebe A.: Cornwall collection at, 12, 97; Peter Cornwall and, 101–2, 103–4, 121

Hellenism, Hellenization, 188, 189

Hit, bitumen from, 116

Højgaard, Karen, 108

Horemheb, *192*

human remains. *See* burials; crania; mummification; skeletal remains

humerus varus deformity (HVD): causes of, 113–15; on skeleton 12-10146, 109–*10*, *111*, 112

identity, 31, 47, 200; ethnic, 63–64; social, 3–4; in Tombos, 206–9

Imhotep, veneration of, 190, 191

"Immortality of Writers," 190, 191

Indus Valley, and Dilmun, 106

infants, 80, 100, 172, 176, 226

Ingharra complex, human remains from, 76, 77–78, 90(n4)

Inherkhau, ancestor veneration, 189–90, 191

Iran, 106

isotopic analyses, of Tombos burials, 196–97

Israel, 8

Israel/Palestine, 113

Jericho, 120

jewelry, 81, 227

Joint Oxford University–Field Museum Expedition to Mesopotamia (JOFME), 65–66

Jordan, 2, 11; Early Bronze Age in, 13, 133, *134–37*

Jordan Valley, 13

Karnak Temple, 210

Kawa, 186

Kerma, 186, 194, 198, 199, 207

Kermian period, burials of, 205–6

Kfar HaHoresh, 46, 52

kin groups, and charnel houses, 135

kinship: Early Bronze Age, 13; memorializing, 207

kinship units, 6–7

Kish, 6, 12, 64; A "Cemetery" at, 61, 62; bioarchaeology of, 70–76; biodistance studies of, 76–79; ethnicity at, 85–88; excavations at, 65–67; historical records of, 68–69; mortuary treatment at, 79–85

Kish Project, 75

Kiya, 221

knock-knees, on skeleton No. 12-10146, 110, *111*, 112

Kurru, el-, 208

Kush. *See* Nubia

Kuwait, Dilmun in, 105

Larsen, Clark Spencer, 5

Late Dilmun period, 105, 113

Levant, 14; Early Bronze Age, 133, 136–37

life cycle, and burial of objects, 47

lineage, 7; at Bab edh-Dhra', 133

literary texts, 7; Egyptian, 190–91

Littleton, Judith, Early Dilmun demography, 107–8

living individuals, and object burial, 47

London, epidemic disease victims in, 236–37

Lower Nubia, 194

Lower Site (South Tombs Cemetery), 223; burials at, 225–26, 227

Lugalzagesi of Uruk, 69, 89(n2); and Kish, 69, 86

MacDonald, Robert, 103

Mackay, Ernest, 67, 75

males: from Cornwall collection, 100; Mound A (Kish), 78, 85–86; from Tell el-Amarna, 234–35
Malinowski, Bronislaw, 9
material culture, 3; and cultural memory, 28. *See also* grave goods/furnishings
matrilocality, at Kish, 86
mats, at South Tombs Cemetery, 229, 230
McCown, Theodore, 101, 102
Mean Measure of Divergence (MMD): in biodistance studies, 73, 75, 76–77, 78, 158, 164, 170–71(table), 174, 175
memorialization, 3, 201; in Egypt, 189–93
memory, 2, 6, 8–9, 28, 204; cultural, 188, 189–90. *See also* social memory
memory work, 9–10, 11
Memphis, biological data from, 194
Mentuhotep, Nebhepetre, 190
Meritaten, 221
Mesopotamia, 2, 12, 14, 106, 120; ethnicity in, 61, 64–65; Neolithic, 30–34
Middle Bronze II, 138
Middle Dilmun period, 105
Middle Kingdom, 198, 231
migrants, Amarna residents as, 239–40
minimum number of individuals (MNI), 144; of Bab edh-Dhra' assemblage, 162–63, 165(table)
MLNI. *See* most likely number of individuals
MMD. *See* Mean Measure of Divergence
MNI. *See* minimum number of individuals
Morquio syndrome, 113–14
mortuary practices/treatment, 3, 6, 190: at Bab edh-Dhra', 135, 137–42, 173–74, 175–76; in Dilmun, 107–8, 116–*18*; at Kish, 79–85, 86–87; of migrants, 239–40; New Kingdom Egypt, 240–41; South Tombs cemetery, 229–30
most likely number of individuals (MLNI), 144; in Bab edh-Dhra' assemblage, 157, 165(table)
Mound A (Kish), 67, 69, 82, 86, 89(n1), 90(n4); analysis of human remains from, 70–76; biodistance analysis of burials, 76–79; mortuary treatment in, 79–85
Mound W, human remains from, 76, 77, 90(n4)
mucopolysaccharidosis, 113–14

mummification, mummies, 229; in Nubia, 200, 204, 206
Mursili II, "Plague Prayers" of, 237

Naga-ed-Deir, 119, 231
Napata, 186
Napatan period, 13, 185; Nubian identity during, 207–8; Tombos burials, 188, 201, 203–7
Nefertiti, 221
Neolithic, 14, 28, 113; burial processes in, 51–54; funerary practices, 30–34; in Turkey, 1, 12, 27
newborns, 120, 176
New Kingdom, 6, 203, 233; commemoration and memorialization in, 189, 190, 229–31; Egyptianization during, 188, 194; mortuary patterns, 240–41; social memory of, 191–93, 207, 208; Tell el-Amarna cemetery in, 13–14
Nile River, water from, 197
Nimah, 120
Nippur, footed ceramic jars in, 83
North City (Akhetaten), 221
North Tombs (Tell el-Amarna), 221, 241
Nubia, 13, *187*; Egypt and, 185, 186, 188, 198; mixed identity in, 206–9
Nubian dynasty, 201
Nubians: bioarchaeological analyses of, 194–97; burial practices, 200–201
Numeira, 140
Nuri, 208

Old Kingdom, 199, 231
Oman Peninsula, 106
Opening of the Mouth ritual, 204
Opet Festival, 190
orchards, at Bab edh-Dhra', 133, 140
Other, people with disabilities as, 119
ovens, Red Terrace and Ditch (Domuztepe), 42

paleopathologies, 4, 6, 107; causes of, 112–15; skeleton 12-10146, 108, 109–12; Tell el-Amarna individuals, 233, 234–35
Panehesy, 186
parry fractures, 197; forearm fractures at Tombos, 197
pastoralism, seminomadic, 138
performances, funerary ritual as, 10–11, 31, 193–94